PENGUIN BOOKS

If Learning is so Natural, Why am I going to School?
A Parent's Guide

Andrew Nikiforuk was *The Globe and Mail*'s popular
and controversial "Education" columnist for three
years. An award-winning journalist, he is the author
of *The Fourth Horseman: A Short History of Epidemics,
Plagues, Famines and Other Scourges* and, most recently,
*School's Out: The Catastrophe in Public Education and
What We Can Do About It*, which was short-listed for
the Gordon Montador Award. A parent and former
teacher, he lives in Calgary, Alberta.

If Learning is so Natural, Why am I going to School?

ANDREW NIKIFORUK

Penguin Books

PENGUIN BOOKS
Published by the Penguin Group
Penguin Books Canada Ltd, 10 Alcorn Avenue, Toronto, Ontario,
Canada M4V 3B2
Penguin Books Ltd, 27 Wrights Lane, London W8 5TZ, England
Viking Penguin, a division of Penguin Books USA Inc., 375
Hudson Street, New York, New York 10014, U.S.A.
Penguin Books Australia Ltd, Ringwood, Victoria, Australia
Penguin Books (NZ) Ltd, 182-190 Wairau Road, Auckland 10,
New Zealand

Penguin Books Ltd, Registered Offices: Harmondsworth,
Middlesex, England

Published in Penguin Books, 1994

10 9 8 7 6 5 4 3 2 1

Copyright © Andrew Nikiforuk, 1994
All rights reserved

Manufactured in Canada

Canadian Cataloguing in Publication Data

Nikiforuk, Andrew, 1955-
If learning is so natural, why am I going to school?

ISBN 0-14-024264-3

1. Education, Elementary - Canada. 2. Education, Secondary -
Canada. I. Title.

LA412.N5 1994   370'.971   C94-931460-9

To all parents who walk the extra schooling mile,
Margaret Nikiforuk, who did just that,
and John Asmussen, who helped to show the way

ACKNOWLEDGMENTS

Many hands and hearts made this book possible but without the organization and patience of my wife and best friend, Doreen Docherty, little would have been accomplished. While I madly rowed, she coolly navigated.

Of the many parents that contributed directly or indirectly to this book over the years, I would particularly like to thank Debra Kerr, Meredith Poole, Dan Levson, Brenda Geise, Elsje de Boer, Maureen Gosling, Maureen Beebe, Sue Careless, Diane Malott, John Pippus, and Dr Joe Freedman, school reformer extraordinaire. For the thousands of other parents that wrote or phoned, my grateful thanks. You kept me informed, corrected my mistakes and gave my columns a truly populist voice:

Several teachers, principals and academics also deserve warm thanks for their continued support and influence. They include Carl Bereiter, Doug Carnine, Bonnie Grossen, Mark Holmes, Walter Scott, Marilyn Jager Adams, Dorothy Pullan, Ron Wallace, Mat Oberhofer, Charles Ledger, Paul Bennett, Nancy Lowden, Peter Coleman, Barry Anderson, Helen Raham, Larry Booi, Ada Kallio, Deborrah Howes, David Hogg, Michael Moloney, Marilyn Dumaresq, Keith Stanovich, Jim Gallagher, Ed Barbeau, Percy

Ciurluini, Jack McCaffrey, Lorne Hicks, Dennis Raphael, Carl Kline, David Carter, Leif Stolee and many others.

I, too, wish to commend several copy editors at the *Globe and Mail* and *Chatelaine* magazine for their attention to detail: Constance Schuller, Phil Jackman, Cheryl Cohen, Cathy Callaghan and Elizabeth Parr.

Last but not least I salute the editor of this project, Barbara Berson, and the staff at Penguin for sharpening a manuscript that kept growing.

We need better government, no doubt about it. But we also need better minds, better friendships, better marriages, better communities. We need persons and households that do not have to wait upon organizations but can make necessary changes in themselves on their own.

Wendell Berry

CONTENTS

INTRODUCTION

Dear Readers,

You phoned and wrote by the thousands. You railed and lamented; you chafed and confessed. And then you asked question after question.

You wanted to know what the research said on whole language. You didn't understand the purpose of "invented spelling" or "co-operative learning." You asked about the quality of French Immersion programs, and wondered if private schools were really better than public schools. You asked who Maria Montessori was and what Waldorf meant. You said that your school had tested its pupils on math but wondered why they never released the results. You pleaded for information on "outcome-based education." Talk straight to me, you said.

This practical guide is my answer to these and many other questions. It begins with Absentee Parents and ends with Year-Round Schooling. In between you can find stories, examples or research on topics as varied as Reading Recovery, Television, Bullies and Self-Esteem. There are short entries and long ones as well as sources and phone numbers. You can use this guide as a dictionary or simply go browsing. As a guide the book invites further inquiries. The accompanying appendices, rich in anecdote and opinion, directly compliment the entries by providing examples of good report cards or school policies. There, too, are numerous essays by principals, teachers and parents that are alternately sad, wise and angry.

I compiled this guide (much material has been drawn from my *Globe* and *Chatelaine* columns) on the premise that there are a lot of good schools out there but they are often hard to find; that parents, first and foremost, are responsible for their children's education, that school reform is largely a community-based activity and that there are so many new ideas, interests and innovations in the schools that parents need some help sorting the chalk from the dust.

After three years of writing about schools I remain, as ever, an informed layman and concerned parent. This guide is dedicated to creating more informed citizens capable of initiating changes on their own, whether the powers-that-be agree or not.

The public school system that exists today is a much different and larger creature than the ones our parents and grandparents attended. And I have increasingly come to the conclusion that it now resembles North America's tattered military-industrial complex. Large institutions, be they banks or corporations, aren't terribly respectful of communities or families, and the public school system seems at times to be no different. Over the years it has lost sight of its original mission—to place citizens on common ground in a democracy—and has become just another complex committed to its own growth and aggrandizement. It has developed its own professional jargon, impenetrable bureaucracy and utopian missions.

The industrial educational complex, a $55 billion business in Canada, comes with an ever-growing set of experts: equity police, testing bodies, teachers' unions, faculties of education, textbook committees, whole language consultants, analysts, social workers, inventive spellers, multicultural experts, paper-washed administrators, real police and hi-tech salesmen. The profiteers and careerists in this group alternately work in ministries of education where policy is set, only to return to the system as superintendents where they eventually implement their own bad ideas.

Not surprisingly, America's military-industrial complex behaved in the same incestuous manner: Pentagon workers drifted to General Dynamics only to return to the Pentagon and then back to the boardrooms of defence contractors.

When school policy becomes the captive of the people running schools, strange and dangerous things happen. Parents and teachers are ignored. Tests become ridiculous tools and standards go missing. Content becomes a dirty word and process becomes the name of the game. As John Gatto, an award-winning New York teacher, recently admitted, the truth also becomes a casualty in the complex. "If you don't keep your word in a community everyone finds out, and you have a major problem thereafter. But lying for personal advantage is the operational standard in all large institutions; it is considered part of the game in schools. Parents, for the most part, are lied to or told half-truths, as they are usually considered adversaries. At least that's been the true in every school I ever worked in.... Whistle-blowing against institutional malpractice is always a good way to get canned or relentlessly persecuted. Whistle-blowers never get promoted in any institution because, having served a public interest once, they may well do it again." A great many Canadian teachers would nod in agreement with Gatto.

No complex would be complete without an ideology,

and the reigning theories and philosophies in education at the moment make strong arguments against schooling. When educators daily proclaim that reading is a natural act, that math is a matter of discovery, that writing is scribbling, that spelling is an invention, and that teachers are mere facilitators, parents have rightly asked, "Why am I sending my kids to school?"

Most parents know a bill of goods when they are being sold one and intuitively know that learning is not as simple as breathing for most mortals. And most recognize that some of their children will need more and better teaching than others. Carl Bereiter, a very fine Canadian educator, once observed that parents generally subscribe to the folk belief that if "you teach it, they will learn it." This idea underestimates the difficulty of motivating kids, but comes much closer to the truth than the "Let them discover learning" creed of the complex.

But like its military-industrial cousin, the educational fraternity has developed its own elaborate defence system. Whenever a parent questions the "learning is natural" doctrine, the system automatically invokes elusive rhetoric, complex excuses and damning accusations. Because the complex fancies itself as a liberal and progressive institution, it often labels those that question or challenge its practises as evil, stupid or politically suspect. The military complex tried this trick too, painting its critics as Reds or subversives.

Many parents have encountered this behaviour from the technocrats now managing the system. The teachers are generally not part of this racket and want to do a good job. For the most part they are parents' natural allies and are just as handicapped by the complex in their teaching as parents are thwarted in finding a meaningful role in their local school. If nothing else, this guide encourages parents and teachers to talk and keep on talking.

In addition to blowing the whistle on a great many questionable practices, this handbook should also help parents understand some of the nonsense they hear from educators. But teachers who pick up this guide will be glad to see that I have not ignored "the parenting deficit." The numerous references to absentee parents, bad parents and violent children pointedly underscores the difficult reality that many teachers face today. For if the public school system has turned its back on its original mission, so too has society turned its back on the schools. Rarely does anyone ask what society owes schools. We have paid dearly for this neglect.

As this guide repeatedly illustrates, good schooling is not about "learning outcomes" or "adaptive problem-solving." It is, as T. S. Eliot eloquently wrote, about preparation for life, work and community. A healthy democracy needs good schools as much as it needs working marriages, true communities and virtuous citizens. What schooling we offer our children should directly present them with the best ideas, proven methods and worthy skills. To offer less but better schooling is not only desirable but necessary. As a people we need to wean ourselves off the complex and turn once again to nurturing our own families and communities. This is, perhaps, the only strategy that stands any hope of neutering the complex's bad practices and self-centredness.

Readers should not treat this guide as the first or last word on schooling. It may help explain things, good and bad, or help you complain about inane practices, but it was not designed as a solitary companion. Nor is it complete. It contains no entries on music, sport, art or motivation. If this book strikes a chord and enjoys long shelf-life, I hope to add them.

I wish to thank the parents and teachers who wrote and phoned over the years. Your letters and inquiries have driven my column for *The Globe and Mail* for a long time now and truly explain its unexpected popularity. This book is very much of your making. I hope it answers your important questions, makes a small difference for a great many children, and ultimately echoes your voices, the citizens of Canada, with respect and care.

Andrew Nikiforuk
Calgary, 1994

If Learning is so Natural, Why am I going to School?

A

ABSENTEE PARENTS   In modern society, far too many parents have been seduced by the sexy sirens of consumerism. They have, in short, opted for more things, more gadgets and more toys than what matters: a healthy relationship with their children.

When parents put their own goals, work or interests ahead of their offspring, the children, the community and the school all suffer. Whether one glances at statistics on daycare, child abuse, poverty or academic achievement, they all point to a new reality: cultures showered with affluence and distracted by rapid technological change neglect their children.

Dr Thomas Millar, a child psychiatrist in West Vancouver, gives a name to this generation: "the Big Chillies." Spoiled by their own post-war parents, the Big Chillies have managed to produce a generation of children that has expanded the horizons of sexual revolution to include elementary school sex and date rape. "While their parents were content to occupy the dean's office and smoke his cigars, today's children have principals cowering in the cloakroom and have taken over the playground. They terrorize the community and when they are apprehended, plead unhappy childhoods to youth workers as naïve as themselves."

To understand how the Big Chillies accomplished this feat, Millar looks at how they approached their child-rearing duties. "Remember, the Big Chillies were ne plus ultra individualists ... and anti-authoritarian to the core. But disciplining children is as important a part of parenting as loving them.... Unreared children have two strikes against them. They have not received enough love to teach them the world is a giving place, and they have not received the consistent discipline that trains. Add to that a bad education and they are heading for a lifetime in the welfare dugout."

Millar paints in broad strokes, and does not account for the economic realities that have turned one-income families into two-income families. Nevertheless, it often seems that time and care are no longer the essential staples of parenting. In 1965 mothers and fathers spent an average of thirty hours a week with their brood. Today that figure has dropped to seventeen hours. The average urban teenager has three minutes alone with Dad, and half of that time is spent in front of the TV set. And so on.

The Big Chillies' pursuit of the Good Life, debts and all, has not been good for children. An American study of grade eight students that compared kids actively cared for by adults to those who took care of themselves more than 11 hours a week is sobering. The "latch-key" kids were twice as likely to drink alcohol or use drugs. Noted the author of the study, social scientist Jean Richardson: "The increased risk appeared no matter what the sex, race or socio-economic status of the children." They were also one and a half to two times more likely "to score high on risk taking, anger, family conflict and stress."

Attachment to parents is also a powerful indicator of how far a child will stray off the beaten path. According to several studies on delinquency the bottom line reads something like this: "The closer the mother's supervision of the child, the more intimate the child's communication with the father, and the greater the affection between child and parents, the less the delinquency."

There are few tasks as demanding and as social as

raising children. "To enter parenthood is to cross a cultural divide from the domain of self to the domain of civil society," writes U. S. social critic Barbara Dafoe Whitehead in the *Utne Reader*. Parents must recognize, as all sustainable societies have recognized, that if there is to be a future worth having, children must come first.

ACCOUNTABILITY   Few North American educators have as solid a reputation for straight talk on schooling as Dr Barbara Bateman. For more than a quarter-century the sixty-year-old lawyer and professor of special education at the University of Oregon has led the good fight against the serious decline in North American schools.

She is also one of the continent's leading authorities on "academic child abuse," the "use of practices that cause unnecessary failure in foundation skills and knowledge areas."

According to Bateman, bad reading instruction in the early grades is simply unforgivable in the face of research that has clearly identified how to teach virtually all children how to read. When school boards ignore this research, they engage in abuse. A child who hasn't learned how to read by grade two often loses his self-esteem, develops bad attitudes about school and is forced to take "special" treatment that subjects both the child and family to much labour, pain and expense.

In Bateman's judgment the perpetrators of academic child abuse are not teachers but administrators. Bateman assumes that teachers "are doing the very best they can do (or are permitted to do) and that they simply serve as the medium for transmitting the decisions made at the district level." Administrators are often guilty of "élitism" and a "one-size-fits-all mentality." As a consequence they often force their schools to adopt programs or innovations that succeed with less than one-third of the school population.

The reason for such bad decision-making lies in education's avoidance of exact and demanding science—the imperfect world of measuring differences and results. The level of thought among educators is simple and polarized, notes Carl Bereiter, an educational psychologist. "Science has trouble making inroads because the thought of educators is basically moral thought about good and bad. It's not whether something is true or false. And this precludes a critical and accountable pedagogy."

Bateman, like Bereiter, strongly believes that education as a discipline is still in a pre-science state, as was medicine in the nineteenth century. As a consequence the profession will turn to "magic bullets" and fads to solve problems rather than seriously study the evidence or research on what works. This is not to say that education can or ever will be a perfect science, but good research can and should direct it.

Bateman argues that good controlled research on what's effective in the classroom (such as systematic phonetic instruction) could better our schools if implemented wisely by administrators. But educators often don't even know what good research is, says Bateman.

Consider, for example, the current educational trend of ungraded, multi-aged classrooms where children proceed at their own pace and in their own style. "We have a lot of literature and opinion pieces in *Phi Delta Kappan* and *Educational Leadership* where John Doe asserts that this must be a good thing," says Bateman. But opinion, anecdote and fuzzy rhetoric about schools imitating the extended family do not make a reliable research base. "If someone asked me if we had a significant data base to justify the disruption of the entire educational system by switching to multi-aging, I'd say 'No. Not for a moment.'"

Although Bateman has no doubt that multi-aging may well prove to be advantageous for some children in some classrooms, she takes a grim view of pedagogical experiments without responsible controls. Adds the educator: "I'd rather wait for the research to know what the advantages and disadvantages will be. I want some balance."

She also raises similar concerns about destreaming ("detracking" in the United States) or "the refusal to group children according to their performance level." She says the research on this practice is decidedly mixed. In fact, most of the educational "innovations" implemented in North American classrooms for the last twenty years have no hard data to support them.

Parents should know that most of the textbooks and programs chosen for a school have *never* been field tested with a variety of children over long periods of time. So don't assume that your school has chosen what works. Educators are likely to pick a reading series just as they would pick a cereal ("Wow, that looks good!"). Reading the research on the effectiveness of different programs is still a novel idea for many administrators. It often takes a committed parents' group, armed with good studies, to change school practices that penalize a majority of children.

For more information on accountability and academic child abuse, contact the International Institute for Advocacy for School Children: 296 West 8th Avenue, Eugene, Oregon 97401, 503-485-6349.

See also **MULTI-AGED CLASSROOMS, "INNOVATIONS" vs. "REFORMS," PHONICS, DESTREAMING** and **DEVELOPMENTALLY APPROPRIATE PRACTICE.**

ADMINISTRATORS   The people who run school boards are an élite who work hard at distancing themselves from ordinary working people. They are largely responsible for what is known as the Great Educational Divide. This piece of geography is much wider than Saskatchewan's grasslands and much deeper than Great Slave Lake.

Mark Holmes, a former professor at the Ontario Institute for Studies in Education and now an education consultant, has mapped this peculiar territory by exploring the beliefs and values of Ontario's chief education officers (CEOs). After comparing their responses to an eighteen-page questionnaire with replies from non-professionals he found a rather startling ideological gap between the educators and the parents. Their contrasting views go a long way towards explaining public dissent about public schooling today.

According to Holmes's research, the Educational Divide begins with the basic character of Ontario's CEOs, which really doesn't reflect the community at large. Most are fifty-year-old white men who vote liberal and attend the United Church. There is not much colour in this crowd and even fewer Baptists, Buddhists or Marxists.

These industrious CEOs classify their work as demanding, exciting and political, but not pedagogical. In fact, most devote *only* 20 percent of their time to delivering and assessing school curricula and personnel. The majority of their day is devoted to paperpushing, public relations, bus schedules or other "busy-work." "That's sad, isn't it?" says Holmes.

But their inattention to results accurately reflects their nice-sounding educational philosophy, the progressive or "child-centred" kind. Progressive thought holds that schools should help children feel good by providing them with lots of individualized feel-good opportunities. Results don't matter so much, as long as everyone is feeling OK about what they are doing.

There is nothing new about the progressive idea except that it now dominates educational thinking. Holmes's survey predictably found that a majority of CEOs ranked the progressive philosophy first or second out of six educational models. Other philosophies such as preparing people for work (technocratic), developing their intellectual and cultural lives (cultural) or even their character (traditional) just didn't appeal to the CEOs.

In stark contrast to Ontario's school bosses, the people selected either the cultural or technocratic philosophies as their first choice. Progressive ranked fifth, because the prevailing folk-wisdom says that schools should cultivate intellectual and social skills as well as prepare students for good citizenship and livelihood in a democracy.

The Educational Divide also pops up in attitudes towards testing. Only 11 percent of the CEOs thought annual testing of students on basic skills is necessary, whereas nearly 60 percent of the non-educators supported routine assessment.

Like most monopolies, progressivism shamelessly promotes itself. Holmes notes that "an applicant without progressive sympathies will have difficulty obtaining promotion to principal in a climate where progressivism is so strongly held by system leaders." Pluralism has no place in our schools.

The NDP solution to this regressive quagmire is to hire CEOs of different colour and sex. Although this is a laudable idea, the educational system will make sure that the new recruits share the same ideological blinkers as their predecessors. The experts, after all, know what's best.

To Holmes the only sure way to breach the Educational Divide is to provide real school choice. Provinces can do this either by funding private and religious schools or by requiring school boards to provide education that respects the needs and values of local communities.

That doesn't mean the death of progressivism, just some healthy competition that respects the pluralistic interests of ordinary Canadians as opposed to the deadly cultural paternalism of our élites.

A Good Administrator

As a social problem, the decline of educational standards is unique: there is no one with a vested interest in its continuation. I have yet to hear anyone try to make a case for bad schools.

—James Enochs

In an age when many school administrators don't even own a library let alone read books, James Enochs stands out as an unorthodox and literate leader. The radical superintendent of California's Modesto City Schools District not only admires Albert Camus but can quote e. e. cummings and discuss Arthur Schlesinger Jr.'s recent bestseller, *The Disuniting of America* (a critique of multiculturalism), all with equal passion.

In addition to his cultural literacy and profound commitment to public schooling, Enochs is probably the only school superindentent in the Golden State who doesn't belong to the Association of California School Administrators. "I quit," he says, "after conference after conference was either on early retirement or investment for the future, and this when the whole system is falling apart." He defines school leadership, by the way, as an "act of elevation, the elevation of standards, performance and satisfaction."

Enochs' departure from the status quo began in a big and public way in 1976 when he served as Modesto's assistant superintendent. At that time the school district served a largely white and affluent community beholden to the fruits of irrigated farming in the San Joaquin Valley. Enochs, an early supporter of Cesar Chavez and other populist causes, could see standards in North America's public schools floundering ("In California the future comes earlier"). He decided to act before Modesto became another casualty in the continent's undeclared war to make all public institutions worthless boxes.

To restore common sense and public confidence Enochs published an eight-point plan, an Eight Commandments of education. It remains as timeless today as it did more than sixteen years ago when Enochs nailed it to the door of every Modesto school.

1. Schools must state unequivocally what they believe in and stand for, how they will measure success or failure and who is responsible for the results. ("It is a worthwhile exercise to remind ourselves occasionally that the schools belong to the people.")
2. Good schools require community involvement.
3. The public school loses its dignity as an armed camp and should not have to serve students guilty of serious and persistent crimes.
4. Students have rights as well as responsibilities.
5. High performance takes place in a framework of high expectations.
6. The full responsibility of learning cannot be transferred from the student to the teacher.
7. Requiring students to do things that are demonstrably beneficial to them is not undemocratic.
8. In order for a good academic program to succeed it

needs continued support over a reasonable period of time.

Enochs then supported the plan with basic school reforms, or what he calls "the machinery that often defeats" educators. It included a basic-skills competency plan from kindergarten to grade eight. District teachers defined minimum competencies as "the lowest acceptable level of attainment required for reasonable progress at the next grade level." Grade six teachers told grade five teachers, "You shouldn't send me a pupil who doesn't know ..." And so on down the line. Competency was assessed yearly in reading, writing and math with standardized tests or plain old written exams. Although Modesto established a floor for student performance, it set no ceiling.

Enochs also prepared written student conduct codes from kindergarten to grade twelve. The conduct codes, brief and to the point, provided for evaluation of students' "citizenship." Students who were tardy or came to class unprepared now risked losing certain athletic privileges that could be regained each quarter by improving their "citizenship."

To complement the behaviour codes, Enochs also introduced in the early grades a "character education program." Noted the administrator at the time: "The program is simply predicated on the belief that there are still some values upon which all reasonable people can agree." These values included courage and conviction, generosity and kindness, honesty, honour and justice.

The program worked so well that student scores and spirits soared. Struck by the populist strength of the Modesto Plan, the Reverend Jesse Jackson adopted it for EXCEL, a special inner-city school project for black students. In spite of Enochs' proactive savvy, the community of Modesto neither cheered nor booed. And then time passed, the community changed and North America's school crisis deepened.

Since those heady days Modesto is no longer the suburban middle class community it once was, and James Enochs is no longer the assistant superintendent.

For eight years now he has been the super, and as a result the Modesto Plan, with its focus on doing what schools do best—teach and learn—remains essentially intact. "I still believe that most of it is really working pretty well," reflects the fifty-eight-year-old Enochs. But his schools, like most urban Canadian schools, have been changed by events around them.

More than a quarter of Modesto's thirty thousand students are now what Americans call "limited English proficient." The immigrants filling Modesto's schools hail from Mexico, Thailand or Cambodia. Nearly a fifth of the board's pupils live in poverty. Stanislaus County, where Modesto is located, has one of the highest rates of unemployment and teenage pregnancy in California. Thirty-four active gangs own parts of the city, while in 1993, police made four hundred arrests on or near school grounds.

"I spend more money on security and anti-truancy programs now," says Enochs. That's money that went to educational programs in the past. "But I can't teach them if they aren't there and if the schools aren't safe." Adds Enochs, "I've seen stuff in school that I thought I would never see. Fifth- and sixth-grade Cambodian students who are pregnant. Children from homes with fifteen people sharing two bedrooms. Kids who come to school with their teeth rotting out of their mouths.... It's crazy."

But unlike many of his contemporaries, Enochs has not abandoned Modesto's standards or its Fourth R:

responsibility. "We have to integrate certain social services into the system. You can't teach hungry children. You deal with that, but then the education must begin."

The district's emphasis on reading, writing and math still gives it one of the best performance records in the state as well as an attendance rate in the high 90s. Modesto stands alone with no process goals (feeling as content work), and annually releases a 250-page report on the status of its schools, good and bad.

But to maintain this accountability the stubborn superintendent says "No" more often than "Yes." He has, for example, steadfastly kept "the self-esteem crap" out of his schools, believing that a healthy sense of self flows from academic achievement and not vice versa. (In contrast, most of the state's one hundred school districts have swallowed the New Age line of a 1990 California education task force that magically defined self-esteem as "something that empowers us to live responsibly." The panel then urged mandatory work in self-esteem in the "total curricula," even though its own commissioned research directly refuted such practice.)

Enochs has also fought the "Me First" brigades, from the religious right to feminists, who "want to shape the schools in their own image. It's really hard to stay on top and not go down one of the side streets."

As for the future of schooling, he's ambivalent and often discouraged. Since he issued his call for a restoration of standards some sixteen years ago, teachers and administrators have merely repeated a three-point mantra: "They are demoralized and cynical. They assign blame for their plight to others, and the solutions they propose impose no personal sacrifices or hardships." The dangerous circle of irresponsibility that prevents people from caring and making a small difference where it matters has gotten wider, not smaller, says Enochs.

He laments that the school voucher system might soon arrive in California, spelling the end of an already sick public system. He's not sure what separate schools for the poor and for the rich will mean for North American life, but he doesn't approve. Given that high school diplomas now range "from the sublime to counterfeit paper" he would like to see national standards that define what skills and values an American citizen should hold at the end of school. He does not expect them soon.

In the meantime he will lead the Modesto schools through their social storms, defending standards, not with bland formulas or glib manipulations but "with common sense, character and good old-fashioned guts." As a rebel administrator he rarely gets invited to education socials, but he takes pride in the fact that his district constantly gets requests for its materials on curriculum and assessment. "And that," says Enochs, "speaks a lot more than being one of the boys."

ATTENTION DEFICIT DISORDER   This is the newest and most fashionable expression for hyperactivity. Anywhere from 3 to 10 percent of all Canadian children allegedly suffer from this condition and scores of books have been written about it.

The essential facts are these: nobody seems to know much about the disorder, or if it is really a disorder at all. Hyperactive boys seem to outnumber girls by four to one. Some children seem to grow out of the condition; others internalize it.

Behaviours associated with hyperactivity include fidgety hands and feet, excessive talking (at the most inconvenient times) and difficulty following instructions and sustaining attention. The big one, of course, is being easily distracted by noises, colours or even changes in routine. Educators are rarely consistent in their diagnosis. What one educator or psychiatrist might pronouce as hyperactivity another might call an emotional disturbance.

The causes of hyperactivity are uncertain but probably stem from a combination of factors: bad diet, compulsive TV viewing, family genes, chemical sensitivities (allergies to paints, formaldehyde and cleaners), punitive child-rearing practices, poor classroom placements and real biochemical imbalances.

Although many doctors recommend medication, such as Ritalin, as a first resort, drugs should come last, if at all. Rather, the school environment is a place parents should look to for help. Research has shown that hyperactive children perform best in environments where they are provided with more feedback and more choices, and where they are given work in which they can pace themselves.

As a teacher, I often gave parents a shopping list that identifies teaching methods that work with hyperactive children. Montessori schools, by the way, model many of these practices.

1. Give this student more positive reinforcement than the average child for work well done.
2. Teach this student responsibility by assigning tasks with the clear expectation that the student will carry them out.
3. Assign work that is at the student's level of mastery so that he or she experiences success and continues learning.
4. Divide assigned work into units, such as three ten-minute assignments rather than one thirty-minute

assignment. The student should be allowed to complete one activity before proceeding to another. If possible, check work immediately. This student needs more feedback than the average student.

5. Reinforce verbal instructions by writing assignments on the board. Have this student repeat instructions or directions more often than other students.

6. Prepare this student for sudden changes in routine. He may need a simple schedule on his desk to learn and follow a daily routine.

7. Do not overwhelm this student with too much work. If the student writes slowly, decrease the length, don't simplify the content, of written-language assignments. Make appropriate accommodations on tests.

8. Find opportunities for movement for this student. Sustained sitting will lead to loss of concentration and the appearance of behaviours that drive parents and teachers to distraction, so schedule lots of breaks or activity periods in daily routine for this student.

9. A small class size or high adult–student ratio is a must for this student. His desk and area should be free of distractions, located next to quiet students, the teacher or a corner. An opaque screen or study carrel may be effective for screening out distractions.

10. This student will not learn from teachers who only talk, talk and talk. Teaching should be fast-paced and should use short instructional commands. Hands-on assignments, where appropriate, are a must. Lessons should be logical and admit only one interpretation—the right one.(Sloppy teaching can confuse a hyperactive kid pretty quickly.)

11. This student will need more repetition than the

average student. Short daily drills over a long period of time will be more successful than long drills over a short period of time.

12. Be consistent. Spell out what is acceptable and unacceptable work (number correct or completed). If necessary, provide a model of acceptable work. Make sure the student understands these expectations.

See also **RITALIN.**

B

BULLYING   Both schools and bullies have evolved together. Although classroom lore assigns an almost sanctioned status to the bully (and the bullied), educators needn't treat them as a natural part of schooling. Such laissez-faire attitudes underestimate the damage bullies can do and does nothing to correct the problem.

Nearly twenty years of ground-breaking research by the Norwegian psychologist Dan Olweus has shown that bullies can and should be put in their place. Believing that every child has a democratic right to attend school without harassment, Olweus has developed an effective model for curtailing bullying in schools by 50 to 70 percent. His approach, which is now being tried in some Toronto schools, takes little money or time but, rather, a perceptual shift on the part of educators.

According to Olweus, the typical bully doesn't fit any class stereotype. Most bullies don't come from the proverbial "wrong side of the tracks." Nor are bullies insecure kids. They are generally confident students who have a strong need for power and dominance. Olweus contends that too little love and care (the characteristics of many families, irrespective of class) and too much "freedom" in childhood all tend to make remarkable browbeaters, bulldozers and tyrants. (See **ABSENTEE PARENTS**.)

Not surprisingly, a school career in bullying often leads to a career in crime. Olweus found that 60 percent of the boys who bullied their peers between the ages of eleven and fifteen had been convicted of a crime by the age of twenty-four.

Contrary to popular belief, bullies infrequently pick on the fat, the ugly and the bespectacled. In fact, the majority of victims seem to be fellow students who are more anxious and insecure than their peers. Male victims tend to be physically weaker. The victims have many friends and are quiet and cautious. They are often singled out because of their reluctance to retaliate or mount an effective defence. Being bullied as a child has links to emotional instability, suicide and violent death in adulthood. Notes Olweus: "Depression and poor self-esteem in later life can often be traced back directly to the victim's experience of being bullied."

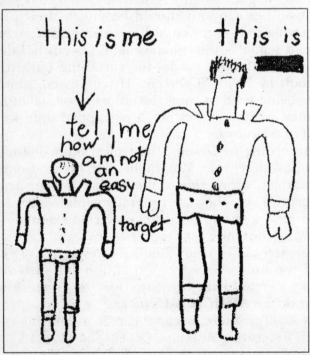

Sarah's Plight: Her parents eventually placed her in another school.

Minister of Education
Dear Mr. Cook,

   I am   and I go to
              and I am in Grade 3 I
have been repeatedly bullied by
          and I would like it to stop.
He has no right to do this and
the school isn't doing much about it
and I think my principal is telling
me that I am lying.   has
been doing this to some of my friends
too and he will not stop no matter
what. Can you please do something
about this now or else it will be
too late. I am scared to go to
school and that should not be
happening because I have the
right to go to school and be safe.

Every time I go to school or think
of   I get a stomach ache
and I DO NOT WANT THAT
AT ALL! My opinion is
          should go to a different school.
          may have some problems
but that does not give him the right
to take it out on kids like us
We   have not done anything
so why should we put up with this?

P.S. If   the school
doesn't do something
soon I will keep writing
to you and then I go to
a different school because
I am fed up

IT has got
TO stop
NOW.

Olweus's program of intervention (described in *Bullying at School—What We Know And What We Can Do*) begins with a questionnaire that establishes the extent of the problem. Nearly half of all Toronto students, for instance, reported being bullied more than once during a school term. These findings are first discussed at a community level. Then teachers and students work together to create a caring school environment where the adults set firm limits on unacceptable behaviour. Every incident comes with a consequence, and witnesses of bullying are responsible for intervening or getting help. If necessary the school will contact parents and provide protection for victims.

The program is now being used in Canada (Toronto), the Netherlands, Belgium, Italy, Germany and Norway. European school districts that no longer accept bullying as part of schooling have recorded substantial drops in vandalism, fighting, drunkenness and truancy.

See also **SCHOOL VIOLENCE** and Appendix 14.

C

CHARACTER EDUCATION

To say that all beliefs are equally deserving of tolerance is to admit they are all equally unimportant.
—Christopher Lasch

One of the subjects often absent from the debate about school reform is moral education. Its absence is not only distressing but ominous. For unless public schools reclaim their former roles as serious centres of moral learning, as opposed to client-based entertainment modules where values change as frequently as television channels, our children will remain at risk.

Such is the weighty theme of a new and excellent book by William Kilpatrick, a professor of education at Boston College. *Why Johnny Can't Tell Right from Wrong* details not only how schools abandoned character development in the 1960s in favour of "decision-making abilities," but the soulless and painful consequences for both school and society. (A maverick Toronto author, William Gairdner, mines a similar vein in *The War Against the Family*.)

In the course of examining how educators have let children become the moral guardians of schools, Kilpatrick presents a telling scenario. Imagine for a moment that you are a parent and have been presented with two models of moral education for a grade five class.

Model A, the one championed by educators since the late sixties, encourages children to develop their own values. Teachers present students with ethical dilemmas, packaged in game-like TV show formats with fun (and real) names like "Me-ology," "Quest," "Decide," "Here's Looking at You" and "Values and Choices." Students are openly encouraged to debate and exchange opinion in an environment where there is no right or wrong, because children and adults should suspend all judgment when it comes to values.

Model B follows the educational path that traditional cultures such as the Blackfoot, Lubavitchers and the Amish have always chosen. It specifically calls upon the whole school to model and teach specific virtues and character traits such as courage, justice, self-control, honesty, responsibility, charity and obedience to lawful authority. After these concepts have been introduced and explained by a teacher, they are illustrated with memorable examples from history, literature and current events. The teacher not only lives by these virtues but also encourages students to practise them in their own lives.

Kilpatrick has no doubt that the vast majority of working class and middle class parents would choose Model B, "because they have a better grasp of what is at stake, and because it is their own children who are in question." In contrast the author finds that many teachers and most educators would opt for Model A, because it is "more fun" and less worrisome. Maintaining and upholding principles, virtues or beliefs implies hard work and consistent thought.

The educational establishment's continued commitment to "values clarification" and other exercises in relativism is rather strange, given that recent studies on "affective" or feelings-as-the-source-of-morality programs such as Decide and Quest have found that these programs actually led to increased drug use among student participants. Research on value-free sex education programs reveals that their graduates engaged in more sex. They also had little impact on pregnancy rates or the use of birth control.

"What sex educators have in the back of their minds," writes Kilpatrick, "is a picture of some imaginary Scandinavian town where, by the miracle of social engineering, life is lived with much rationality ... and where healthy, honest and guilt-free boys and girls sample the joys of sex.... That is the idyllic/utopian vision, but the actual result of their programs looks more like a vision from Kafka."

Equally disturbing—and equally ignored by educators—is the disavowal of these "humanistic" programs by many of their original authors. The eminent psychologist Abraham Maslow belatedly recognized the anti-intellectualism implicit in human potential psychology and made it very clear it was not intended for children. So,too, did Carl Rogers. The most outspoken of all, however, is Mr William Coulson.

The Confessions of William Coulson

William Coulson, a sixty-year-old psychologist, travels the continent making apologies.

A celebrated past drives his expiatory mission: three decades ago the man championed "the human potential movement," worked alongside Carl Rogers and Abraham Maslow and edited several texts on "getting in touch with your feelings."

But Mr Coulson now defines this part of his life as a grand mistake. The apologetic lectures, says the staunch Roman Catholic, are all "part of my penance."

Critics, however, have branded the man a "kook," a right-wing fanatic and a nasty denigrator of his friend and co-worker, Carl Rogers. Although Mr Coulson's politics probably veer towards the right, the psychologist deserves none of these labels.

His story begins in Wisconsin where he and Rogers

applied non-directive, non-judgmental therapy to schizophrenics in 1963. When the good citizens of that state said they didn't want to volunteer for therapy in a similar project for normal people, the psychologists set up shop in La Jolla, California. "There we picked on school children because they were the most compliant."

The experimenters introduced their program to the six hundred nuns and several thousand children in fifty-nine schools. When they had finished with their message of self-actualization, "openness to experience" and "doing what you choose is liberating," none of the nuns were still teaching and only two schools remained in the system.

This result troubled Coulson, as it did Rogers, who later referred to affective education incorporating group experience as "that pattern of failure" and "that damn thing."

Coulson also witnessed the therapy's potent effects on fellow practitioners. Practising personal growth with pimping, pandering, prostitution and pornography, one of Coulson's former associates, Hal Lyon Jr.—once the U. S. deputy assistant undersecretary of education for the gifted and talented—actualized himself into a state prison.

Abraham Maslow also began to notice that Dionysian-type education didn't respect his Jewish heritage of books and libraries. His private journals, released in 1979, contain almost 1,300 pages of regrets about "doing your own thing." He even concluded that self-actualization does not occur in young people because they have not learned enough about evil in themselves and others, and they lack wisdom.

Despite these growing misgivings, affective education began to invade the schools as self-esteem courses, values clarification, and so-called anti-drug programs like Quest.

As Coulson tirelessly explains to largely parent audiences, the research says that non-directive sex and drug programs teach kids a very confused and frightening logic that goes like this: "I'm a wonderful person. Smoking cigarettes, taking drugs or sleeping around aren't so bad because I do those things, and I'm a wonderful person."

By 1977 Coulson, the father of seven, couldn't stomach any more of affective education's legacy of violent, confused and illiterate children. Ever since then he has effectively challenged the use of simple-minded Rogerian techniques in schools, ranging from peer mediation to self-esteem courses.

"When a person writes a good essay or wins a race, their self-esteem goes up," notes Coulson. "But when people write a bad paper or lose a race they feel bad about what they did and ought to. That's Nature's way of getting us to do a better job tomorrow."

The psychologist also was the first to blow the whistle on Quest's "Skills for Living." Partly funded by firms like R.J. Reynolds, a cigarette manufacturer, the program shunned traditional morality and assumed that kids "should be allowed to make their own choices"—just the kind of attitude a marketer of drugs, alcohol or condoms would appreciate.

A 1989 study on the program found that participation in Quest was followed by striking increases in the use of drugs and alcohol. Although now revised with a more direct message, Quest still reaches an audience of two million Canadian and American students a year. "Capitalism," adds Mr Coulson, "has jumped upon the bandwagon of bad education."

During a recent five-country tour of Europe the chastened psychologist outlined the American experience with affective education to attentive audiences. The Swiss and Irish seemed most responsive, he says. One

Zurich psychologist explained his concern this way: "We have no natural resources here except the minds of our young people, and we can't afford to lose that."

The solutions that Coulson and Kilpatrick detail for schools and parents are rooted in history and are realistic and deeply moral. The school, he advises, must create a counterculture to the amoral and image-diluted society around it by saying, "Here's where we are and what we stand for." And to build character it might very well have to employ what traditional societies have always employed: epics, stories, songs and rituals that remind children that the virtuous path is the most difficult but the most rewarding. Parents and teachers must tread this path together.

See also **SEXUALITY AND SEX EDUCATION, SCHOOL VIOLENCE** and **VALUES CLARIFICATION**.

CHARTER SCHOOLS   When a group of parents approached a school district north of St Paul, Minnesota, four years ago asking for an elementary Montessori school, the district hemmed and hawed. Montessori teachers are hard to find, the administrators complained, and transportation would be a major pain. Where would we find a building? they asked.

Then Minnesota's state government levelled the playing field. It passed charter school legislation, granting public bodies other than a school board the power to set up autonomous, performance-based public schools under a state charter.

Armed with the new legislation, the Montessori-minded parents went back to their district and said, "We're going to apply for a charter." Within a week the district had reconsidered. Suddenly there was no shortage of Montessori teachers, an empty school just

happened to be available and the busing issue had a
simple solution: a shuttle from the central bus depot.

To Ted Kolderie, a Minnesota-based policy analyst
specializing in charter schools, the story illustrates the
power of a good idea. "Charter schools carry tremendous dynamism," says Kolderie. "They can affect the
whole behaviour of a district and move it towards doing
something better for children.... They are a wild card."

This is a bold claim for what is only a three-year-old
experiment in the United States. But Minnesota pio-
neered the charter idea after failing to change its
schools with a host of other reforms. The rationale of
the politicians was pretty radical: if the state can't
force schools to be better, then it will give them a good
reason to change on their own. Now twenty states have
followed Minnesota's lead, including California,
Michigan, Massachusetts and Colorado. With the
exception of Michigan, all have placed limits on the
number of schools that can receive "charter status."

According to Kolderie, the uncompromised charter
idea (professional educational bodies have watered
down the concept in some states) honours several
basic principles.

1. It breaks the school board monopoly on public education by permitting a body besides the local
   board—a university or municipality, for example—
   to run a public school.
2. The sponsor either honours a set of perfomance
   objectives for its students over a three- or five-year
   period or loses its charter. Charter schools must
   also respect the fundamentals of public education:
   no religious bias; no fees; open admissions; no
   racial discrimination; and no enrolment of only
   "nice" kids. (Massachusetts, for example, limits its
   charters to poor communities.)

3. Management on site becomes a real and potent force, because a charter effectively makes a school a legal entity. Accountability cannot be passed elsewhere in such an institution.

4. A charter ends the school board game of "dealing" with schools. According to Mr Kolderie, the all-too-predictable ethic of "We don't give you autonomy; in return, you don't give us accountability" gets a quick burial. A charter shifts the emphasis from the board's obsessive control over how things are done to a school's natural concern about what is being learned.

5. Using a funding formula set by the government, the state pays the school directly. Teachers have the choice of being employees, owners or members of a co-operative. If employees, they may choose to bargain as part of the teachers' union or just with the charter school. The National Educational Association, America's largest teachers' union, recently formed a committee to study the charter idea after vigorously opposing the legislation in three states and suffering three successive defeats.

The implications of charter schools are mostly good. A community of autonomous schools, for instance, could shift big urban school boards away from being fat providers of mediocre administrative services to the lean buyers of instruction that has proven to be effective. Wrote one Colorado school board administrator, who initially opposed the charter idea: "Moving away from the role of exclusive [producer] of education may be a blessing in disguise."

Although the charter school is a young and imperfect idea (there are no data on the performance of these schools or how this approach may strengthen or weaken ties between elementary and secondary schools), it does go to the heart of the problem. "School is supposed to be about learning and the interests of kids ...," says Kolderie. "But for the districts and the adults in them the system pays off whether the objective is accomplished or not," because the state assures the district its customers, revenues and jobs, no matter how dismal the results.

Kolderie doesn't think it is smart "to expect performance from an institution in which the rewards are provided whether the mission has been accomplished or not."

Across Canada, parents are now either applying for charters or lobbying their provincial governments for charter school legislation. To date Alberta is the first and only province with such legislation. Dr Joe Freedman, a tireless school reformer, recently sent a ten-page proposal to the country's anglophone school boards as well as fifty-one deans of education.

The proposal: given that the educational system is in a nasty and self-defeating gridlock, real change seems, at best, improbable, and at worst, impossible. The answer, says Freedman, is "an alternative model school."

Much like the United States' charter school, Freedman's alternative model would operate in a "free education zone" established by a public school board— a sort of private school with a public school conscience.

As such, the "model school" would offer the following guarantees. Its enrolment would reflect the make-up of its local community and thereby "avoid the criticism of élitism," says Freedman; spending per pupil would be the same as or lower than that in nearby public schools; the charter school would operate autonomously, free of the control of the local school board, teachers' union and extreme parental self-interest, whether religious or political.

The principal and teaching staff would be committed to teaching techniques, whether progressive or traditional, that large-scale empirical research has identified as the best, particularly for the disadvantaged. As a "living laboratory," the school would feature a well-considered research protocol from the beginning, which would allow comparisons with public and private schools. Perhaps the key question to be answered by these disclosures would be this: "Compared to existing public schools, how did this school do with its disadvantaged children?"

The school would also respect the simple pedagogical truth that strong consensus plus shared responsiblities leads to strong results. Parents will have to agree on behaviour, discipline, appearance, homework and academic expectations. And teachers will have to agree on teaching methods, academic expectations and assessment, as well as a core of values.

Freedman's proposal is a bold one, and it challenges all the laws of existing school governance. If the board ascertains that there is community and financial support of "the alternative model," then Freedman asks for a three-year trial from kindergarten to grade three or six, because "schooling goes wrong early."

At this point, a community board of governors would be established and school board representation would be limited to one seat only. The board of governors would select a principal, and the principal in turn would select the staff. All participants would know that they are involved in a trial whose results would be closely and publicly scrutinized.

Once the character of the school has been determined, a community education campaign would follow. It would inform parents of the nature of the charter and what the school would expect of them should they apply. A random lottery of the applicants would ensure that the children honestly reflect the community.

Establishing a model school would cost money. To fund the information campaign and research protocol, Freedman suggests that school boards solicit support from the federal government, universities, businesses or charitable foundations.

Freedman has no doubt that boards participating in this national project will benefit in two ways. The charter school will help clarify and focus the board's purpose and will give the board some well-earned status as a supporter of an educational research project that could make a difference for the nation's children.

For parents, the model school idea offers a common sense way of getting involved in their children's education: home support of a school's clearly defined mission and obligations. According to Freedman's design, a model school wouldn't shy away from reminding parents that they should be reading to their children, enforcing daily routines, surpervising homework and controlling the amount of time spent watching television.

The intent of Freedman's proposal is revolutionary. If successful, his charter school idea could point towards better ways of educating children in a pluralistic democracy and release the gridlock holding back the public education system. If unsuccessful, a score of model schools would represent only the failure of a well-defined experiment, as opposed to the failure of a whole system.

For copies of Dr Freedman's proposal, send $4.00 to the Society for Advancing Education Research, 57 Allan Close, Red Deer, Alberta, Canada T4R 1A4.

For more general information, *The Charter School Chronicle* is an invaluable source. For a subscription to the Michigan-based monthly, phone or fax 517-772-9115.

Charter school pioneers in Colorado recently published a useful primer called *Planning a Charter School: One Colorado Group's Experience*. It is available from Angel Press, 534 Detroit Street, Denver, Colorado 80206. Send a cheque or money order in U. S. funds for $9.00. Add $2.00 for postage and handling.

See also Appendix 12.

CHILD-CENTRED LEARNING   The American philosopher John Dewey is the modern father of this form of pedagogy, although its roots go back to the eighteenth-century French essayist Jean-Jacques Rousseau. Dewey, a sort of "socially responsible reporter-reformer," essentially reacted to the extreme formalism and rigidity of schools in the 1890s and demanded that things should be done differently.

Dewey, who was also rebelling against his own strict religious upbringing, believed that schools should "adjust" children to the social world with a much broader free-market type of curriculum. He viewed schools as instruments for social change and hoped they could eventually humanize North American capitalism. Deploring the traditional emphasis on reading and math, he called for more "learning by doing."

Dewey, too, introduced the notion that process was more important than product. He wrote that "the educational process has no end beyond itself; it is its own end." He believed that "growth was the characteristic of life" and that education "is all one with growing." This liberal technocrat viewed life and education as a series of endless problems to be solved, forgetting that the joys and tragedies of life cannot be so easily quantified through problem-solving.

His legacy in North American education is awesome; it explains why he is often rated as the most important educational thinker since Plato. The advocates of the open classroom, whole language, values clarification and individualized teaching all cite Dewey as their inspiration. "Proficiency in learning comes not from reading and listening but from action, from doing and experiencing," he wrote. As every parent with schoolchildren knows, the key tenets of child-centred learning are "readiness," "choice," "needs," "play" and "discovery."

This naturalistic credo is an inherent argument against public schooling. "If each child is unique, and each requires a specific pedagogical approach appropriate to him or her and to no other, the construction of an all-embracing pedagogy or general principles of teaching becomes an impossibility," notes the British educator Brian Simon. "And indeed research has shown that primary school teachers who have taken the priority of individualisation to heart, find it difficult to do more than ensure that each child is in fact engaged on the series of tasks which the teacher sets up for the child; the complex management problem which then arises takes the teacher's full energies. Hence the approach of teachers who endeavour to implement these precepts is necessarily didactic [telling kids what to do] since it becomes literally impossible to stimulate enquiry or to lead from behind."

Although the progressive model can work well in some settings, it has severe limitations. Howard Gardner, a Harvard educator and author of the theory of multiple intelligences, recently spelled out these constraints in *The Unschooled Mind: How Children Think and How Schools Should Teach* (published by Basic Books).

After noting that progressive education required well-trained and dedicated teachers, he plainly defined the approach's bias: "Progressive education works best with children who come from richly endowed homes, whose parents are deeply interested in their children's education and who arrive at school with motivation and curiosity." It is optimistic, he adds, to expect success with children who come from other neighbourhoods and backgrounds. "Progressive education ought to be fused with an approach that can offer more nuanced kinds of help and support to students who are not independent-minded, to students who lack self-discipline, and to students who exhibit distinct learning disabilities as well as to students who have unusual strengths. A large and possibly growing number of students need the kind of help, support, modeling, and/or scaffolding that has often been seen as antithetical to the unstructured atmosphere of progressive education."

Studies of progressive or child-centred classrooms have indeed found that they yield unequal results, favour the advantaged, widen learning gaps between rich and poor children and generally mirror the same amoral outcomes of any laissez-faire approach, whether applied to economics or parenting. The lucky, in other words, get what they need. In fact, progressive schools rarely get the progressive results that Dewey yearned for.

In later life Dewey often despaired of the excesses practised in the name of child-centred or progressive education. He did not want schools to become havens of anti-intellectualism, but his ideas were implemented that way. "Progressive schools," he noted, "set store by individuality, and sometimes it seems to be thought that orderly organization of subject matter is hostile to the needs of students in their individual character. But individuality is something developing and to be continuously attained, not something given all at once and ready-made." Last but not least he saw progressivism becoming such a dogmatic ism that its reaction to other isms prevented its followers from even thinking about education itself.

In 1981 Carl Bereiter, one of North America's leading educational psychologists, gave this honest assessment of child-centred teaching in the journal *Interchange:*

> Child-centered approaches have evolved sophisticated ways of managing informal educational activities but have remained at a primitive level in the design of means to achieve learning objectives.... The conceptual analysis of learning problems tends to be vague and irrelevant, big on name-dropping and low in incisiveness.... Child-centered educators have evolved a style of school life that has much in its favor. Until they develop an effective pedagogy to go with it, however, it does not appear to be an acceptable way of teaching disadvantaged children.

Or a great many other children for that matter.

See also **CONSTRUCTIVISM**, **MONTESSORI**, **GRANT**, **SUMMERHILL**, **CHARACTER EDUCATION** and **WHOLE LANGUAGE** and Appendix 16.

CHILDREN'S LITERATURE   Few modern children's authors have been as popular as Dr Seuss and for good reason. His whimsical stories not only respect a child's moral imagination but provide a true example of the power of fine writing.

> Your Majesty, please.... I don't like to complain,
> But down here below, we are feeling great pain.

I know, up on top you are seeing great sights,
But down at the bottom we, too, should have
rights.

—Mack, the turtle

Dr Seuss, who died in 1991, wrote many splendid
books for children but his greatest achievement was
the cold-blooded murder of Dick and Jane (North
America's first deconstructionist couple) and their
insipid pet, Spot.

Although most parents and kids fondly remember
Dr Seuss as the fanciful inventor of "logical insanity"
and such ridiculous characters as Yertle the Turtle and
the Cat in the Hat, the good doctor did much more
than write humorous verse.

The artist and latter-day Aesop not only exposed the
banality of "look-and-say" basal readers but defiantly
promoted the importance of phonics for teaching
reading. Children, he reasoned, loved language patterns whether they be "red fish, blue fish" or a "mouse
in a house." (See **PHONICS**.)

He also championed a literature for kids that
emphasized the three R's—"Rhyme, Rhythm and
Reason"—and never apologized for the profound
moral tone of his books. In his words, "Either the
good guys win or the bad guys win." To his last illustration the populist resolutely avoided sugarplum bun-
nies, and more than 200 million parents dearly loved
him for it.

Born in Springfield, Massachusetts, in 1904 to
German immigrants, Theodor Seuss Geisel originally
intended to become a teacher. But after the undergraduate merrily illustrated his way through
Dartmouth College, he found that Oxford University's
panjandrums had no funny bones. When its august
press turned down his proposal to illustrate *Paradise*

Lost with an archangel sliding down a sunbeam, oilcan in hand, Geisel switched his English studies to Jonathan Swift.

After a professor dryly advised the student to investigate Swift's teenage years, the only period during which the satirist didn't write a single word, Geisel threw up his arms and wisely forsook the idea of formal education altogether.

However, he added "Dr" to his middle name so as not to disappoint his father, the superintendent of a zoo. "I figured by doing that, I saved him about ten thousand dollars," he once said.

During the 1920s Geisel penned cartoons for various magazines, where his zany animals caught the eye of a Standard Oil executive. He employed the young man to promote Standard's then popular bug-killer, Flit, and Geisel's "Quick Henry, the Flit" soon made advertising history.

In 1936 Dr Seuss wrote *And To Think That I Saw It on Mulberry Street,* a book whose catchy title was inspired by the musical rhythm of an ocean liner's engines. Originally rejected by twenty-seven publishers, the story of Marco and his ever-growing imagination put Dr Seuss on the literary map.

He followed this success with a string of tight stories peopled with fantastic characters, including the artful Bartholomew Cubbins, the greedy Grinch and the compassionate tree-sitter, Horton. But he had yet to make his greatest impact on children's reading when, in 1954, a searing critique of North America's bland Dick and Jane readers in *Life* magazine pointedly invited Dr Seuss to help prevent kids "from bogging down on the First R."

Seuss's lively antidote to the "Run, Spot, run" school of reading took a mischievous cat, 223 rhyming words and one long year to write. Educators initially ruled

The Cat in the Hat frivolous, but Rudolf Flesch of *Why Johnny Can't Read* fame immediately recognized its brillance and subsequently called Seuss "a genius, pure and simple."

Seuss never abandoned his belief that phonics mattered greatly for beginning readers (a sentiment supported by reading research) and followed the Cat's popular acclaim with a series called Beginner Books. Shortly afterwards Bennett Cerf, Geisel's publisher, cheerfully bet the artist that he couldn't write a book with only fifty words; Dr Seuss replied with *Green Eggs and Ham*. "It's the only book I ever wrote that still makes me laugh," said Geisel before his death at the ripe age of eighty-seven.

But Seuss was never satisfied just with the endearing magic of egg-hatching elephants or rapping Wumps. Like his favourite childhood mentors, Dickens, Stevenson and Swift, he felt it was impossible to tell a story without a moral. Hence Yertle, the domineering turtle, is a caricature of Adolf Hitler; Marvin K. Mooney, a parody of Richard Nixon; and the Lorax is an ecological parable that appeared long before green-minded tales were popular.

Geisel, a cat-loving perfectionist who entertained few vanities other than smoking and fossil-collecting, never had any children of his own because he didn't think he could write with kids peering over his shoulder. He often told parents, though, that if "you have 'em, I'll amuse 'em."

He kept that promise with a wink, I think.

COMPUTERS

Where is the wisdom we have lost in knowledge?
Where is the knowledge we have in information?

—T. S. Eliot

When it comes to buying the sweet-sounding promises of technological progress, educators often behave like hurried consumers: they ask few questions, read little research and then spend lots of other people's money on bogus products. The short but troubled history of computers in our schools clearly illustrates this short-sightedness.

Beginning in the early 1980s, educators, business people and many parents championed the machine as a revolutionary cure-all that would create higher-achieving students, more dynamic schools and a more competitive workforce for the Information Age. Some exuberant propagandists even suggested that the computer would replace teachers altogether.

Given these bold claims, it's not surprising that nearly every elementary classroom now owns at least one computer. In addition, most Canadian high schools now come equipped with between twenty-five and fifty machines, while as many as a dozen experimental schools across the country have gone totally high-tech with a computer for each pupil.

But this ten-year trial and status game has failed to deliver on its promises, proving once again that educators (and parents) should not jump on bandwagons and adopt new teaching tools unless they have good evidence that they can improve student performance. And given an appalling absence of good research, solid guidance or useful software for computers, the machine remains a classroom trend without a solid educational mission.

To date, what the research shows is that computers can do only a few things well. Educators have learned, for instance, that computers seem most effective with underachieving students, particularly males, in teaching basic skills. This seems largely due to software programs that provide better step-by-step instruction or more positive feedback than the average teacher. One program, known as Pals (Principles of the Alphabet Literacy System), provides such a highly structured approach to reading and writing that struggling high school students can make up three grades' worth of material in just twenty weeks. Yet, in spite of such evidence, most inner-city schools in east Montreal or Winnipeg's North End rarely see such programs, let alone the computers needed to run them.

In addition to drill and practice, computers can also sharpen critical thinking skills, such as the ability to develop a logical argument. But few software programs address this kind of higher-level learning in an effective or systematic manner.

These limited benefits do not justify the unrestrained entry of this innovation into the nation's classrooms. A 1989 University of Alberta survey of three thousand secondary school students, for example, found that fewer than 2 percent ever used a computer for actually learning a subject such as math, science or English. For the most part, the machines simply sat in computer labs as expensive tools for teaching computer literacy. Yet given the rapidity with which computers and software become obsolete (a well-known truth in the computer industry) such basic keyboard skills could easily be taught on a typewriter or in the workplace where the skills will be used.

One reason so many computers become little more than glitzy typewriters in the schools is a serious lack of useful software. Computers can't perform good work without good programs, and most existing programs provide little more than a basic format into which teachers must enter the questions and guidelines they want their students to follow. A Canadian-designed program such as CESILE can effectively help students learn how to construct a hypothesis the way a real scientist thinks, but it requires constant supervision and lengthy input by the teacher to achieve its purpose.

Given that most software packages are not designed by teachers or people who understand the nature of learning, it is not surprising that the vast majority of programs end up gathering dust within four months of their purchase. In many cases, teachers simply don't have the time or the skills to do the hard work necessary to make them effective. And therein lies the second reason computers have failed to deliver: most North American teachers have had fewer than ten hours of computer training. Only the most skilled and able instructors have integrated the machine into their teaching lessons.

But even when teachers have tried to use computers to enhance writing, reading or problem-solving skills, the results have been decidedly mixed. In math, for example, computers seem to increase student achievement best as an adjunct rather than as a replacement for conventional teaching. Even then, computer use seems better suited to improving students' attitudes towards computers than towards the specific subject being taught.

There is also a very real and little-debated danger that computers may eventually flood classrooms, as they have many newsrooms, with more meaningless data than most teachers or students could use in a lifetime. As the educator Theodore Roszak has observed in *The Cult of Information* (Pantheon, 1986), "the mind thinks with ideas, not with information." If the principal task of education is to teach young people how to deal with ideas, then classroom dependence on data-processing machines might actually be a hindrance.

Furthermore, computers have routinely compounded existing inequities in the classroom. While the machines rarely find their way into the classrooms of the disadvantaged where they've proved useful, in middle class schools, according to a University of Alberta high school survey, the machines merely exacerbate other differences. Boys typically log more time on classroom computers than girls for word-processing, subject review and making spreadsheets. More than 70 percent of the female students never turned on a computer in an average week, compared to 55.9 percent of the male students. Males also dominated attendance in computer courses by a ratio of 60:40. This inequity was repeated in the home, where boys were two or four times more likely than girls to use a computer once a week or more. The study concluded that the current situation in most Canadian high schools was still "one of inequitable use and opportunity."

Now, none of these findings or philosophical questions suggest that computers can't be powerful teaching tools. But they do indicate that educators have a frightful tendency to adopt expensive approaches without any evidence to suggest they can make a healthy difference in learning.

The computer boondoggle could have been avoided had educators exercised some prudence. For starters, no school should spend a lot of money on new technologies unless it has solid evidence that they will result in improved student learning. Nor should any new tool be adopted without specific projections about its effectiveness, such as higher achievement scores in math or a lower failure rate. The act of making projections, of course, demands that educators then monitor new programs to see if they actually live up to their promises. This is the only way to keep the system honest and fiscally responsible.

Had educators followed these reasonable ground

rules for computers, they would have quickly scaled back their grandiose expectations, reduced their purchases by half and recognized that the tool has very limited classroom uses given the current state of teacher training, the short lifespan of the machine and the low quality of computer software for classrooms.

If parents and educators ignore the costly mistakes made with computers, then they will be likely to repeat the same errors again and again. Now that even more expensive high-tech tools such as video discs and multi-media equipment (computers, television and phones all in one unit) are being primed for classroom use, it's time that parents and educators learn to ask the only two questions that matter: Can this new tool make a real difference for learning and teaching? And where's the proof?

To keep abreast of the changes the computer revolution will make in our schools (the public has no choice in this regard), I recommend three different journals.

WIRED is a colourful and critical monthly that covers the electronic age with humour, detail and punchy commentary. If your teenagers are computer savvy, and you're not, get this journal. Subscription is a steep $64 (U. S.) a year, but worth it. Call 415-904-0660.

TECHNO is a glossy quarterly that accurately reflects what North America's status quo in public schooling is thinking about virtual reality and "internetworked schools." A one-year subscription is $24 (U. S.). Phone 812-339-2203 or fax 812-333-4218.

TEACH is a popular Canadian journal about schooling with a lot of high-tech information. A subscription costs $18.95 plus $1.32 GST. Phone 416-537-2103 or fax 416-537-3491.

CONSTRUCTIVISM   This educational theory, which purports to let children construct meaning by and for themselves, has made deep inroads in public schooling in the last decade. The idea is probably as old as the ancient Greek proverb that says "The bird sings sweetest that has not been taught."

First advocated by a university élite, "constructivism," when translated into the classroom, looks and sounds an awful lot like Social Darwinism: those who can construct meaning become intellectual contractors and those who can't just dally in the sandbox. Formal instruction is considered unnecessary and even bad. A constructivist seeks to provide a safe environment in which children can make choices about their learning. Hence constructivists see their role not as instructors but as facilitators of exploration. As a consequence they regard the curriculum not as a body of knowledge to be learned but as a set of activities from which knowledge can be blocked, cemented and hammered by the student into his or her own individual framework.

In a true constructivist classroom, children will follow their talents and motivation; meanwhile, the untalented and unmotivated will construct themselves into special education classes. In schools following a strict constructivist agenda, disadvantaged children are often at risk of learning nothing.

Although the idea of constructing meaning may be of some use (many children do learn this way in different situations), it has big theoretical holes, the biggest being what Canadian psychologist Carl Bereiter calls the "learning paradox": "If one tries to account for learning by means of mental actions carried out by the learner, then it is necessary to attribute to the learner a prior cognitive structure that is as advanced or complex as the one to be acquired."

Bereiter is merely saying that a child's ability to construct meaning is determined by what he or she already knows, which in turn is influenced by a variety of factors including chance, imitation and the child's learning support system. The latter is the degree to which parents or grandparents naturally teach what the child is ready to learn.

Consider, for example, the case of children exposed to two different reading programs. One group gets a basal reading program featuring excellent literature while the other struggles with an image-rich package of formatted texts, all conforming to "readability indexes." Not surprisingly, the children constructed what they had been systematically exposed to: the good reading program produced varied writing styles of high quality; the bad reading program yielded Dick and Jane writers.

The great weakness of the constructivist camp is that it views schooling as either being good and student-centred or bad and teacher-centred. However, as one American educator recently noted, "learners can construct meaning while being instructed by a teacher." The supposed incompatibility between constructed and instructed knowledge, discovery and practice, innate understanding and the workmanlike mastery of rules is false. Learning requires all of these in balance.

See **DEVELOPMENTALLY APPROPRIATE PRACTICE**, **CHILD-CENTRED LEARNING** and **WHOLE LANGUAGE**.

CONTINUOUS LEARNING   The admirable intent of "continuous learning" or "program continuity" is for children to progress at their own rate in their own style with a personalized learning program designed by the teacher.

According to various ministry of education proposals, "individualized educational planning" is facilitated
by replacing the traditional classroom with an ungraded setting where "learners" of varying ability and interest can "retain autonomy and initiative" by building
self-esteem "with personal relevance of new knowledge."

But in Alberta, program continuity rapidly lost all its
continuity as soon as the ministry decided in 1987 that
it would be implemented in all elementary schools by
1993. In the rush, the idea quickly came to mean so
many different things to so many different administrators (from "multi-aged classrooms" to "collaborative
learning") that Alberta's minister of education, Halvar
Jonson, put an end to the resulting mishmash by
killing the scheme in 1993.

British Columbia's experiment in "continuous
learning" (see **YEAR 2000**) could well follow Alberta's
discontinued example if its ministry doesn't heed
Alberta's hard-learned lessons.

Alberta's first and most fatal mistake was to latch
onto an idea without any solid research base. In a 1989
master's thesis on program continuity for the
University of Alberta, Maureen Lemieux discovered
that the province's education ministry did only two
research studies on the innovation, neither of which
examined its effects on teaching or learning. This
omission prompted one teacher to observe in the
magazine *Alberta Report*: "If I were buying a consumer
product I would check the consumer reports to see
which one to buy. Where is the research on program
continuity?" The question remains unanswered.

The government's second error was its edict for
wide-scale implementation. Instead of allowing pro-
gressive-minded teachers, principals and parents the
opportunity to create a series of non-graded but perfor-

mance-based schools where product counts, with all the appropriate controls of an honest social experiment, the ministry tried to impose one wispy idea on everyone, providing little in-service training. In so doing, it ensured the reform's demise.

Alberta's educrats then muddied the waters of classroom continuity even more by deciding in mid-stream to push for great achievement and accountability, with departmental exams in grades three, six and nine. Torn between the call for results and for individualized instruction (not incompatible goals), teachers didn't know whether administrators wanted them to focus on product or process, subject or student.

Last but not least, the ministry failed to question program continuity's two key assumptions. The first is that children should be allowed to learn at their own pace. Some people are faster learners than others, but there are very few households—or offices, for that matter—that allow people to crawl around at their own speed. As Margarete Wolfram, an educational psychologist at York University, recently noted: "Mother Nature has equipped us with a mechanism called arousal which allows us to shift gears to live up to challenges.... Unless one lives in a greenhouse, pace is largely determined by what is required."

The second faulty assumption made by program continuity was that the school, which was created to teach pupils in groups, could somehow champion the aristocratic ideal of private tutoring for thirty pupils per class without burning out teachers or going bankrupt at the same time.

In a sharp summary of teachers' reactions to Alberta's ill-designed experiment, Maureen Lemieux recorded a deep frustration among experienced teachers who took the reform seriously and a paranoia among administrators who recognized that the whole mess was "beyond their capacity without direct access to the computers at Cape Canaveral and the gold in Fort Knox." Long before the ministry pulled the plug, she also identified a growing consensus that the program would fall, like the open classroom, into the crowded dustbin of educational fads.

Leif Stolee, a former teacher and administrator, writes a wicked column on education for *Alberta Report*. His parable on continuous learning also speaks volumes about the current mindset of public education:

> Imagine two shepherds each given the task of moving a flock of thirty sheep from the valley to the summer pasture in the mountains, a two-months' journey. Fuji, working for Shumo Sheep Inc., eyeballs the map, and thinking about the watering holes, the grazing, the streams, the hills and passes draws up a General Trek Plan and sets out on the journey. Once the flock is moving steadily, he looks for strays, untangles those stuck in thickets, occasionally carries one that is hurt, monitors the pace by either slowing the van or prodding the laggards. After grazing and at the rest-stops he checks those needing personal attention to their hooves, hide or horns. The sheep are weighed and measured as they go through certain gates by professional scalers, and if he needs special information he checks his handbooks, Guiding a Flock, Sermons for Sheep or Mastermind Mutton In Mass. In the evenings he sits in the pub singing "Oh, for the life of a shepherd."
>
> In contrast Frazzled Fred, working for Ovine Outcomes and Attitude Adjusters Inc., starts by preparing 30 Personal Progress Plans tracing out

detailed paths for each sheep. They all proceed at their own rates; so at any given time some are feeding, others are resting, sleeping, marching, munching, drinking, or "mooning" Fred, who has been de-sensitized by extensive courses in Sheep Creativity. Convinced that "a sheep knows best" Fred lets them devour grass, grain, bark, thistles, legumes, loco weed, or leaf, as and when they see fit. Fred spends his time rushing from sheep to sheep in different stages of distress or dalliance, periodically weighing them on portable bathroom scales, using the findings to update the Personal Progress Profiles and alter the Personal Progress Paths. Fred's frequent confusion is helped by the handbooks: Sheep is Singular, Forget the Flock, The Self-Directed Sheep. When stress overcomes him, Ms. Peep, a popular consultant affectionately called "Bo" inservices him in self-hypnosis and stress reduction techniques, while crooning softly "Let them alone and they will come home wagging their tails behind them."

CO-OPERATIVE LEARNING This fashionable teaching method has been so badly implemented in so many schools that the basic idea of students working together in teams runs the risk of being thoroughly discredited.

As a teaching strategy, co-operative learning is nothing new. Good teachers have judiciously employed it in classrooms for centuries. Its basic premise is simple: by working together in pairs or small groups (the maximum size should be six) on specific projects that require students to practise good social skills, students improve their overall academic performance in, say, history or science.

In good hands, co-operative learning demands both group and individual accountability, actively teaches students how to co-operate effectively, and involves meaningful work in engaging subject matter for all participants (in other words, one student doesn't do all the writing or thinking). Five conditions must be met if co-operative learning is to have any value:

1. Objectives for the lesson are clearly stated.
2. The teacher makes decisions about student placement before the lesson is taught.
3. The teacher provides students with clear explanations of the task, goals and nature of work.
4. The teacher monitors the effectiveness of the groups (making changes if necessary) and intervenes to provide help.
5. The teacher evaluates group and individual achievement and guides students through a discussion of how well they achieved the goals and how well they collaborated.

In the hands of inexperienced or badly trained teachers, co-operative learning too often looks like this: a poorly matched group of students who chat away while one does all the work, which the other students then copy. Ill-trained teachers also tend to hand out assignments that should be done individually rather than co-operatively. Many teachers and principals also wrongly define co-operative learning as simply sharing math textbooks or drawing castles together.

To Dave Pollard, such abuses undermine the value of co-operative learning as a supplemental teaching technique. He is an elementary school teacher in Scarborough, Ontario, whose version of co-operative teaching is featured in the well-known instructional video, "Together We Learn." But he integrates co-operative learning with direct whole-class instruction and small-group work. He illustrates the system's overindulgence in co-operative learning with this scene from a grade three class.

The two students in a spelling team are correcting each other's work. One student has crossed out his partner's incorrect spelling and substituted another mistaken attempt.

"Who checks your work?" asks Pollard.

"My partner," replies the co-operative learner.

"But what happens if your partner can't spell?" continues Pollard.

"Well," replies the perceptive pupil, "I guess I'm out of luck."

This scene unfortunately represents the state of co-operative learning in far too many classes and is a prime example of "academic child abuse."

Pollard, who talks to teachers regularly about the wise and improper uses of co-operative learning, emphasizes that co-operative learning must be part of a balanced instructional approach, not the entire program. "We, as teachers, invite criticism when co-operative activities are limited, unimaginative, simplistic and poorly structured. Without planning, co-operative learning often becomes no more than a pooling of ignorance. Many parents plead the case that in the 'real world' children also need to know how to work independently, yet these opportunities, in the eyes of many parents, seem to be disappearing with the advent of more so-called progressive interactive learning. The question teachers should ask themselves is this: 'If you are providing co-operative learning programs, how much of your day do you also devote to allowing children to learn independent work skills that are equally important?'"

A balance of other strategies, adds Pollard, is the key to successful co-operative learning. "Few parents question the need for pupils to learn about themselves by interacting with others. There is little doubt that co-operative learning is still the best way for pupils to learn how to work in positive interdependence. At the same time, we can no longer naïvely accept the long-standing belief that any one teaching model can do it all."

When employed as part of a balanced program that includes whole-group and individual instruction, co-operative learning can play a positive role in fostering higher student achievement, greater collaborative skills and other worthy educational ends. Its wise utilization demands the mastery of basic skills and challenging instructional objectives. Older students should get more of it than younger students.

Based on my own experience, this strategy should not be used extensively until after grade four. Nor should it be forced on any teacher who has not had lengthy in-service training in how to do it properly. If co-operative learning is the only activity your school endorses, withdraw your child and find a school with a more balanced approach to teaching and learning.

CRITICAL THINKING   Every provincial school curriculum highlights critical thinking as a desired "outcome." But the notion that all children should leave school as bona fide "critical thinkers" is purely utopian.

Critical thinking may result from good schooling but, like wisdom, it is an end, neither a means nor a beginning of education.

Real critical thinking demands that children be exposed to ideas and to history. People don't expect carpenters to perform good woodwork without a saw or hammer, yet schools somehow expect children to think critically about the world without any broad knowledge base. "Critical thinking," notes the American educator Jacques Barzun, "can only be learned by the discussion of an idea which is part of a subject, under the guidance of an able thinker. Thinking is like piano playing: it is shown, not taught."

A school that teaches critical thinking as an entity separate from the teaching of history, science or art is missing the point and abusing its mandate. Parents should critically challenge such practice.

CURRICULUM

The sense of continuity, of one step leading to another, of details fitting gradually into a larger design, is essential to education, and no sequence of individually isolated experiences can possess this.

—Northrop Frye

A good curriculum is a clear and systematic presentation of ideas and concepts that teachers should teach and students should learn. Good teachers always aim at a level of learning that goes way beyond the curriculum.

Every school has at least four curricula in reading or math: the curriculum that is mandated by the province or board, the one that is actually taught by the teacher, the one that is learned by students and the one that is eventually tested. All four needn't mesh.

Siegfried Engelmann, an exceptionally talented curriculum designer in Oregon, has often argued that curriculum makes the difference between school success and failure: "When the curriculum fails, the teaching will fail. Period. This is not to say that if an excellent curriculum is in place, the teaching will automatically succeed. It means simply that the curriculum is like an automobile. The teacher's behaviour is like driving the automobile. If the car is well designed the teacher has the potential to drive fast and safely. If the curriculum is poorly designed, it will break down no matter how carefully the teacher drives." (British Columbia, for example, does well on international and national math tests because of its sequential and orderly math curriculum.)

Canadian schools suffer from two curricular diseases. First, they try to teach too much, a symptom of a "crowded curriculum." Second, they offer students two unequal curricula. Typically they offer a traditional curriculum for university-bound students and a progressive curriculum big on relevance, utility and free choice for everyone else. Given that the nation's future will be determined by the 80 percent who don't go to university, this educational scenario does not bode well for the future. As historian and long-time school critic Diane Ravitch noted several years ago, North American schools offer a schizophrenic curriculum: "At one extreme, the perfervid traditionalists have been content to educate those at the top without regard to the welfare of the majority of the students; at the other, the perfervid progressives have cooperated in dividing and diluting the curriculum, which left the majority with an inadequate education. Most schools and teachers are not at the extremes, but they have little ability to blunt the lure of either progressivism or traditionalism, particularly to an indiscriminate media and to hyperactive policymakers. Pedagogical practise follows educational philosophy, and it is obvious that we do not yet have a philosophical commitment to education that is sound enough and strong enough to withstand the erratic dictates of fashion."

Ontario's Common Curriculum illustrates these criticisms frighteningly well.

Ontario's Common Curriculum

Employing inflated rhetoric, Ontario's Common Curriculum spells out the province's new program of study from kindergarten to grade nine.

The guide comes in a simple Dick and Jane version for parents and a more technically worded one for educators. The document, written by bureaucrats and teachers, is part of Premier Bob Rae's "restructuring" of the province's schools. According to the government, non-educational events such as global change, broken families, violence and the information revolution have prompted the need for a new curriculum.

The new curriculum assigns schools the difficult task of helping in "the elimination of poverty, illiteracy and violence" with a hodgepodge of notions called language, the arts, self and society, and mathematics, science and technology. What the document says and doesn't say about this new subject matter and the quest for social justice has also alarmed a great many teachers and parents.

For starters, words like *mastery, achievement* and *competence* appear rarely if not at all in the document, while notions like "relevance" pop up regularly. Math, science and technology, for example, "is best acquired in a learning environment that promotes hands-on and relevant problem solving." The document's collective authors assume here that these subjects come with no difficult knowledge to be mastered, but only relevant problems to be solved.

(Education's celebration of relevance, which the guide dutifully reflects, often alarmed the great Canadian teacher Northrop Frye. The Nazis championed the idea of relevance in education, says Frye, and in so doing destroyed the sciences and art in Germany. Education, he often wrote, is "a matter of developing the intellect and imagination," tasks that are always reality-based but rarely relevant to consumer society and not always exciting.)

In addition to calling for more relevance, the key aim of the guide appears to be integrating curricula and helping kids make connections between them—subtle and worthy ends that good teachers work towards all the time. But the guide again assumes that integration and "holistic viewpoints" can be achieved by putting the end before the beginning, that kids can in effect learn to swim, play water polo and gossip all at the same time.

Consider the melding of math, science and technology, three related but distinct courses of study, in one problem-solving, cross-curricular pot. Even educational research does not support such bold experiments in discontinuity. In 1973 a major study on science education conducted in nineteen countries by Elsie Comber and J. P. Keeves found that school systems such as Japan's, which taught science coherently as a subject, achieved good results among their students, but those such as Scotland's, which had integrated the subject across the curriculum, had poor results.

Ontario's new curriculum, like British Columbia's Year 2000, also sends history and geography to the dustbin by creating a social science, psychology and physical education hybrid called "self and society." This new program defines "historical understanding" as "helping to show how unequal relations of power contribute to the evolution of social prejudice and conflict and how principles of freedom, equality and solidarity have evolved." No good historian would stomach such a simple-minded dogma.

The new guide has not won unanimous acclaim.

Most parents still want to see an actual body of Canadian literature for study (it is absent from the guide) and to have writing well be given considerably more weight than outcomes such as "pursuing information from a wide variety of sources."

Notes Martha Harron, a Toronto parent: "One of the more disturbing things about this curriculum, which purports to be 'outcomes-based,' is that it says less about what facts children are expected to know than it does about what children are expected to think. Surely the goal of education should not be to teach children what to think, but how to think for themselves. There are frequent references to children 'being able to demonstrate satisfaction and enjoyment,' and 'demonstrate interest,' as if attitudes can be made compulsory."

Ultimately, the Common Curriculum will please parents who think school should help kids "encounter change with confidence" or fight racism and sexism. It will not please those who understand the limits of any good school: teaching and learning a few things well.

Martha Harron's advice on fighting bad curricular ideas is pointed: "Participatory democracy only works if we participate. Call or write your local trustee and your MPP, and tell them how you feel about the way our tax dollars are being spent. Above all, please write to the Minister and tell him you want a reality-based curriculum, written in English instead of Schoolspeak, with realistic, specific outcomes of performance, not attitude."

See also **YEAR 2000** and Appendix 4.

DAYCARE   In the Western world, debates about day-care are usually reduced to one question: how can governments provide more of it?

In her latest book, *Children First* (published by Knopf), Penelope Leach, renowned author, psychologist and social activist, denounces this technocratic agenda, because it places more value on economics and labour markets than it does on the real issue: the care of small people. Moreover, the case for universal daycare, she argues, travels with a great many false assumptions about parents and children.

For starters, much of the media and many special-interest groups contend that all parents want strangers to care for their kids. Not true. In most Western countries, the majority of children are still raised at home or by a relative. Even in Sweden, where universal daycare is available, either the mother or the father will routinely opt to spend the first eighteen months after their child's birth at home.

In illustrating how the case for daycare is grossly overstated, Leach cites a 1987 Labour Force Survey by Statistics Canada. It reported that 60 percent of women with children below school age worked for pay, while 40 percent toiled at home with no pay. The statisticians thus assumed that 60 percent of Canadian parents required daycare. But once part-time workers and small home businesses had been subtracted from the total, only a 30-percent figure remained, "with no information on the level of actual demand."

The media also report selectively on the research on

daycare. While a reporter might well champion daycare's effectiveness by quoting the classic 1978 study by Jerome Kagan, he or she will more often than not ignore Kagan's formidable provisos: unlimited funding, professional expertise, highly trained staff and middle class parents.

Although largely unreported, a host of recent studies have raised some troubling questions about daycare. Edward Zigler, for example, has found that daycare can foster such traits as sociability and independence to excess: "From the research carried out to date, a tentative consensus emerges that ... children who have experienced early group care tend towards assertiveness, aggression and peer rather than adult orientation."

This is not to say "that either a pro-daycare or anti-daycare stand is tenable," adds Leach. The effects of daycare will vary from child to child depending on the personnel of the institution, the child's background and the character of the children being cared for. But to say that daycare is "OK for kids" and that all they need is more of it is insulting. It also ignores the experience of other cultures. Israeli kibbutzim, for example, are dismantling their high-quality collective daycare centres because, as one social scientist noted, the experience has taught them that "even a limited disassociation of children from their parents at a tender age is unacceptable."

Leach's thoughts on what children really need is bravely unequivocal. Until the age of three they need a parent, Mom or Dad. "Whoever it is who cares for infants, they need to have permanence, continuity, passion and a parent-like commitment that is difficult to find or meet outside the vested interests and social expectations of family roles, and cannot be adequately replaced by professionalism." She disparages "quality time" (another technocratic image) as a cruel joke and tells parents the simple truth: "The more you are around, the better, and the younger the child, the more it matters."

There is a place for preschools for children three years or older, but Leach does not make a case for universal care. She considers mothers who take other children into their own homes as the most likely form of daycare to meet the needs of infants. She concludes that the search for alternatives to parental care is just as absurd as the popular belief "that there must be widely available alternatives because parents cannot and do not want to care for their own infants."

The solutions, she says, can be found in common sense and Scandinavia. Why not support parents to nurture their children at home, as the Norwegians and Swedes do? Why not grant mothers and/or fathers long work leaves? Why not give parents a six-hour day until their children reach the age of eight? Why not expect mothers and fathers to be equally responsible for the well-being of their children? Why not shift the debate from daycare—an agenda basically tied to employing more adults—to a debate about the care of children?

Why not, argues Leach, put children first?

See also **PERRY PRESCHOOL PROJECT**.

DESTREAMING

School failure is not the failure of kids, and often not the failure of teachers. It's the failure of a sick system that places more value on the whims of adults than on the obvious needs of children.
—Siegfried Engelmann, American educator

In Ontario, few initiatives have caused as much concern among parents and teachers as "destreaming," a practice that is now common in most provinces.

Destreaming: A Four-Part Educational Play

Act 1: Officials at Ontario's ministry of education wring their hands. Genuinely dismayed by the appalling number of poor, black and disadvantaged kids dropping out of high school, they identify the villain: the practice of "streaming" or "tracking" teenagers into basic, general and advanced courses that respectively lead to a dead end, community college and university.

Having discovered the obstacle to equity and access to education, the bureaucrats devise a strategy. End streaming by removing all the course labels, they say. Take all grade nine students, regardless of ability or performance, and put them into mixed classes. The experiment to remove barriers that "dead-end" students begins in sixty high schools across the province.

Act 2: After passing through several handlers, the task of overseeing this controversial venture falls on the desk of Dianne Pennock, an education officer in the curriculum policy development branch. She reports that there is a "foundation of information" that leads the ministry to believe that destreaming will "enhance student self-esteem" and give some students a better crack at entering academic classes in grade ten.

Pennock says the ministry has no time to wait for the results of what is really a four-year experiment and is proceeding on the basis of one-year results from the pilot projects. "There is an indication the kids [the disadvantaged ones] will improve. There seems to be a body of research that indicates this will come about." The professional decision to destream all grade nine classes in 1993 "is based on qualitative data." The province will monitor the results every year, but given the demands of the modern world it can't put off destreaming "indefinitely."

Pennock does recognize that "the integrated approach" of teaching kids with varying reading, writing and oral skills all in the same class will place new demands on teachers. To this end, the province has set aside $2.7 million for teacher in-service programs on "teaching/learning strategies ... relevant to a diversity of learning styles." Pennock calls the approach "collaborative learning" and says "there was something good happening" when she tried it.

Act 3: Teachers, the first to implement the policy but the last to be consulted, now begin to ask basic questions about destreaming. Where is the quantitative research to support the policy? Will teachers get smaller classes to make the policy work? Will higher-performing students spend their time teaching the poorer performers? Will standards be lowered? Why not wait for the results of the pilot projects?

When one Toronto elementary teacher asks these pointed instructional questions, her superintendent tells her to get out of his board and out of teaching. A Toronto high school teacher raises similar concerns and is told by his superintendent to "f—k off."

The forty-thousand-member Ontario Secondary School Teachers' Federation concludes that "destreaming or delabelling" will jeopardize the very students it is supposed to help. Without proper resources, smaller classes, retraining and a new curriculum, destreaming will be nothing more than a form of musical chairs.

Act 4: Far from Ontario, Siegfried Engelmann, an American researcher and teacher, wonders why

Canadians "copy the crap we Americans do." He says that the research on destreaming shows that it penalizes all kids academically and socially, and "rips off" the higher performers the most. As for self-esteem building, when non-readers get grouped with literates, it becomes brutally clear to the lower performers that not only are they failing but failing badly.

The problem, he adds, is that policy makers confuse the institutional act of streaming with the instructional tool of grouping kids in order to teach them efficiently what they need to learn. With good teaching, kids move from group to group. The issue, he adds, is really not to destream or stream, but to teach all kids the skills they need to succeed. Homogeneous grouping is the best way to achieve this end, he concludes.

"The teachers are right and the decision makers are the bozos."

In principle, destreaming is a good idea. Slotting rich and poor children into different streams for academic classes or dead-end activities is not an admirable practice. Most Asian countries, for instance, do not segregate their students until the age of sixteen. George Radwanski, in his famous but little-read 1987 study on education, found Ontario's policy of streaming "a social injustice, a theoretical error and a practical failure."

But there are ways to destream and ways not to destream, and Ontario appears to have chosen an imprudent path that not only has antagonized its secondary teachers, but may well promote more "social injustice" if not outright educational abuse.

In his landmark report, Radwanski did not make destreaming a case against grouping kids according to ability within subjects. As Robin Barrow notes in *Reform and Relevance in Schooling*, a collection of essays published by OISE, destreaming should not mean denying "the existence of personal differences between students at various stages which can neither be overcome by treating them all alike, nor allow us to treat them as if they were all alike." To deny a child who is good in math the chance to advance, for whatever reason, would take "a mindless fear of individual superiority." The education ministry, which has seemingly confused destreaming with heterogeneous grouping, seems to have developed this fear.

The International Institute for Advocacy for School Children, a U. S. group of educators, describes "heterogeneous grouping for instruction" as a "prima-facie discriminatory practise." It observes that in presenting the same lesson to children of varying ability, including minority kids, heterogeneous grouping demands that minority kids learn unreasonable amounts of material, at a rate that is unreasonably fast, and in a setting with students who master the material with far less effort. As now practised in Ontario, destreaming expects students with achievement levels ranging from grade three to grade ten to do the same work in grade nine.

Although ministry documents contend that ability grouping "has few, if any, benefits for student achievement," the research on homogeneous or ability grouping speaks otherwise. In a 1985 analysis of 102 ability-grouping studies, Chen-Lin C. Kulik, an American researcher, concluded in a presentation to the American Psychological Association that homogeneous grouping "is often beneficial for talented students, may improve achievement and self-esteem of slow learners, and has little effect on the achievement and self-esteem of average students." In other words, homogeneous grouping discriminates against no segment of the population.

According to Dr Mark Holmes, an educational consultant and former OISE professor, destreaming could achieve real equity for disadvantaged kids if the ministry introduced "a clearly sequenced program for the first eight grades ... and minimum standards for entry into grade nine courses." The government began destreaming grade nine without these reforms. Adds Holmes: "This Asian style of destreaming implies setting up preparatory programs in grade eight, in summer school and in high school, for those who have not achieved, say, end-of-the-sixth-grade norms in reading, language and math, by the end of grade eight." The Ontario ministry of education does not appear to be moving in this direction; nor is it collecting hard data on the comparative achievement of disadvantaged kids in streamed and unstreamed classrooms.

To visualize what destreaming can mean in the classroom, consider this observation from a grade six math teacher in Nova Scotia. She had the ideal-sized class of twenty students. But four couldn't multiply or divide while another four could have completed a grade six or seven math program in a year: the remaining twelve ranged "from low- to high-average ability."

"Guess who suffered?" asked the teacher.

"To protect us all from the disruption four frustrated boys would have caused, I taught to the bottom end of the class. To assuage my uneasy conscience for neglecting my bright lights, I handed them an enriched math book to work on independently when their classwork was completed.... The result? My top students, who could have advanced at the rate Asian students progress at, were cheated of instruction."

Ontario's secondary teachers make a good point when they argue, as does Jeannie Oakes, a leading authority on destreaming, that "simple structural changes imposed from above do not result in increased equity." They might also add, as the ministry has neglected, that equality of access does not guarantee equality of outcomes.

See **SELF-ESTEEM**, **"INNOVATIONS"** vs. **"REFORMS"** and **ACCOUNTABILITY**.

DEVELOPMENTALLY APPROPRIATE PRACTICE (DAP)

In 1987, the National Association for the Education of Young Children (an American organization based in Washington, D.C.) published a document entitled *Developmentally Appropriate Practise* (DAP). Like many documents about schooling, it reads like the panacea for educational ills. In both Canada and the United States, educational administrators with little or no teaching experience are pressing teachers to adopt DAP's theoretical principles. British Columbia's controversial Year 2000 program encorporates many features of DAP.

DAP asserts that children should be allowed to follow their own blissful interests through play. It contends that children "construct knowledge as a result of dynamic interactions between the individual and the physical and social environments [not as a result of planned teaching]." And it argues that learning, playing and constructing take place best in open, unstructured and non-graded environments.

A typical DAP classroom promotes "discovery" math and "discovery" science, encourages children to move at their own pace, emphasizes the development of self-esteem, employs whole language and provides children with a host of activity centres where they are expected to work by themselves or in small groups. "Learning should not be inhibited by adult-established concepts of completion, achievement and failure."

Bonnie Grossen, the editor of the journal *Effective*

School Practices, recently critiqued DAP with this observation: "The idea that children often learn from the activities they initiate is perfectly reasonable. The idea that children should also have ample opportunities to take initiative is also acceptable. However, the idea that a teacher cannot possibly initiate and direct learning effectively requires closer examination. It may be that child-initiated and teacher-initiated learning both have an important place in education."

DAP, however, does not take such a reasonable position. It simply condemns as inappropriate the following validated classroom practices: an organized curriculum based on core subjects, the correction of errors, teacher-directed reading groups and the presentation of math as a separate subject scheduled every day.

The theoretical underpinnings of DAP ostensibly derive from the works of Jean Piaget, Erik Erikson, Lev Vygotsky (a brilliant Soviet educator) and Maria Montessori. It is unlikely that any of these educators or philosophers would agree with DAP's totalitarian tone or strict prohibitions against diversity in classroom practice. In fact, DAP contradicts much of Montessori's research, which found that most children were ready to read between the ages of four and six: DAP states that most children will learn to read by the age of seven.

Although some upper middle class children coming from language-rich homes will do just fine in DAP classrooms, this approach openly penalizes handicapped or disadvantaged children by deliberately denying them a structured and coherent curriculum as well as direct instruction.

Given the unsound and theoretical nature of DAP, parents should press schools that have succumbed to this innovation to offer a more teacher-directed program along with the DAP stream. Parents should also demand full disclosure of DAP's philosophical biases and limitations, as well as student test data in reading and math. Its experimental nature suggests that parental consent be an essential component of this program.

Parents who identify with many of the philosophical premises of DAP should seriously consider a Montessori program. In many respects DAP is very much a blind man's version of Montessori without a Montessori curriculum.

Some thoughts from DAP:

"Formal, inappropriate instructional techniques are a source of stress for young children."

"Annie, we agreed not to hit. Take a time out at your earliest convenience."

Susan Jerde

"The curriculum is integrated so that learning occurs primarily through projects, learning centers, and playful activities that reflect current interests of children. For example, a social studies project such as building and operating a store or a science project such as furnishing and caring for an aquarium provide focused opportunities for children to plan, dictate, and or write their plans (using invented and teacher-taught spelling), to draw and write about their activity, to discuss what they are doing, to read nonfiction books for needed information, to work co-operatively with other children, learn facts in a meaningful context, and to enjoy learning."

"Children need years of play with real objects and events before they are able to understand the meaning of symbols such as letters and numbers."

"The classroom is treated as a laboratory of social relations where children explore values and learn rules of social living and respect for individual differences through experience."

See also **CONSTRUCTIVISM, PIAGET, MONTESSORI, OPEN CLASSROOM, NON-GRADED CLASSROOM** and **YEAR 2000**.

DIRECT INSTRUCTION (DI)   Good teachers have been using this method for centuries to maximize student learning in the basics. It is also known as teacher-directed, formal or teacher-centred learning.

Unlike constructivism or child-centred learning, which posits that students can make their own meaning in an unstructured environment, DI is direct and purposeful. According to Douglas Carnine, the author of

Direct Instruction Mathematics (published by Charles E. Merrill), DI "provides a comprehensive set of prescriptions for organizing instruction so that students acquire, retain, and generalize new learning in as humane, efficient and effective a manner as is possible."

The proponents of DI—who are few in North America as a result of the dominance of progressive teaching theories—accept three classroom truths:

1. A well-designed program and a good teacher will not produce significant gains if the instructional time is limited or eroded by self-esteem courses.
2. A good program taught regularly will not be successful if the teacher is not skilled.
3. Routine periods of study plus the hard work of a skilled teacher won't perform wonders if the program reads like a television guide or comic book.

Teachers using direct instruction techniques for math or reading generally follow nine steps:

1. They specify goals clearly.
2. They aim to teach higher thinking skills as opposed to memorization.
3. They determine necessary pre-skills—what students must know in order to tackle a new concept successfully.
4. They sequence skills carefully from the known to the unknown.
5. They select the right teaching approach, whether it be modelling a rule to be learned or demonstrating a series of sequential steps for solving a problem.
6. They choose their words for presenting ideas that are clear, consistent and unambiguous.
7. They select appropriate examples to reinforce new concepts.

8. They provide practice and review.
9. They pace their teaching in a lively and animated manner.

The effectiveness of this approach has been well documented since 1976. In a 1988 review of teacher effectiveness studies, G. Patrick O'Neill, a researcher at Brock University, reported that "increased learning gains among primary children from working and middle class backgrounds is a common, almost universal conclusion of recent research" on direct instruction.

Like any solid educational tool, direct instruction shouldn't be used all the time, but it should be a central ingredient of every elementary school program.

See also **PROJECT FOLLOW-THROUGH** and **CHILD-CENTRED LEARNING**.

DISCIPLINE   In Calgary, a local high school principal recently chastised three boys for setting off firecrackers in the schoolyard by ordering them to write long, apologetic essays.

Then the administrator dutifully phoned each student's parents and demanded to know what they were going to do about their child's behaviour. The phone call suggested that parents impose a "real" brand of discipline. The parental responses were sadly predictable.

Parent One thanked the principal for the information, but didn't know what action to take.

Parent Two told the principal to mind his own business, and "buzz off."

And Parent Three reacted to the news by promptly grounding the boy for six months and cancelling his birthday party.

This haphazard approach to school discipline,

which guarantees unequal if not improper results, aptly illustrates the disorderly state of many public schools today where inept administrators often ask parents to do what they themselves have failed to do: establish a set of limits and rules that make for a warm, caring and orderly learning environment.

Now, consider the example of Woodbridge College, a public Ontario high school located north of Toronto. It neither defines discipline as a coercive tool for keeping order nor as an ad hoc procedure where parents are asked what to do with students who misbehave. For at Woodbridge, discipline means a clear set of well-defined behaviours and expectations for all members of the school.

"Discipline is a nice frame upon which teachers hang their love for kids and love of learning," explains Jim Garrow, the former director of special education at the College and the original framer of much of Woodbridge's approach to discipline. And that frame includes a uniform code of conduct and even an educational contract. "It's what makes our school work."

At Woodbridge shooting off firecrackers or swearing in the classroom would bring fair, immediate and consistent consequences. The school might advise parents of disciplinary measures, but only if such communication would support a desired change in student behaviour. "But we certainly would not have asked the parents what to do," adds Garrow.

Woodbridge College, however, didn't always provide its students or parents with such direct messages. Before remaking itself as an academy with high expectations and academic standards in 1991, it was just another decaying basic high school whose enrolment had declined from 752 students in 1978 to 300 in 1990. Nearly a third of these students were eighteen years or older (as opposed to 18 percent in neighbouring schools), and trouble and the police visited the school on a daily basis.

"There was a lack of discipline," recalls Julie Anne Philips, now a seventeen-year-old in grade twelve and a co-chair of the student council. "Students came as they chose and it was disheartening to go to a place everyone referred to as Last Chance High."

But this poisonous atmosphere changed radically when principal John Buell and vice-principal John Sims turned the school around with the practical help of Jim Garrow, a former vice-principal who has advised twelve different school boards on how to establish a clear-headed approach to effective discipline.

To Garrow, a forty-two-year-old educator and former marriage counsellor, the onus for establishing a disciplinary framework to deal with firecrackers or knife play falls squarely on the school. "We are the professionals who have received the training, so we have to try to be professional educators and situation managers."

That doesn't mean parents aren't part of the collegial team that nourishes school discipline, says Garrow. It's just that the school must be consistently direct about what it expects from both its teachers and kids. A school staff that says "Do as I say and not as I do" not only undermines itself but sets the conditions for destructive power plays with kids. "What works for the goose has to work for the gander."

To achieve this fair balance, Woodbridge College plainly spells out its expectations in a student handbook. The rules include behaving and speaking in a manner that demonstrates common courtesy, showing respect for property, completing homework, attending classes punctually and wearing the school uniform (grey slacks or skirts combined with white or blue shirts).

To ensure everyone understands the school's priorities, parents and students are asked to sign an innovative, six-point Letter of Commitment that they are then required to uphold "as a condition of enrolment." The letter, which is supported by consequences (both negative and positive), also prevents many discipline problems from ever arising by simply erasing doubt about the school's purpose.

"If you have no standards or are always changing them, then kids will always challenge you," reports Garrow. "They want and need to know what the limits are."

This basic piece of school wisdom, which research on effective schools repeatedly underscores, is also readily accepted by most students. Notes Philips: "I think Woodbridge's contract is a really good idea.... It just reinforces proper social skills."

With an enrolment of six hundred (plus a long waiting list), Woodbridge's uniformed denizens now walk around freely, laughing and chatting with staff and even applauding the police at student assemblies. "We've got a lot more students participating, and people are happy to be here," adds Philips.

For a good disciplinary regime to succeed in any school, it requires swift and consistent reinforcement as well as constant communication with parents. As a general rule Garrow believes that a school administrator should never phone parents to complain about their kid's behaviour if the administrator hasn't first established that he cares about that kid by saying something good about him or her. "You don't have the right to phone negatively if you haven't phoned positively. You've just lost it.... Parents need to know that their kids are worthy." And a two-minute phone call to a parent celebrating a child's genuine achievement is perhaps the best investment a school can make in terms of building a healthy disciplinary environment.

It is also one way of guaranteeing, adds Garrow, that when a teacher or vice-principal does phone to say that "Johnny lost it today in class" or shot off a bunch of firecrackers, the parents will listen and "not adopt an adversarial view."

Schools like Woodbridge College ultimately teach parents what discipline should always mean in a good school: "We care about your child."

See also **EFFECTIVE SCHOOLS** and Appendix 15.

DROPOUTS   According to Statistics Canada, 18 percent of Canada's youth empty their school lockers each year and perform an act of almost political significance: they drop out.

Contrary to wild-eyed public images of tough kids, complete with leather and motorcycles, dropouts come from all classes and walks of life. And their exits are usually tied to one of two rational realizations: they are either bored silly (the reason they themselves most often cite) or don't have the basic reading skills to make staying a rewarding experience.

Governments regard this exodus as a rather serious matter because of the dollars and cents at stake. According to their ledgers the social and economic costs of dropping out all too often include unemployment, welfare, crime or that evil of all evils—"decreased spending power." (It's no accident that the rate of dropping out mirrors the health of local economies: the impoverished Maritimes reports a nearly 30 percent dropout rate; the West, just 16 percent.)

Faced with such losses, governments often respond irrationally to school leavers by conducting well-intentioned stay-in-school campaigns that encourage students to remain in places that are, for them, hostile or mindless environments.

Hear out three students at Calgary's Alternative High, an alternative public school for students who have bombed out of traditional programs. Their stories suggest that dropping out is sometimes a very necessary choice—if not a wise one—for all concerned.

Let us begin with the story of Julie, an eccentric, outspoken and confident eighteen-year-old. In 1991, she would have pulled the plug on an erratic school career had she not found Alternative High, a small, democratically run school with high standards.

"I've always had a hard time adjusting," explains Julie, whose early school years included anti-social behaviour—the legacy of an ultimately successful battle with autism. "But three years ago I was attacked by a bunch of girls with sticks at my school because they thought I was a Satanist." She was not, but the incident convinced her to leave anyway.

Realizing that sitting at home and watching TV was almost as cruel an option as staying in school, Julie applied to Alternative. How many times do you want to hear Geraldo "interview Eskimos living in Cyprus?" she asks with a laugh.

Accepted as just another student, her average moved from 49 in grade ten to an 81 in grade twelve. "Students drop out because they find the work either too hard or too easy ...," adds Julie. "And then there is the student pressure. If they don't like you, they'll go out of their way to make your life a living hell."

Then there's Skye. Sporting shaved and blonde-dyed hair, the eighteen-year-old describes herself as a "punk rock Earth Mother Goddess," and then adds, "I don't know, I'm just me." She started to fade out of a grade eight French Immersion program in Saskatoon.

Routinely described as a student with "high potential" and "OK grades," Skye slowly lost interest, credits and credibility for a variety of reasons. "I was very bored and thought the classes were just wasting my time. My self-esteem was low and I was dating a rotten guy, and most of the time I just wanted to go out for a cup of coffee...." Problems at home added to the brew.

By the time she quit, most of her teachers would have gladly shown her the front door. "I had come to a point in my life where I wasn't taking on the challenge of finishing high school," she says.

After leaving home and sharing a house with five guys ("It was hell!"), she heard about Alternative High. She moved to Calgary and is now determined to meet the challenge (as Julie is) with a balance of academic and community volunteer work.

To Skye, most dropouts have had the misfortune of attending "loose" elementary schools with no standards and "tight" high schools with no flexibility. "I would raise expectations quite a bit," she says. She would also allow students to move through the system much more quickly than the standard twelve-year ticket now permits.

The last story belongs to Paige, a straight-talking seventeen-year-old. She was a good student in junior high but then began to disappear in high school. "I felt the teachers were constantly comparing you and trying to get you to the top of the class." She fell into a clique experimenting with drugs and soon her peers all arrived at the wrong conclusion. Paige dropped out of school for five months and then applied to Alternative, where "teachers care about what you are doing."

She feels that most high schools are way too large ("It's total babysitting at the big high schools") and believes that students must take more responsibility for their learning. A high school with a democratic charter, she adds, makes students "feel they are more part of the system rather than just moving through it."

Behind these tales of wasted time and dull activities in school there is a greater awareness that the high school diploma doesn't mean much in the market-place anymore. If you know "you'll end in a dead-end job pushing ketchup," as one student put it, the incentive to finish high school loses some of its power.

See also **HOPE**.

E

EDUCATOR   A somewhat glorified and much misused noun that is loosely applied to professors, administrators, textbook writers, consultants or anyone who doesn't spend much time in a classroom. Jack McCaffrey, an Ontario high school English teacher, supplies this honest definition: "Educators are often teachers who escape the classroom and shortly thereafter begin to have brilliant ideas which they would like other people to carry out. I have had the experience of getting away from teaching for a half year or so, and have found that after a few weeks two things happen: we forget what it is like to be in the classroom, and we start to see with startling clarity just what teachers should be doing. Upon returning to the classroom, we find that the ideas which seemed so clear and obvious are difficult, if not impossible, to carry out. This latter experience is unknown to the educator, and is one of the key things that separates an educator from a teacher."

Clearly, too many school systems suffer from an abundance of educators and a shortage of teachers. Parents should use this term selectively and only use it to describe teachers or administrators who are extraordinary instructional leaders. See also **PRINCIPAL.**

EFFECTIVE SCHOOLS   For more than twenty years now, a small band of researchers in Canada, England and the United States have worked hard at defining what makes one school a garage for the mind and another a developer of sound intellect and civic virtue.

Known collectively as "the effective schools research," these radical studies have generally received little media attention, and have had even less impact on how North Americans run their schools because of their very unradical conclusions. Creating and sustaining an effective school, it seems, demands neither sexy nor expensive innovations but lots of good will and hard work.

The methods used to identify these effective places, which probably represent no more than 10 percent of all schools, have been decidedly thorough. In England, Canada and the United States, researchers sat down in private, Catholic and public schools, in rich and poor neighbourhoods, and compared student achievement. Then they investigated pairs of schools with low and high academic results to observe how life differed in these places.

What all these studies found, whether dealing with single institutions or entire school districts, was that effective schools hummed with energetic purpose fuelled by approximately six shared characteristics. Because these essential values read like common sense, parents can generally spot them or their absence a mile away by interviewing the principal, visiting a classroom or talking to other parents with kids in the school.

Here, then, are the most spottable practices commonly associated with good schools, public or private:

1. A focus on teaching and learning: Elementary schools that make a difference tend to concentrate on the mastery of basic skills (reading, writing and math), while effective high schools limit instruction to a dozen basic subjects, as opposed to countless electives.

Unlike poorly performing schools, which may boast lots of sandboxes or a lot of extracurricular activities such as peace or global education, the good ones don't come with many frills. Although teaching methods may vary, good schools seek out academic programs that get good results and abandon those that do not. Notes Mark Holmes, an educational consultant in the Maritimes: "The evidence overwhelmingly shows that the degree to which the school aggressively works toward academic goals is related to its success in achieving those goals."

But in keeping such a tight focus on academic learning, good schools are not technocratic, boring or authoritarian. Effective schools, in fact, understand that regular physical exercise, art, music and laughter are life-affirming activities that feed the soul and complement the pursuit of high achievement.

2. Regular and meaningful homework: The kind and amount of homework a school assigns is purely a reflection of its commitment to academic goals. Good schools don't send home mindless mimeographed sheets or busy-work. They do, however, make a point of regularly assigning exercises that are respectfully corrected or commented upon the next day.

In a study of 1,015 Catholic, public and non-religious private schools, the American sociologist James Coleman found that regular homework assignments partially explained why students at Catholic and private schools outperformed public school students by one academic year. Catholic and private students did one to two hours' more homework per week than their public school peers. These nightly assignments not only built on what had been taught during the day but were corrected promptly.

3. An orderly and safe environment: There isn't a lot of talk about "parent rights" or "student power" in effective schools. That's because a healthy and caring school climate is the responsibility of *all* participants, including teachers, parents, students and administrators.

   As a consequence, effective schools usually have a clear charter of agreed-upon conduct and expectations (ask for one at your local school) that is both well known to the school community and is applied fairly, swiftly and consistently to all of its members. When everyone knows the rules, as well as the goals, truancy and deliquency don't become problems. (See **DISCIPLINE**.)

   Not surprisingly, high-achieving schools often regard learning time as sacred. For this reason they don't tolerate classroom disruptions or sexual or racial threats against teachers and students. Studies of good inner-city schools show that it takes no more than one-tenth of a percent of the student body acting as troublemakers to pollute the learning environment.

4. Assertive on-the-spot leadership: The presence of able administrators committed to achievement clearly separates good schools from bad ones. Parents can generally judge a good leader when they meet one because the good leaders value community and put the health of their school first in all decisions.

   Good principals typically set a climate of high achievement by focusing on the quality of instruction and on the performance of teachers and kids. Unlike many who literally hide behind mountains of paperwork, the effective principal spends half the day in the hallway or classrooms. He or she selects teachers carefully, infuses them with a team spirit and spends more time, say, on grouping kids properly for instruction or addressing the language needs of immigrant students than answering board memos.

When the principal is weak in a good school, a cadre of inspired teachers or the superintendent will often fill the leadership gap. Like effective principals, able superintendents work long and hard to shape and direct a shared commitment to excellence among teachers and kids. In a study of twelve British Columbia school districts, researchers Peter Coleman and Linda Larocque, ultimately found that the best administrators made a difference "more by modelling high standards of professional conduct than by exhortation." (See **SCHOOL BOARDS** and **PRINCIPALS.**)

5. Accountability: A good school can typically explain in clear language what its program is, what it expects in academic and behavourial performance, what happens to those who succeed or fail and how changes in performance are monitored.

   It evaluates all programs on the basis of pupil achievement and reports progress or lack of it regularly, honestly and meaningfully. Effective schools not only tell parents when children are experiencing difficulty, they forward a plan of action. Good schools also share and explain the results of local and district-wide tests to parents.

6. Dedicated teachers: When led by caring administrators, teachers will walk the extra mile in the classroom. In effective schools, teachers believe that all children can learn and feel they have failed when a student has not obtained minimum mastery of a subject.

   In good schools teachers often collaborate and share lesson plans in order to achieve continuity in the curriculum. In bad schools, teachers often "work in a classroom with a bunch of kids where the building becomes a bunch of rooms where people are only connected by a common concern about parking," reports Peter Coleman. "But in a good school there is a sense of collective responsibility."

Although researchers haven't yet established if these characteristics are the cause or the effect of good schools, they know that these special features cannot be mandated or sold as some kind of ready educational mix. Attempts to do so in the United States have repeatedly failed for two reasons: teachers perceived them as "top-down" developments and principals treated "effectiveness" as an administrative fiat.

But schools can become effective only when all of their participants, including teachers, students, parents and administrators, collectively choose to build a shared ethos of high achievement. This has never been a tidy process nor one that money or legislation can advance. "It is not that we do not know what to do, and not that we do not know how," concludes Mark Holmes. "The problem is one of will."

While locating a quality school, then, has always been a bit like spotting an eagle among pigeons, creating one has always has been a difficult human struggle to either extend a community's sense of purpose to the classroom or, in the absence of neighbourhood, to invent a caring place with a communal sense of purpose.

A Traditional Example: St Francis of Assisi

Jennifer Edghill, the mother of three children, never thought it could be this way.

"My children have attended three different schools," says the thirty-four-year-old. "But this is the first time I've been in a school where I felt they cared about my kids and wanted them to grow and excel and do well. I didn't know a school could be something so good."

Mike McEvenue, the father of two boys, sings similar heartfelt praises. "There is a sense of honour and respect in this school that I haven't felt since I was a boy.... We lucked out. We were biting our nails down in Toronto, but I don't feel that way now. I see opportunity and hope now."

Hymns to a private school? As the parents will attest, St Francis is just one of thirty-one English elementary schools in Ontario's Simcoe County Roman Catholic Separate School Board. Although it officially opened in January, it has already become a model of what good public schools can and should be if there is a will to develop high levels of achievement for all students.

In my three years as an education columnist I've never encountered a school for predominantly lower middle class children where 81 percent of the grade one class (that's fifty-one out of sixty-three students) are reading fluently and where the rest of the students are decoding and almost on their way.

Or where children in kindergarten demand homework and shun the sandbox during activity periods because, as the senior kindergarten teacher Ron Koll reports, "they want to work with words and numbers; they want to feel they are learning something."

Or where the anecdotal report card abruptly got axed, much to parents' relief, only to be replaced with a meaningful document that actually reflects the school's priorities in reading, math, science and French.

Or where the steadfast forty-seven-year-old principal, Ada Kallio, will ride school buses, visit classes and regularly send home a newsletter that proudly announces great student achievements as well as reporting the latest pedagogical research on what works.

Or where parents like Ms Edghill and Mr McEvenue, after years of wandering in Ontario's pedagogical wilderness, now confess that they feel part of their own children's education in a way they never felt before.

So what is going on here? How did a school population previously known for low levels of achievement, lack of motivation, schoolyard rowdiness and a large contingent of "high-needs" children suddenly become a place where a thirteenth-century expression, "Peace and All Good," means what the patron saint of the poor intended it to mean: a respectful community where students strive to do all good in everything they do, whether it be ecological work or schoolwork.

The real transformation of St Francis began not when 525 students entered its doors in January 1994 but when the principal and her dedicated staff, veterans of all kinds of methods and schooling, jointly decided that they would create an effective school. In so doing they took to heart the admonition of Ronald Edmonds, the father of North America's effective school movement: "We can, whenever and wherever we choose, successfully teach all children whose schooling is of interest to us."

This endeavour appropriately started with the selection of an effective reading program. Ada Kallio, a principal for seventeen years, chose Open Court, a sequential reading series that integrates spelling, grammar, writing and the study of good literature all in one kindergarten-to-grade-six package. But without letting her teachers know her preference, she sent them down to the library at the Ontario Institute for Studies in Education to choose their own. After examining scores of reading programs they, too, picked

Open Court. Nothing even came close to matching its consistency and intelligence, they reported.

Open Court, long a favourite of radical inner-city school teachers, was developed in the 1960s by an American businessman and immigrant, Blouke Carus, who was appalled by the Dick and Jane readers his own children brought home. So he hired some of the best and the brightest educators to design an effective program that was big on the systematic teaching of phonics until the end of grade one but even bigger on the presentation of good literature. (See **PHONICS**, **WHOLE LANGUAGE**.)

As a consequence, the first graders at St Francis now read and write about Aesop's fables, Leo Tolstoy, Christina Rossetti and Robert Louis Stevenson. By grades four and five students ably graduate to the likes of Thoreau, Shakespeare and Swift.

"I have twenty-four kids and they are all reading," proudly says Jackie James-Hussey, a grade one teacher. But in September, one-third of her children couldn't even recite the alphabet. "To know that I'm doing something worthwhile and not just killing five hours every day," adds the twenty-five-year-old native of Newfoundland, "that makes my day."

In most schools only 65 percent of the children achieve reading fluency by the end of grade one, but at St Francis that figure is an impressive 81 percent. (This school, remember, draws none of its charges from Ontario's professional classes.) Having observed the effects of all kinds of reading methods, Kallio knows a good thing when she sees one. "My grade ones would equal a grade three in most other schools."

Debra Cinelli, who teaches a grade six/seven class where students perform *Romeo and Juliet* or study Thornton Wilder's *Our Town*, says the results for teachers and students alike are invigorating: "The school is built on Open Court and its consistency makes this place tick. We have taken what is good in whole language, the exposure to good literature, drama and writing and given our kids a solid base to work from as well."

Open Court has given the staff an ecological map to follow and complement from kindergarten to grade six.

"There used to be a lot of lonely teaching going on," notes Ron Koll, a senior kindergarten teacher who has taught around the world. "But now this school is unique."

The secret of St Francis's success is not confined to a core curriculum of reading, French, math and science. Students can be found drawing with Macintosh computers or learning from practising artists who regularly visit the school. "I feel strongly about the arts," says Kallio, "because it's a wonderful way for children to express themselves." When children read about Beethoven in the Open Court series, the music teacher naturally plays a little *Moonlight Sonata*.

And then there is the issue of discipline. Parents and visitors alike delight in the school's serenity and creative energy. But before opening its doors Kallio had been warned that the student population was so volatile that courses in conflict resolution and trained peer mediators would be necessary.

The principal said no to such methods, and yes to fair and consistent rules. If children fight or swear they are suspended. If they disrupt a class they are detained after school. "I'm pretty black and white," adds Kallio. "I don't ever get angry and I don't carry things over. This is a safe school, and I want parents to feel comfortable when they leave their children here for five hours."

And how do students react to adults judiciously

exercising their authority in a school? "There are limits, and we know what they are. We know exactly what we can and cannot do," says one grade six student. Adds another: "It is strict, but I like it that way. People play more fairly and nobody gets teased in the yard."

The school also has a habit of surprising parents with direct and honest communication. Kallio recently replaced anecdotal reports with a nifty document that (surprise!) actually reflects the school's curriculum. A separate report for students in kindergarten has categories on language, math, and social and creative development; it even identifies whether a student uses left to right sequence for reading or can add. "The parents all said 'I'm very surprised, but this is great,'" says Koll.

Unlike far too many schools today parents really matter at St Francis. Kallio even prepares a regular newsletter that highlights student work, explains how parents can help with homework, and documents the latest research in what works. "I just want to help parents understand, especially if they have had bad experiences in and don't want to step into a school."

And respond they have. "I feel that I'm finally part of my children's education," says Jennifer Edghill. Adds Nancy Smith, a single parent: "I often talk to the teachers and they often phone me. I know what's going on every day. In other schools you just wouldn't see that closeness."

Of course, it helps to have a principal who "walks her talk," rides the buses and keeps individual notes on the performance of 565 children in reading and math. "What makes this school different is Ada's high expectation of children, staff and parents," says Christa Lane, a grade four teacher and veteran of seven schools. "She expects the parents to work with us. It's a whole-team approach."

A Progressive Example: Huron Street Public School

A number of crayon drawings with invitations and thank-yous pepper Nick Puopolo's bulletin board, but the most telling is a small card that describes Toronto's Huron Street School as "the doors of friendship."

"We have an open-door policy which makes our school distinct," says the soft-spoken but authoritative forty-eight-year-old principal. "Parents are welcomed at any time. I try to get to know as many as I can."

But openness at the 102-year-old school does not mean openness to everything or anyone. Although Puopolo is always prepared to listen, he is not always prepared to bend to the educational inanities and bureaucratic politics that paralyse so many schools in a Sargasso Sea of listlessness. "You have to intercede and intercept on behalf of the teacher and the kids to protect that special learning time," emphasizes Puopolo. "That's a big part of my job."

Although the school is squarely committed to child-centred education, successful learning counts more than dogma. If a particular student–teacher match fizzles or a program such as "creative spelling" fails a child, solutions are found and implemented quickly.

"Creative spelling doesn't always work," notes Puopolo. "So, I'll order some traditional spellers for my teachers. You've got to be prepared to use what works." His unwritten motto, "the kids come first," permeates the school's entire well-balanced agenda— from productions of *The Wizard of Oz* to a research project on the country's most innovative computer education program. The motto also sums up the ethos shared by both the school's twenty-nine teachers ("I wouldn't change one of them") and the local community.

Unlike many of the nation's schools, Huron has

long been part of a very distinct, racially mixed neighbourhood. The school is located in a middle class corner of Toronto called the Annex. Here administrators,
academics, artists and the well-to-do live in stately old
Victorian homes and take a very serious interest in
their children's education.

Although the majority of the school's well-mannered
students come from maple-lined streets, about a fourth
of the kids are drawn from city-wide daycare programs
and four hostels for battered women. Many of these
kids spend eleven hours a day away from home. "The
only real adult interaction they have is between the
teacher and daycare," notes Puopolo.

Given such social realities, innovation and flexibility
have become part of Huron's signature. To accommodate the fact that only seventy of the school's children
now go home for lunch, the school converts its gym
into a noon eating area each day, and even sells
reusable non-littering sandwich bags. When classes
end, Huron also offers seventeen after-school courses
to accommodate the taxing schedules of working or
single parents. Puopolo, himself the father of two, even
spends a lot of time waiting for tardy parents, because
"I wouldn't want anything to happen to these kids."

These non-educational challenges now comprise
nearly a third of Puopolo's duties. "The board expects
us to be curriculum leaders, and I think we do that
well, but you can only devote so much energy to that
when you are taken down these other directions," he
explains. "The board will add a new social program,
but nothing is ever taken away."

Yet Puopolo and his staff continue to meet these
challenges bravely, without forgetting the bottom line:
high levels of student learning. He, too, spends a lot of
his time in the classroom teaching science. "It's surprising how the kids view you differently after that."

But half of Huron's success truly belongs to its involved parents. The school's seventy-member Parent Guardian Association takes little for granted and actively debates such substantive issues as the curriculum and even the placement of portable classrooms.

While members of the PGA agree that Huron listens seriously to its parents, many add rather wistfully that they wished the school did not end at grade six. In some fellow institutions, parents often have to scream to get attention; Huron works the other way, says Huron parent and university administrator Beata FitzPatrick. "They spotted a reading problem with my daughter that I hadn't noticed, and we worked together to solve it ... and she took off a mile per minute."

An Alternative Example: Alternative High

We have decoupled rights from civic responsibilities and severed citizenship from education on the false assumption that citizens just happen. We have forgotten that "public" in public schools means not just paid for by the public but procreative of the very idea of a public.
— Benjamin Barber, U. S. school critic

Deep in the heart of Preston Manning's Calgary riding sits an exceptional high school housed in a very ordinary box of concrete and glass.

But, Alternative High, with its student murals and painted lockers, long ago transcended its architecture by establishing a prairie-wide reputation as a school that offered dropouts or potential dropouts a demanding and safe place to drop into.

Now celebrating its twentieth year—a formidable achievement for any alternative school—the institution also boasts a democratic charter. Notes Jim Hoeppner, the school's long-time principal: "We are one of a kind, the only democratic high school in the province." (A similar school just opened in Red Deer.)

The academic refugees that enter Alternative's doors each morning come in all stripes and fashions. There are short-cropped punks and long-haired hippies as well as the omnipresent devotees of baseball caps, nose rings and loose jeans. In addition to horrendous school histories, this diverse and largely white student body shares a healthy respect for learning and an earnest desire to finish school and get on with life.

The relatively small scale of Alternative honours a little-understood principle of political economy. With no more than 120 students and 10 teachers, Alternative re-creates all the blessings of a Hutterite colony. Its size allows for a community of individuals to be recognized as visible participants with responsiblities. Any change in scale would probably see more people arguing about work than working.

Not surprisingly, most of the school's students dropped out of cliquish, impersonal and often violent high schools where student populations of 1,500 or more violated the very principles of scale Alternative respects. "If you looked at someone the wrong way at my old school," says Julie, an eighteen-year-old with a penchant for black clothing and accessories, "they'd go after you." At Alternative Julie is just another budding mortician eager to finish her studies.

Although democracy at Alternative means "one person, one vote," it is also an apprenticeship in liberty. Students are not only expected to participate in "democratic meetings" every Friday but to abide by town-hall "agreements." According to Colin James, who has taught at the school for eighteen years, "the students have invariably voted for tighter controls than the staff would—with the exception of smoking."

Students, too, manage the school store or help run

new programs like Catalyst—a local spin on Alberta's mandatory Career and Life Management course. Alternative's version actually encourages students to take part in learning outside the school and in community service, whether it be an environmental cleanup or reading to the blind.

Because Alternative's Jeffersonian version of democracy makes its students owners of the school, the place has no vandalism or violence. New students must be jointly approved by staff and pupils and pass a six-week probation period. For individuals who have trouble honouring commitments there is a four-point "step program" that firmly reminds pupils that actions have consequences, including dismissal.

In contrast to many avant-garde public schools that have failed, Alternative has increasingly tightened its structure and focus on academics over the years. The basics and a beefed-up arts program matter here, because they remain the roots of critical thought.

In the math program, students generally move at their own pace, provided they have mastered the material at hand. English includes both group and individual sessions with pointed instruction in the differences between a description, an analysis and a judgment. No one can earn the right to say "Shakespeare sucks!" until he or she has read and studied him.

Although Alternative is not a model for every high school, it is an alternative that every urban high school system should offer students alienated by the normal scheme of things. The school costs approximately $200,000 more to run than one of its regular cousins, but its yearly twenty-four graduates leave as citizens, not as expensive wards of the attorney general.

More tellingly, the half-dozen students I interviewed spoke uniformly of what works at Alternative and what is exportable. Their recommendations for the system included three bold dares:

Dare to challenge students with high expectations and stand up to them when they initally object to hard work.

Dare to involve students in the democratic governance and maintenance of the school and the life of the local community.

And last but not least, dare to trust students to be more than they seem to be.

See also Appendices 5, 8 and 9.

ENGLISH AS A SECOND LANGUAGE (ESL)   In Montreal, Toronto and Vancouver, nearly half the school kids speak a language other than English. While some of these young immigrants hail from stable countries, others arrive from battlefields and ecological disaster zones. The burden of educating these children falls upon the local school board. Current immigration policy remains blind to the task of teaching children English or even the rudiments of Canadian culture.

It can take non–English speakers anywhere from two to four years to acquire the fluency they need to tackle a regular program. Students from Colombia, France or Italy, for example, can usually learn English much faster than students from Taiwan or Thailand. Very little research has been done on how to teach these children. Many schools use the total immersion (sink-or-swim) approach. Others will segregate the newcomers until their English is good enough to participate in the regular program. The following story about a school in Etobicoke (Metropolitan Toronto) aptly illustrates the problems posed for schools by a federal immigration policy that ends once the immigrants have arrived—and the triumphs that can be achieved.

A Somali School

God willing, it will be well with us.

My heart is not the heart of a sheep.

—Somali proverbs

By any measurement, it is a long way from war-torn Somalia on the Horn of Africa to Ontario's not-so-Golden Horseshoe and the predictable order of suburban Etobicoke.

The distances, both cultural and geographic, extend from drylands to paved farmlands, from Islam to the gods of materialism, from the Somali language to English, from pastoral huts to concrete apartments, from camels to subways and, last but not least, from poetry to Orwellian "newspeak."

These great divides all meet in six dirty, white condominiums on Dixon Road, and in particular at Kingsview Village Junior School. Here, principal Naomi Emmett presides over a burgeoning elementary school under construction (plus twelve crowded portables) where 50 percent of the school's 650 students come from a Somalia broken by civil war and drought. The rest of the school's students boast thirty different countries of origin.

Like many urban Canadian schools, Kingsview has become the first official welcome-mat for immigrants and the front line for federal immigration policies that often ignore the cultural, financial and pedagogical consequences of immigration on schools.

In the last several years, waves of political and now economic refugees, primarily from Somalia, have doubled the school's population, forcing Emmett to reorganize Kingsview as many as four times in one year. "We have had kids come the day after they arrived from Somalia," says the energetic forty-three-year-old principal. "Kids with no English and kids who have never been to school, kids whose siblings have been murdered, kids who have taken the weapons off dead soldiers and sold them...."

Because the federal government provides no direct financial support for translators, teachers of English as a Second Language or even for background papers, the innovations and accommodations reached at Kingsview have been achieved by Emmett, her dedicated staff and the Etobicoke Board of Education.

With a little federal foresight, a simple immigration report could have alerted the school to Somalis' love of verse (the country teems with poets), their tendency to treat each other as equals (in Somalia, bus drivers and cooks attend school meetings on curriculum) and their habit of greeting hardship with an uncanny spiritual calm (most are Sunni Muslims).

No such briefing ever arrived, so Emmett and company discovered these realities on the job. When a Somali child fell to his death from a highrise condo, the teachers were more upset than the students. "The kids thought it was his time and not their place to question it," recalls Emmett. "We spent a day trying to get our teachers to understand that."

It also took some time for the Somali parents to learn that getting a phone call from the teacher didn't mean their child had misbehaved; it was just a symbol of Kingsview's determination to work with the home.

Given the racial tension present in the overpopulated condominiums feeding the school, Kingsview exudes a remarkable harmony ("This is a safe haven," declares Emmett). It has created this climate by offering logical rules with fair consequences; Emmett has sent home many an errant kicker and stone thrower with full parental support. She has also learned how to say "no" in Somali: "Maya."

The school's academic program combines activity-based learning (an Etobicoke staple), direct instruction and individual tutoring with full immersion for non-English-speaking children. "If you didn't do your stuff in Somalia, you would get a beating," explains one ten-year-old in a busy grade five class. "Here if you don't do it, the teacher will just get mad." (There are, adds Emmett, other consequences, too.)

Aiding Emmett and thirty-seven teachers in forging a healthy school community is a full-time Somali-born assistant, Habiba Aden. The twenty-three-year-old models the kind of poise and elegance Somali women are famous for, and notes that it is difficult to compare old-style Somalia schools influenced by British or Italian colonial policies with Canadian ones. The former teacher adds that a few educated Somalis have trouble understanding the nature of Canadian schooling. "Gee, what are they doing? All they are doing is playing," they tell her. "But they forget there are some consequences and forget all the expectations.... Most parents are satisfied in every way."

Determining how tight or loose, direct or indirect a pedagogy should be for Somali students remains an ongoing concern for Emmett. "I'm trying to find out about schools in North America that have dealt with these issues. Even in the literature there isn't much there. Even the experts say they don't know."

For this very Canadian challenge the Somalis typically have a verse: "To be without education is to be without light." And there is much light at Kingsview.

See also **RACISM AND MULTICULTURALISM** and **EFFECTIVE SCHOOLS**.

ENVIRONMENTAL EDUCATION   One of the greatest enthusiasms to have swept through North American schools in the last five years has been environmental education.

Although teachers deserve credit for taking an important civic issue and integrating it across the curriculum, the enterprise has not been wholly successful or always educational.

Garrett Hardin, professor emeritus of human ecology at the University of California, is one of the world's most respected ecologists. He has been writing about multiplying humans, bad economics and the death of the natural world since long before most people thought it all mattered.

Speaking bluntly, of course, is one of his trademarks (Hardin infuriates environmentalists and politicians alike). He believes, for example, that much of what passes for "environmentalism" today is really a bunch of thoughtless "enthusiasms." Like eighteenth-century English intellectuals, Hardin understands an "enthusiast" to be one who "acts as if directed from a god within, and that's why the eighteenth-century English didn't trust enthusiasts of any kind."

Given such a perspective, Hardin also believes that the environmental movement and environmental education have "gone off half-cocked" in far too many dubious directions. ("A decade from now new wrong paths will open up.") Adds Hardin: "The general attitude of the conservative—let's look it over before we embark on saving the world—has been missing."

His solid antidote to so much haste and waste is something he calls "filters against folly." These are, in effect, three distinct thinking strategies: "the literate filter, the numerate filter and the ecolate filter." If the seventy-eight-year-old had his way, secondary teachers and their pupils would routinely apply these filters to the major controversies of the day.

The first filter, literacy, has been a traditional school staple. By literacy, Hardin means skill in either written or spoken language. To pass a subject through this filter is to ask "What are the words?" and "What are the most appropriate words?" It is to know that language has two functions—"to promote thought and to prevent it"—and to ask the question: "Is this writer merely being eloquent?"

The second filter, numeracy, has long been the language of scientists. To ask "What are the numbers?" is really to ask what follows from such questions. Such inquiries, adds Hardin, are as old as Galileo. The famous Italian once noted that if you put three dogs on top of each other, the bottom one would do just fine. But if you stacked three elephants on top of each other, the results for the first animal would be very bloody.

In numerate terms, scale always makes a difference, whether it comes to the strength of long leg bones or to the size of schools. A high school with seven hundred students remains a community; a high school with two thousand wards becomes an alien mall selling credits. "There are always scale effects involved," says Hardin, and this perspective is science's greatest gift to critical thinking.

Unfortunately, economists seem to have learned only half of this lesson, says the scientist. The culture's premier number crunchers devote great treatises to economies of scale and how countries like Monaco can't support an automobile industry. "But they don't notice the diseconomies of scale or how some things get worse when they get bigger." Democracy is a perfect example of a diseconomy of scale, notes Hardin. "The more populated the nation, the thinner and thinner its representation."

The third filter, ecolacy, is a bit vaguer than the other two. Time and its consequences are its essential concerns. To pass an idea through an ecolate filter is really to ask "And then what?": is this idea sustainable, stable or destructive over time? According to Hardin it's the question most often missing in any economic or environmental debate.

By definition the ecolate filter is profoundly conservative. For example, neither a literate nor a numerate analysis alone would have led scientists to conclude that every antibiotic or every pesticide eventually selects for its own resistance. Yet an ecolate view, which understands that humans can never do one thing in isolation, would have predicted that DDT would breed DDT-resistant mosquitoes and that pencillin would eventually breed penicillin-resistant streptococci. The question "And then what?" is generally not welcomed by enthusiasts, "whether they be profit-minded promoters or altruistic reformers," says the ecologist.

In sum, Hardin sees a good environmental education as really being a good general education that ultimately teaches students to ask "What are the words? What are the numbers? And then what?" No one filter is adequate for understanding the world or predicting the consequences of human actions, but all three at least can give us some humility.

F

FRENCH IMMERSION French Immersion is Canada's most celebrated educational experiment. It began in the 1960s, when a group of English-speaking parents expressed their dissatisfaction with the quality of traditional "hammer-the-grammar" French instruction in Montreal schools.

What they proposed instead was a program that would develop kids' fluency through lots of talk and listening, with little emphasis on boring stuff like nouns, verbs and their proper use. The movement quickly spread throughout anglophone Quebec, Ottawa, bilingual parts of Ontario and eventually the western provinces. Sixteen hundred schools now offer the program; nearly 300,000 children are enrolled. Though demand seems to be waning, parents still line up to get their kids into the schools.

A typical immersion program offers middle and upper class English-speaking students (that's what the demographics say) all their instruction in French until grade three or four. Once French has been mastered the students begin to study other disciplines in both languages.

Immersion owes its popularity to a number of factors. Of chief importance is its sound goal of having children become competent in a second language. But most parents simply regard French Immersion as a type of publicly funded charter schooling with a more intensive academic program, where the students are all eager to learn.

A sensation in Canadian schooling, French

Immersion has often been called "the most successful innovation in Canadian education" and is much admired in Europe and abroad. Studies have consistently shown that the program's students learn much more French, while achievement in other subjects remains constant or soars. However, the quality of the French learned is the subject of considerable debate.

Since 1975, research reported in *The Canadian Modern Language Review* has consistently found that many French Immersion students can indeed talk quickly as well as listen and read French well. But their ability to communicate accurately is seriously impaired because they speak a strange pidgin known as "Frenglish." Far too many French Immersion graduates write and speak French ungrammatically because inaccurate language use, when not formally corrected, becomes fossilized. (Francophone students—kids coming from French households and French-only schools—make only one-third to one-seventh the number of grammatical errors that French Immersion pupils do.)

French Immersion has demonstrated that a communication-oriented curriculum that focuses on lots of oral practice will no more produce accurate and proficient second-language speakers with consistency than a traditional language program. What many French Immersion programs have failed to do, notes researcher Rebecca Valette, is "combine the advantages of the grammar-based curriculum [accuracy] with the advantages of a comprehension-oriented program."

French Immersion programs aren't the only ones making this mistake. An associate professor of French at the University of Toronto recently reported this finding: of twenty-seven students enrolled in her first-year course, one was dyslexic and couldn't spell a word in French; ten were functionally illiterate in both official languages; four had serious problems in French and in understanding basic grammar; eight were at course level; and four were too good for the course. Of these four, three had been educated in old-fashioned schools in Africa and Mauritius. Noted the instructor: "In French the lack of attention in our schools to grammar, vocabulary and memory-training techniques (such as repetition and drill) has produced, in the words of one of my colleagues, a generation of unteachables, virtual functional illiterates in both French and English."

A formal 1988 study of high school students entering universities confirmed that there are real differences between French Immersion and Core French programs: "(a) immersion graduates tend to perform functions well but at the expense of accuracy and (b) students from a core program (French for an hour a day) who take a six week course, show fewer discrepancies in their speaking skills and obtain ratings only slightly lower than those of immersion graduates."

A great many critics have also faulted French Immersion as an élite program for middle class students. Strong social and class divisions are very evident in many French Immersion schools. In this regard the Canadian experience differs markedly from the American experiment with bilingual Spanish programs, which were designed for primarily poor children whose mastery of English and Spanish is weak. But, not unlike French Immersion, these programs have tended to reduce language competence rather than enhance it. They have also had other unhealthy effects. Notes the historian Arthur Schlesinger, Jr.: "Bilingual education retards rather than expedites the movement of Hispanic children into the English-speaking world.... It nourishes self-ghettoization and ghettoization nourishes racial antagonism."

French Immersion hasn't created the fabled bilingual class it promised. Most graduates are not eager to continue in French at university or to work in bilingual positions (these still go to Quebecers). One Manitoba study found, for example, that girls graduating from immersion programs were much more likely to study the hard sciences or engineering than French at university.

There is also a wide and little-reported variation in French Immersion schools: the most successful and academically inclined seem to be based in British Columbia and Alberta, and the least successful and most experimental seem to flourish in Ontario. Schools that are more analytic in their approach to teaching French do much better than schools that use indirect or holistic approaches. Because the analytic schools focus more on proper use, the use of English and correction of errors, their graduates speak both French and English well. (The Lycées or International French Schools tend to do this job much better than the average French Immersion school.)

Depending on one's reading of the research, French Immersion is either Canada's first successful charter school franchise (phenomenal growth, wide popularity and high academic performance) or a disastrous failure (social divisiveness, a high dropout rate at the high school level, and a decided failure to produce a large body of bilingual adults).

The future of French Immersion is as problematic as that of any Canadian school program. Quebec's separation, if it comes, will probably kill much but not all of the public enthusiasm for immersion. But it could remain a potent force in Canadian education, provided that French Immersion schools continue to excel academically and make their French instruction more systematic.

Hector Hammerly, a professor of applied linguistics at Simon Fraser University and a long-time critic of the unsystematic pedagogy used in many French Immersion schools, offers this advice to parents. He says that the natural and most desirable approach for learning a second language is to surround a two-year-old child with native speakers of that language. This experience, however, cannot be duplicated in the classroom. As a consequence, he concludes that "cognitively developed older children and young adults, because of their conscious linguistic awareness, their ability to focus on accuracy, their study skills, their rich experience/memory and their responsiveness to appropriate correction, make better classroom language students than younger children. Children, however, have better motor memory than adults. The best age, then, to begin systematic classroom learning of a remote second language is ten or eleven, when cognitive development has reached an adequate level, peer pressure and inhibition are not excessive and motor memory is still fairly strong."

Hammerly's book on the subject, *French Immersion: Myths and Reality* (Detselig Enterprises Ltd, 1989), is a good investment for any parents interested in enrolling their children in an immersion program. For a less critical review, consult Merrill Swain and Sharon Lapkin, *French Immersion: The Trial Balloon that Flew* (OISE Press, 1983).

G

GRAMMAR   When carpenters are taught how to cross-cut, join, bevel, wedge and frame, no one accuses their instructors of dehumanizing pedagogy. But whenever a teacher gives names to parts of speech (children, by the way, like to name things) he or she stands the risk of being censured by administrators. Grammar no longer exists in most provincial curricula.

The wild aversion to teaching grammar in public schools reflects the progressive disdain for direct instruction, practice or rule-learning. It also stems from the lifeless way in which grammar was often taught in the past.

Progressives are more right than wrong when they argue that teaching parts of speech and how to analyse a sentence will not directly make a pupil a good writer. But as James Steele, an English professor at Carleton University, explains, there are other good reasons for returning grammar to the English curriculum: "It can give the learner a language for talking about language—both one's own and a foreign one. It can enable a student to analyze (when necessary) the syntax of complex statements and to understand the terminology commonly used in dictionaries. There is also evidence that a knowledge of sentence organization can help young children to read better. [Parents interested in pressing this issue at school might want to get hold of an article by Phyllis Weaver, "Improving Reading Comprehension: Effects of Sentence Organization Instruction," *Reading Research Quarterly* 1979 (15): 129–46.] Furthermore, just as a knowledge of arithmetic makes algebra easier to understand, so a knowledge of elementary sentence grammar may facilitate an understanding of compositional grammars that is especially relevant to linking units of information at the level of the clause in the context of a paragraph."

The effects of not teaching grammar are evident everywhere and have driven a great many English teachers in high schools, community colleges and university to distraction. A quarter-century of no structured, sequential teaching of grammar, reports Jack McCaffrey, an Ontario high school teacher, has made it impossible to deal systematically with student writing problems:

"I have been told many times that all the studies show that teaching grammar has no effect on student writing. It is obvious that a knowledge of grammar will not compensate for having nothing worthwhile to say. But even if a student writes something interesting, he may have many technical problems. How is a teacher to deal with these? The meaning of terms such as *verb, noun, phrase, clause,* and *sentence* is unknown to the majority of my students; therefore, any suggestions I might have about their handling of such items are incomprehensible to them.

"I have never understood why a knowledge of grammar should be harmful to students. The educators of the last quarter-century seem to have concluded that almost any discipline is an enemy to creativity. They seem to believe that if students just write a lot, and never have to submit to criticism or be bored by learning certain dry facts, rules and nomenclature, they will learn to write well. By the same logic, if one wanted to be a musician, one should just play all the time, and never submit to the indignity of practising scales or learning musical theory. These are dull, and might crush the creative instinct.

"The problems of trying to teach students to write are exacerbated by the wildly divergent mixture of abilities in the modern multicultural classroom. I know that the good students are supposed to teach the weak ones, but those students who can write do so only by instinct. They have no exact knowledge of the structures of language, and are therefore not equipped to explain anything to their uncomprehending peers. That is why peer editing and proofreading have not, in my experience, been effective.

"What would be effective? I do not pretend to know. But I do wonder if harm would result from a systematic, sequential approach to grammar, with the use of specified textbooks and workbooks—and even exams—to ensure that everyone at least makes an attempt to teach and learn a certain amount of grammar."

A Case Study of Grammarless Schooling
The misapprehension of the language structure used in society was often lead to its destruction.
—an Ontario high school graduate

Each year several Ontario high schools send five thousand fresh and eager faces to Humber College, one of the nation's largest community and technical schools. And each year approximately one out of three newcomers promptly fails a simple English placement exam because of the inability to recognize, let alone write, a blooper-free sentence.

One of Humber's many remedial teachers, Mary Jo Morris, keeps a running tab of these illustrative bloopers, and sampling a few is like reading some English curricula in Ontario's high schools: you don't know whether to laugh or to cry:

After the train was out of the city, the beautiful spectacles passed by me.

We as human beings spend very little time doing the tasks of writing and thinking properly, which is the reason why few people of who we think of having a basic knowledge of understanding do not comprehend at all.

The scene at these types of events have all the glamour and pizzas that one might expect.

Bilingualism, which means men and women getting the same pay for the same work ...

Your local Butterworths Sales Representative has placed you on order to receive an examination copy once it is published. We believe it will be well worth the wait in lieu of your Fall 1992 courses.

As the years progressed with the help of western tech they incorporated some of our food traits.

And on the bloopers march. Morris's extensive list also includes such innovative clichés as "dead beets on ice" and "bombfires on the beach."

She is also somewhat alarmed at being part of an annual million-dollar exercise in raising the communication skills of Humber entrants to the point where they can successfully study what they entered college for. (To calculate the annual costs of remediation for all of Canada's community colleges, simply multiply Humber's bill by 200.)

Frustrated by this phenomenal financial drain (Ontario's ministry of education does not pay for remediation) and a seemingly endless stream of unprepared students, Richard Hook, Humber's vice-president of academics, and Sheila Susini, the co-ordinator of Humber's links with high schools, came up with a subversive idea called the Placement Testing Project.

It began in 1992 when Susini, a former remedial English teacher at Humber, approached feeder high schools with a copy of the College Board Computerized Placement Test for Sentence Skills and Reading. She asked administrators and chairs of English departments if they wouldn't mind entering the multiple-choice test into their computers so that students could, in a "riskless" way, find out what's needed for success in college. She assured administrators that Humber would learn a student's score only if the student chose to tell them.

Because external tests raise red flags in schools, Susini had a hard sell ("principals would be interested but heads of English departments would not be"), but in the end seventeen courageous high schools put the two-dollar test into their computers. "It will snowball for sure now," adds Susini.

As a student motivator the test has few peers. By objectively informing students that they are bound for remedial English classes unless they improve their skills, the test adds new meaning to old tasks such as assembling nouns and verbs into logical sentences. "It opens some marvellous doors," reports Jim Willson, who tries to link Etobicoke's high school programs and activities with the realities of post-secondary education. "It tells students what they have to work towards."

The test also quietly gives high school teachers a clear statement on the minimum English skills expected by community colleges. "It's easy to help the university-bound kids," says Susini. "But for the community colleges, most teachers don't have any idea what skills are needed and we haven't been very clear about communicating those skills."

According to Hook the test is also a local, cost-efficient way to address the erosion of provincial standards that has followed a quarter-century drought. "Even if we spent $100,000 on this project, it's money in the bank," he explains. And that's because the test politely suggests solutions at the problem's source rather than "putting developmental English programs all over the place."

By achieving so many laudable goals with one novel idea, the Placement Test project is a good ecological parable on the silliness of the public school system working in isolated bits and pieces. For as every college remediation teacher can attest, the act of learning how to write strong, clear and accurate prose in high school has economic, psychological and educational consequences far beyond grade twelve.

Or as a high school graduate recently put it, "The exercise that every student should be doing is practising expressive ideas until the right words are formed."

GRANT, GEORGE

All a poet can do today is warn. That is why the true poets must all be truthful.

—Wilfred Owen

George Grant, a chainsmoker who rarely finished a sentence, was a nationalist poet and Christian philosopher, who honoured both traditions by disturbing Canadians with powerful and unpopular ideas.

His most acclaimed book, *Lament for a Nation*, remains just as prescient an attack on Canadian liberalism as it did when it first became a bestseller in 1965 long before the free trade fiasco. (Mr Grant defined liberalism as an anti-ecological creed: "the idea that man's essence is freedom and that what chiefly concerns man in this life is to shape the world as we want it.")

Although Mr Grant died in 1988, no comparable

thinker has replaced his voice or even come close to echoing his thoughtful critiques of modernism and technological society. William Christian's new and wonderful biography of the man (University of Toronto Press) vividly provides the reason for this: Mr Grant was simply an original and demanding critic who defied ideological labels.

The largely self-taught philosopher was also a formidable educator with absolute values. This is not surprising, says Professor Christian, as "education was the family business." Grant's grandfather, for example, was principal of Queen's and his father headmaster of Upper Canada College.

But if education was the family business it was never a very comfortable one for Mr Grant. He despaired of the influence of the shallow American philosopher John Dewey on school thinking and lamented the invention of "multi-versities"—institutions of higher learning that claimed to be "value-free," which only meant they had become the handmaidens of technological progress.

George Grant began his adult life as a Deweyite but quickly disavowed himself from Dewey's pragmatism, which held that schools should create well-adjusted citizens for democratic life with a consumer-like curriculum. He concluded that Dewey, a dour and soulless modernist, was a well-meaning liberal and as such a very dangerous character.

To Mr Grant, education was a much more noble enterprise than solely "life-adjusting" citizens for a life of money, power, technology and sex. He believed that Dewey faltered mightily in assuming that traditional education was cut off from life. Traditional educators taught history, geography and philosophy, he argued, not to distance people from reality but to provide them "with a tough instrument with which to analyze reality." Such work was work, not play. "The fallacy of progressive education is that so often it has believed thought was easy. The material it gave children to fashion their brains on was not tough enough. The result was inevitably sloppy thinking."

Grant, who spent most of his adult life in unversities (McMaster, Dalhousie, York), found a great deal of sloppy thinking going on there too. In a brillant 1967 essay ("The University Curriculum"), the philosopher made it clear that universities had betrayed their traditions by accepting dynamic technology as the new world religion, "value-free" social sciences as the new curriculum, and efficient technicians as the university's new global graduate.

In the process the humanities have lost all heart, becoming mere slaves to "the fun culture" or as Grant put it, "the orgasm at home and napalm abroad." Given the relentless pace of technological life, the public purpose of art "will not be to lead men to the meaning of things, but to titivate, cajole and shock them into fitting into a world in which the question of meaning is not relevant." The new and busy role for humanities is to abet this demanding task.

Grant, being Grant, laid the blame for this mess squarely on the shoulders of modern liberalism. "It has been able to criticise out of the popular mind the general idea of human excellence and yet put no barrier in the way of that particular idea of excellence which in fact determines the actions of the most powerful in society. The mark of education is claimed to be scepticism about the highest human purpose, but in fact there is no scepticism in the public realm about what is important to do."

Mr Grant also had a habit of living what he believed. When a fledgling York University asked him to head their philosophy department in 1960, he tentatively accepted on the grounds that he would have freedom to respect the subject matter at hand, philosophy. But when he was told he would have to adopt University of Toronto's first-year curriculum as well as a limp textbook about philosophy rather than a work of philosophy (Mr Grant always began with Plato's *Republic*), he rejected the offer.

Such a shoddy curriculum, then reasoned the forty-one-year-old with six children, would introduce students to much scepticism and many opinions. But it would not direct them to the real task at hand: fashioning hard and true judgments about ideas.

The beauty of Mr Christian's lively biography is that it reawakens a personal and principled voice that Canadians and Canadian educators need to hear more than ever.

See also **CHILD-CENTRED LEARNING.**

H

HOME-SCHOOLING (HOME-BASED EDUCATION)

When Lois Strom quit her job as a hospital administrator in 1988 to home-school her daughters, Cher and Chelsea, she started off with a collection of desks and chairs in the basement and the collective disapproval of friends. "Your girls will never get a real job in the real world," said the doubters.

Five years later, her eldest daughter, eighteen-year-old Cher, has finished her high school courses and started a job as a consultant at Calgary's KDM Career College—a position she earned because of her superior poise and skills. Her youngest, Chelsea, began a grade ten study program at home. She does her work in a book-studded living room because the girls quickly found the basement setup too schoolish, says Lois. "We started out as school at home and now we are just a normal home where learning happens." And the doubters have become believers, as home-schooling has left the fringes of education and become a popular and doable alternative to lacklustre education in private or public schools.

Although no federal agency keeps an eye on home-based schooling, the world's most durable educational institution, the interest in this pioneering and controversial approach to learning is growing rapidly. According to Wendy Priesnitz, national co-ordinator of the Canadian Alliance of Homeschoolers, her organization received 190 inquiries from parents in July 1991 about home-based education. Two years later the number of phone calls more than quadrupled to 811.

Notes Priesnitz: "Home-based schooling has become a legitimate alternative, and people no longer fear it."

The growing acceptance of home-schooling (it is now legal in every province) has come as more and more parents like Lois Strom and Wendy Priesnitz (she also schooled her two daughters at home) have demonstrated its effectiveness by rebutting the three central arguments often marshalled against the movement.

The first myth says that home-schooling is something only done by misfits or back-to-the-landers. (In 1988 even Strom thought it was something that only granola crunchers did "in the backwoods of British Columbia.") But the parents who have turned their kitchens into classrooms and refrigerators into blackboards come from a diversity of backgrounds. A 1990 survey of five thousand Canadian home-schoolers (an estimated thirty thousand parents now teach their children at home) found that they included professors, farmers, tradespeople, teachers and single moms. The survey also noted that most home-schooling families earned modest incomes ($30,000 or less), were self-employed or lived in the country. Such findings make the home-based education a decidedly lower middle class movement.

The motives to home-school are fundamentally hopeful. Perhaps the strongest is simply a desire to strengthen family values and bonds. About half of all Canadian home-schoolers also hold strong religious beliefs that many public schools no longer honour or uphold. Strom, for example, began home-schooling when Cher, then in grade eight, confessed that she simply didn't care to attend public school anymore because of the social pressures to experiment with drugs and sex. "We also did not approve of the school's philosophical bias." (The Stroms are strong

Christians and objected to the school's brand of "secular humanism.")

The next myth, the argument most often levelled against home-schoolers, is that parents can't teach as well as trained teachers. In fact, recent research on home-educated children clearly refutes this shibboleth. A recent U. S. study of 4,600 children, for example, found that the home-schooled routinely outperformed 80 percent of all other students on standardized achievement tests. Canadian children taught at home have also scored higher on such tests than average. Some American universities, such as Harvard and Yale, actively recruit home-schooled students because of their good study habits.

These positive results suggest that a parent can do in two hours a day what now takes the school system an uncertain six hours to achieve. For at home a parent can focus flexibly on learning, character development and small-group teaching (home-schoolers usually educate more than one child at home) in a way most schools can't afford or have long since abandoned.

The other most common argument against home-schooling is the myth that children taught at home will somehow suffer from uneven social development or gross isolation. But like their school peers, children taught in the kitchen play with friends, take skating, dance or French lessons, attend church clubs, visit museums and so on. Unlike their schooled neighbours, however, they regularly meet and work with a full range of older and younger people and daily confront the real tragedies (as opposed to school-made ones) that make up modern living.

Most home-schoolers, for instance, make commmunity work and service part of their daily curriculum, often working with the aged, sick or troubled in their neighbourhood. Chelsea Strom not only has a part-time job at a cleaner's but also helps out at her neighbourhood teen drop-in centre.

Given the strong emphasis most home-schoolers place on character development, the argument that kids schooled at home are brought up in a bubble and can't cope in the real world just doesn't make sense, says Priesnitz. She taught her two children at home until they reached high school age and says she hasn't yet met a home-schooled child who wasn't well-behaved and self-reliant. "I say to people all the time that the best preparation for dealing with negative things in life are early positive experiences at home."

Although home-schooling is definitely not for everyone (it takes a regular time commitment on the part of one parent each day), it provides a healthy alternative for parents who value strong families and able learners.

Case Study: An Alberta Family

A couple who make a good marriage, and raise healthy, morally competent children, are serving the world's future more directly and surely than any political leader, though they never utter a public word.

—Wendell Berry

Eight years ago, Brenda Giese broke all kinds of social conventions and home-schooled her firstborn. This year she and her husband, Bruce Birney, will teach all of their five children at home in the short-grass town of Brant, Alberta (population 40). And they will do so with the province's blessing and a $1,200 stipend per child from the Cochrane Separate School Board.

When the family started home-schooling, fewer than a hundred families shared their passion; today five thousand Alberta families have chosen to use the hearth as it has always been used, as a place for learning.

Although there is no such thing as typical home "teachers," Brenda and Bruce live and breathe many of the simple values that characterize the home-based education movement, perhaps the fastest-growing and most economical alternative to public schooling available to the country's lower middle class.

Like most of Canada's thirty-thousand-plus home educators, Brenda and Bruce, both native Albertans, live in the country. The family grow their own food organically and get by on one income (Bruce is a school custodian). They profess no particular church allegiance but practise a living Christianity that puts children and community ahead of careers. "We live as close to the earth as possible," says Brenda.

The couple's decision to home-school is as multifaceted as their five-acre prairie homestead, which sustains a garden, a dozen pheasants, two rabbits, three sheep and one horse.

As people with strong spiritual beliefs they knew that public schools are, as Brenda politely notes, "very delicate about moral education." They thought, too, that the family's vegetarianism might not be able to compete against the fast-food culture in the schools. Bruce, then a Calgary taxi driver on the night shift, also realized that he would see little of his children if they went to school.

Persevering with home-schooling took great determination. The grandparents were totally against it and even descended upon the house with the message, "It's not the right way to go." Brenda also had to prove to Bruce that it was feasible. "I was against it too," recalls Bruce, a reluctant participant. "I thought home-birthing was the last home thing I'd be doing (four children were born at home), but then home education reared its head.... But I've come to see that it works, and appreciate all the benefits.... I'm teaching now. I do the math."

Aside from familial opposition, Brenda had to battle her own real fears about visits from truant officers (they never came). But these concerns largely evaporated when the province revised its School Act in 1988, making the traditional freedom to educate at home a legal and increasingly popular choice for Alberta parents.

Although many public school boards remain hostile to the idea, several pioneering and cash-strapped Catholic boards will give parents half of the province's school foundation grant (between $2,100 and $2,500) if the parents register with them for supervision.

The grant money is a blessing, says Brenda. This year, for instance, they will pay for a new computer ("None of us are familiar with the machine—it will be a family study"), textbooks, several courses outside the home (karate, gymnastics and computer instruction) and other instructional odds and ends.

Educating five children at home, however, has "its ups and downs," confides fourteen-year-old Laibrook. It takes not only an enormous amount of teamwork, but instruction that goes well beyond words and numbers. Each child, for example, prepares one breakfast and one lunch per week (Bayden, for instance, a lanky eight-year-old, is the French-toast expert).

Animal husbandry, organic gardening, sewing and carpentry also show up on the curriculum. There is also a rich stream of Biblical stories. "We are teaching them how to live and how to care for themselves in the countryside."

Like most home-schoolers, Brenda does not regard what she is doing as some kind of social panacea. She knows many families that thrive on public schooling.

"But when you think of all the experimental things schools do with children and then look at home-schooling ... at least we do what we do with love and lots of feedback."

As for one of the central arguments that educators muster against home-schooling—that it produces poorly socialized individuals who can't find a steady job, build a relationship, hold a cup of coffee or even write a poem—it is rendered invalid by this family's home-schooling.

Motions

I sit in the mall/ watching people come and go/ I see a blond girl and mouth a hello/ She winks,/ and then cracks a smile/ I run up beside her, and we talk a while/ I walk her home,/ and meet Mister and Misses/ As I leave/ She blows me kisses/ without these small motions,/ we would have never become friends/ and this, my friends is where my poem ends.

—Laibrook Birney

The two girls and three boys run the gamut of emotions and personalities. But having spent a lot of time with adults, they are comfortable in their presence. "They are their own people.... You don't get this attitude of kids being against adults," says Brenda. Adds Bruce: "The whole thing might be a little more problematic in a single-child family."

Laibrook Birney, the eldest, confidently sports the badges of Canadian teenagerhood: a baseball cap, a shaved head and loose jeans. Cressa, shy and cautious, has long red hair, a crush on Bryan Adams and a vocabulary that astounds friends and adults alike.

Like many home-educated children, both Laibrook and Cressa have attended a formal school—an experience that gives them a unique perspective on the whole subject of learning.

"I had more friends at school, but it was not as challenging," says Laibrook, a budding poet. "Things were easier and we worked at a much slower pace. At home, once you have learned something, you just go on to the next thing."

But home-schooling, adds Laibrook, is not altogether excellent. "It has its ups and downs, like anything in life." It requires a great deal of self-discipline and drive. "You don't have a huge social life," he adds with a smile. Yet he admits that local youth groups and courses in karate and computers keep him in touch with teenagers his own age.

Cressa, who was called "the well" at school because of her formidable memory, shares many of her brother's observations. She prefers the relaxed pace of working at home and doesn't care much for all the henpecking in the schoolyard in which "the older grades hit on the younger grades."

The centre for much of Laibrook's and Cressa's learning (both are taking a grade nine curriculum this year) is the family dining room where multiplication tables, a world map and a diagram of the human body adorn the walls.

A crowded bookcase reveals titles as varied as Beka's *God's Gift of Language* (a popular Christian series), books by Farley Mowat, Johanna Spyri, the brothers Grimm and Dr Seuss, the Usborne *First History* series, chemistry and physics textbooks, Orton phonogram cards and a complete writing program designed by the U. S.-based National Writing Institute.

The family's four school-age children all have schedules to follow and home chores to perform. But much work is completed informally. There is also a fair amount of what Brenda calls "out-and-out big-time debates. We have to bash it out sometimes."

The healthy arguments partly stem from the fact that the home-schooled don't respect their parents the same way they would a teacher, says Laibrook. "You know how far you can stretch the limit with your parents. You have always been around them. But with a teacher, you don't know how they are going to react. You watch out." ("Way to go, son," says Brenda, sitting at the kitchen table.)

Adds Laibrook, who has entered the famous age of needing something to kick against: "It's just hard to do what they say without challenging them." Brenda and Bruce, of course, counter with their own challenges.

The family consensus, however, is that home-schooling has strengthened bonds between parent and child, adding to the hearth a climate of strength, competence and humility. As in any endeavour, there have been failures too. "When I see the scratch that passes for a signature in this house," says Bruce, "I wish we had done the handwriting differently."

For families beginning or considering home-schooling, Laibrook offers some seasoned advice: "Spend time with your children. Work with them. Get to know them. It will be a lot of work. Be aware that there will be ups and downs." "Remember," he adds, "you've got to build yourself educationally up before you go out into that rat race."

The governments of Alberta, British Columbia and Saskatchewan are the most friendly to home-schoolers. Ontario's school bureaucrats, who still believe in myths, remain the most hostile. As a general rule, Catholic school boards are much more receptive to the idea than public school boards. It seems that Catholic educators still feel that a child's education is the parent's responsibility.

For more information on the home-schooling movement, I recommend the following publications.

Quest: The Home Educator's Journal. 1144 Byron Avenue, Ottawa, Ontario K2B 6T4. This is a Christian publication designed to promote "justice, integrity and love through the sharing of home-schooling."

The Alternative Press. 195 Markville Road, Unionville, Ontario L3R 4V8. This journal treats home-based education as a worthy lifestyle that goes hand in hand with such pioneering efforts as organic farming.

HOPE   Hope was once the currency of public education. We sent our children to school in the hope they would learn valued cultural traditions, and as teachers and parents we supported our children with the hope that they would graduate as citizens prepared to build a better society. We did all of these things in the expectation that the future would be saner and brighter than the past.

Daily news bulletins on urban decay, rising taxes, aloof élites, polluted food and tribal violence have changed these assumptions. In this age of diminishing expectations few people believe in the myth of progress anymore. And even fewer believe that computers, free markets or time efficiency can replace what we have lost: healthy communities, sound families, wild spaces and sane lives. This pervasive pessimism, notes school critic Leon Botstein, makes schooling all the more problematic:

"Education demands allegiance to the most archaic conception of time. We tell children that if they get through twelve years—maybe more—of school, they'll see the rewards some twenty years down the line. The amount of delayed gratification inherent in education made sense when the society thought in terms of generational time. But kids now grow up in a world in which people change their jobs every few years and their relationships every few months; they assess their success in the workplace and in the economy by the day, if not the minute. Children are left with no sense of permanence and thus no understanding of why they should make a long-term investment in their own education."

Botstein doesn't have a simple answer to this dilemma, but he does recommend that schools slough off their bureaucracies and concentrate on doing a few things well (reading, writing, math and science). He calls for a restoration of hope. "Saying, 'Hopefully, the school system will be better,' is very different from saying, 'I hope the school system will be better.' Because if you say 'I hope,' the next question is, 'What are you going to do about it?'"

I

IMPRESSIONS This is one of the most popular (and controversial) whole language reading series in North America. This anti-phonics program, first published in 1984, has probably sponsored more classroom chanting, chorusing and guessing from Victoria to Charlottetown than any other reading program. According to one of its authors, David Booth, "one out of every two Canadian elementary school children has used books in the series."

Published by Harcourt Brace and Company, the primary reading and language program is an anthology of five hundred stories and poems by well-established authors, including A. A. Milne, C. S. Lewis and Lilian Moore. A Canadian product, Impressions comes complete with small books, big books, audio cassettes, activity books, worksheets and teacher anthologies. The only thing missing is T-shirts. The whole package costs a school $3,300, and that's not including GST.

Booth describes whole language as one of the most effective ways to teach children how to read. "Under such an approach, children initially experience a story—not a text created by a textbook writer, but a real story not intended to "teach" anything—by reading it themselves or by having it read to them by a teacher. After this initial reading, students are directed through activities designed to prompt them to respond to the ideas, the sentences, the words and other components of the story they have just experienced."

Many teachers like this program because it is a

packaged series that can be followed closely or easily
supplemented. The literature is also better than that

From the Impressions *reading series: a grade one reader.*

My Bedtime Rules
by
David Booth

Every night
before I go to bed
I follow my bedtime rules:

1. Ask to watch one more
   television show.

2. Ask to hear a story
   read aloud.

3. Ask for a glass of orange
   juice.

4. Ask for the window open.

5. Dream wonderful dreams
   about not going to bed.

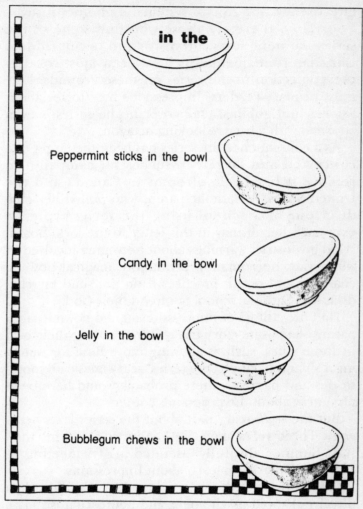

found in most basal reading series. (Remember Dick and Jane!)

But Impressions has set off a many-sided controversy. Among its opponents stand parents and researchers who find the series' just-let-them-read methodology weak, its content somewhat narcissistic and its overall effectiveness inferior to systematic phonics instruction. Then there are those who find some of the series' content scary, offensive and occult-ridden. Christian fundamentalists have been most vocal in their objection to the series on these grounds. Like most primary readers, Impressions has stories about witches and goblins. One cover in the series is even adorned with a bizarre-looking octagon.

As a consequence the series has been the target of a concerted and largely unsuccessful campaign to remove it from schoolrooms in Canada and the United States. A Catholic parent who pulled her children out of a school using the series typically expressed her dismay in this letter to the local board: "God gives strict warnings about becoming involved in witchcraft, necromancy, divination, magical powers, chanting and occult practices. I do not send my children to a Catholic school to offend their God."

Had the editors of Impresssions toned down its anti-parent slant (one story has children setting their own bedtime rules, such as allowing more time for watching TV) and balanced the series' scary tales with moral stories and parables, there probably would have been no outcry about the program's content.

But the *really* scary part about the series is its pedagogy. Three years ago Case Vanderwolf and his wife, Judy Sumner, dutifully attended a PTA meeting in London, Ontario, to learn about Impressions.

"We sat there both totally aghast," says Vanderwolf, a fifty-five-year-old psychologist and neuroscientist. "The method of teaching was foolish. Chanting through books. Looking at pictures. Guessing at words. It's not reading, it's memorizing."

What deeply disturbed these parents was the series' laissez-faire attitude towards reading. For example, the teacher's "resource book" (there is no real step-by-step guide for teaching Impressions) claims that "children become proficient users of language through experience and experiment" and become readers by "interacting" with print.

Compare this with the clearly stated purpose of Open Court, a highly acclaimed phonics series: "to teach children to read and write independently by the end of the first grade."

According to the Impressions resource book, a typical lesson begins with pupils listening to a story read aloud, reading the selection themselves and then doing a lot of colouring or writing with invented spelling.

This child-centred approach, of course, contradicts scores of reading studies that say direct, systematic and intensive phonics get better results. "It seems to me that you have to teach children the sounds of the letters first," says Vanderwolf. "And the research says that's right."

Research or no, the Canadian authors of Impressions don't even recognize a hierarchy of reading skills; they really believe that students learn by osmosis. Given Impressions' disdain for even minimal teaching, Patrick Groff, an American reading specialist, calculates that more than 60 percent of the words in the series appear, comet-like, with no preparation or skill development.

Groff, like many parents, posits a logical question: "How is it possible for illiterate children to read stories by themselves before they have learned to identify the words these stories contain?"

Impressions cites as some of its hallowed goals "appreciating literature" and "recognizing emotion." Contrast all of this appreciation with the clear objectives of Open Court: "learning sounds, blending sounds into words and spelling phonetically regular words."

From the Open Court *reading series.*

The Old Woman and Her Pig

English Folk Tale

An old woman went to market and bought a pig.

Pig had four legs,

But pig would not go.

"Well," said the old woman, "what shall I do?"

━━━━━━━━━━**WORDS TO WATCH**━━━━━━━━━━

market	two	butcher
bought	hours	gnaw
farther	quench	again

To complement Impressions' indirect and incongruous pedagogy, the series offers a frightening dose of 1980s narcissism. Children are admonished to talk, read and write about themselves ad nauseam, a technique that condemns inner-city kids to intellectual and cultural poverty. Open Court demands that students study fine literature (Aesop's fables, folktales,

Christina Rossetti and Leo Tolstoy) and learn how to write for public audiences. Unlike Impressions, with its strong literature bias, Open Court also introduces children to good science and history writing.

Faced with Impressions' many instructional demons and their school board's intransigence in the face of reading research, Vanderwolf and Sumner finally taught their sons how to read at home using the Open Court reading series. Their boys, now six and eight, are independent readers. And that's something Impressions can't achieve with a majority of kids with any verifiable regularity.

Open Court comes with three years of active field testing behind it; Impressions doesn't. But the whole language series does come with lots of feel-good anecdotes.

See also **WHOLE LANGUAGE** and **PHONICS**.

INCLUSION   For most of this century deaf, blind or mentally retarded children have been educated, often abysmally so, in institutions separate from community schools. Only a hundred years ago the administrators of asylums for the mentally retarded eased crowding by hosing their charges down so that some would catch pneumonia and die.

After World War II education in these facilities improved. And during the sixties and seventies many of these children moved into regular schools but remained in separate special education classrooms, often run by specially trained and highly qualified teachers. The current trend—inclusion, integration or mainstreaming—advocates full integration into regular classrooms.

Proponents of inclusion typically argue that a regular classroom should be able to accommodate everybody, no matter what their physical or mental state: "All children have, by law, a right to education.... To isolate any child because we fail to understand their needs is our failure and our system's failure. Our nation needs to become more tolerant of differences, cultural or developmental. What better place than a classroom to learn that tolerance? What better person than a teacher to model tolerance, acceptance and the value of diversity?"

But many teachers and parents, although sympathetic to the principles of integration, have serious concerns about the practice in reality. Their reservations generally stem from the way administrators have abused the intent of the policy and have ignored the ecology of a normal classroom. As a consequence, in many school boards inclusion is driven purely by political correctness or financial expediency: cutting special education classes and teachers is a cost-saving but short-sighted trend in public schooling.

To accommodate one or two students with limited or minor physical disabilities, provided an aide is assigned to take care of their physical needs, is an eminently sane practice and something most teachers are prepared to do. But to integrate children who yell, run around, are incontinent, abuse themselves physically, destroy property or require constant supervision can stretch the limits of both a teacher's training and a group's tolerance for differences.

To sensibly integrate more handicapped children into regular classrooms, administrators must first consider four realities: the current make-up of the class (are there already too many special-needs children in attendance?); the teacher's training (does he or she have the skills and experience to provide an appropriate curriculum? most teachers have no special education credentials); school and community resources (will adequate support such as an aide or special program be granted the teacher and the disabled child?); and the educational needs of the child being integrated (is a regular classroom setting going to improve or retard this child's learning?).

A recent report by the Alberta Teachers' Association, *Trying to Teach*, included the following testimony from an elementary school teacher in Edmonton. Her thoughts accurately sum up the intensity of teacher feelings about this issue and integration's grand administrative failures:

> The short-term and the long-term effects of the integration trend that we are now on, combined with non-retention (the practice of no-fail schooling), has the potential to be catastrophic regarding the education of our students and the continued well-being of teachers. Students who suffered years of failure in regular classrooms are being put back in for the improvement of their self-esteem. What precisely has been changed to suddenly make this a positive experience for them? Class sizes have not been reduced; other students within the class have not miraculously gained humanitarian qualities that will help them accept and help those students who are in their eyes "stupid"; teachers have not been adequately trained to provide for their needs; additional preparation time has not been provided for the teachers in order for them to coordinate the running of multiple programs rather than just one; and funding has not been increased to provide the necessary supports such as aide time.
>
> Behaviour disordered and dependent handicapped children are not funded enough to provide them with a full-time aide. Yet each time one

of these children is integrated, he requires a full-time aide, causing the school to subsidize the salary. Each time this happens, money for the regular classroom children is diminished, which reduces "excellence in teaching." An example is a dependent handicapped autistic student who was integrated in my Junior Adaptation classroom. He was functioning at about a 20-month-old level, with an approximate IQ of 25–30. Although appropriate programs focusing on his level of functioning were available and recommended, his parents adamantly decided it would be better for him to be integrated. The boy had also been integrated in our school for the previous two years. The cost of educating him, taking into account aide time, teacher time, and consultant's time, was between $25,000 and $30,000 per year. In short, it cost between $75,000 and $90,000 to educate him during the three years that he was at our school. Had he been in an ability appropriate program he would not have required a full-time aide and would have cost far less money.

Monetary cost was not the only cost of this integration. It reduced overall preparation time that I had for the other students' program because I was responsible for setting up and monitoring two distinctly different programs. The students additionally "lost out" in learning through the number of disturbances created by this student. He would frequently cry out, make whimpering sounds, bolt across the room, lie upon the floor and giggle, and attempt to masturbate. How does this promote excellence in education?

Educational psychologists have made similar observations. In particular, the combination of inclusion with child-centred education appears to be having a "double-whammy effect" in British Columbia. Writes David E. Carter, the director of the Kiwanis Learning Assessment Research Clinic in Kelowna:

> While I am a proponent of mainstreaming when it is done properly and with the right children, I am alarmed at the policies of many school districts who by fiat declare that ALL special needs children should spend their whole day and receive all of their support in a regular classroom. While this procedure is trumpeted as an exercise in the child's rights to a "typical" education, it often results in the dumping of special needs children into very poor educational environments without adequate support....
>
> The research is abundantly clear. Special needs children, especially learning disabled and mentally challenged children, benefit most from direct instruction. In British Columbia schools and elsewhere, the move into "child-centred" instruction removes most if not all direct instruction. The result is that those children who most need direct instruction receive none at all, while bureaucrats in the system connive to trumpet this process as a notable educational achievement.

Dr Barbara Bateman, one of North America's leading experts on special education and a former teacher, favours integration provided it is exercised prudently and still allows for a variety of alternative educational settings that might be more appropriate for severely handicapped children.

But she is completely opposed to "full inclusion"— the political jargon for integrating all disabled children into ordinary classrooms regardless of the social or academic consequences. "It just doesn't make any educational sense," says Bateman. "A lot of people have falsely applied the lessons of racial segregation and the civil rights movement to the segregation of the disabled. They don't understand that skin colour has never been an educational variable, whereas a disability has always implied different kinds of teaching."

Few schools and even fewer school boards seriously acknowledge this truth. As a group, parents can work with their local school board to ensure that it has a sensible integration policy that respects the educational needs of the child, the training of the teacher and the ecology of the classroom.

See also **LEARNING DISABILITIES** and **DIRECT INSTRUCTION**.

"INNOVATIONS" VS. "REFORMS"   Parents should know that a genuine educational reform is something that actually yields measurable improvements in student learning. A sequenced curriculum in math or a reading program that emphasizes systematic phonics teaching in grade one is a true reform that benefits children regardless of social class.

Innovations are ideas that administrators implement in the hope that they may do some good. Discovery learning, whole language, invented spelling and the open classroom are all examples of nifty innovations that were implemented with no foreknowledge or subsequent measurable proof of their effectiveness. Nonetheless, educators and some parents often mistake an "innovation" for a "reform."

The Oregon Education Association's *Handbook for Site Councils*, which is reproduced in Appendix 19, recommends testing every new method, approach, technology or change with these six questions: Are the approach and its results clearly defined? What evidence exists that the approach is effective? Is an accountability process built into the approach? Is the approach sustainable? Is the approach equitable? Are the costs of the approach and its implementation reasonable? See Appendix 19.

To ask such questions would save schools, teachers, parents and children much money and even more peace of mind.

A Teacher's View

I fail to see how we can cope with new curricula, discipline, coaching, day-to-day teaching, as well as integration, individual education plans, portfolios, continuous progress, program continuity and on and on.... It makes me wonder whom we're serving: students or innovations.

—an Alberta teacher

North America's teachers' unions have always been champions of pensions and salaries, but often poor advocates of good teaching. But the Alberta Teachers' Association has radically challenged this imbalance with an extraordinary publication, *Trying to Teach*, that probably offers the most candid review of current classroom trends and whims—from a teacher's perspective—yet published in North America. As such it is an invaluable resource for parents.

The twenty-seven-page report eloquently documents teacher responses to a host of problematic innovations, ranging from "integration" or "inclusion" (placing children with special needs into regular classrooms) to "program continuity" (a no-fail, learn-at-your-own-rate approach). In so doing the document spells out with street-level honesty the difficulties that innovators can create for students and teachers.

The combined effect of contradictory and often mindless edicts from administrators, notes the report, has often created school environments where "teachers feel suffocated, frustrated, angry and stressed to the point of collapse."

The report, based on two hundred submissions from school staff and individual teachers, begins by stating truths that administrators routinely ignore: that ideas, good in theory, can be implemented so poorly that they become unsound; that some innovations, such as integration, may work well for some students but not for all; and finally, that some classroom practices may work well enough alone but quickly fall apart when combined with other unrelated reforms such as a wild mix of integration, individualization, program continuity and more testing.

According to Larry Booi, the chair of the committee that produced this remarkable study, the source of much unsound innovation can be found in the way educators are promoted. "People get promoted not for running an effective school or supporting their teachers, but for doing new and innovative things. Administrators will push trendy ideas saying they are good for you and then, while teachers are left to pick up the pieces, the innovator gets promoted to another school."

The report asks, for example, if time-consuming "porfolio assessments" (fat folders of student work) are really necessary for all subjects or all schools. On the subject of program continuity it poses this timely question: "How can a teacher require more of a student when the philosophy is 'Let the student find his or her own comfort level'?"

The report concludes with a powerful set of principles that call for a "significant reduction in the expectations" placed on schools, the teacher's right to choose appropriate tools, good school organization that recognizes the constraints of group instruction as well as the limits of individualization, and a proper system for assessing innovations under controlled conditions by independent evaluators. A program's effectiveness should not be judged only by student performance but by its impact on teacher workload and other classroom practices. No ministry of education now practises such common sense.

"Teacher unions go and do things they think are important and sometimes ignore the obvious fires around them," says Booi. *Trying to Teach*, now in its fifth printing, has focused on classroom blazes that matter.

Trying to Teach contains comprehensive information on integration, continuous progress, individual educational plans, increased external testing, portfolio assessments and vision statements. As such, it serves as an excellent guide to these subjects as well as the range of teacher opinion on them as classroom practices. I highly recommend this short and readable report for parents with concerns about any of these issues.

Copies can be obtained free from the ATA, Barnett House, 11010—142 Street, Edmonton, Alberta T5N 2R1. Phone 403-453-2411, or fax 403-455-6481.

See also Appendix 2.

INTERNATIONAL BACCALAUREATE (IB)   Forty-seven Canadian high schools, both public and private, offer this special two-year pre-university course of study. Founded in 1965 with a curriculum largely set at Oxford University, the IB represents a deliberate compromise between those nations that want their children to specialize and those that desire a broad education for their students. The intent, notes one brochure, "is that students should learn how to learn, how to analyze, how to reach considered conclusions about people, their languages and literature, their ways in society and the scientific forces of the environment."

An IB program consists of studies in two languages, the experimental sciences (including biology, chemistry and environmental systems), mathematics, "individuals and societies" (history, geography and economics) and several electives. Community service is compulsory, as is a course on integrating disciplines entitled "theory of knowledge."

Diploma students are required to write a four-thousand-word essay as well as take a very rigorous formal exam scored by educators outside the school.

More and more universities, including Harvard, McGill, Toronto, MIT and Yale, give special recognition to the IB, which is now offered by 350 schools in fifty-three countries.

Parents should contact their local school board to find out if an IB program is available in their community. The IB definitely gives students an edge in ever-tougher competition for university admission. But even if an IB graduate decides not to pursue university studies, he or she still walks away with an education superior to most.

For more information on the IB curriculum, write International Baccalaureate North America, 200 Madison Avenue, Suite 2007, New York, NY 10016; phone 212-696-4464; or fax 212-889-9242.

INTERNATIONAL COMPARISONS   Observing the classroom rituals of other countries can often be an exercise in playful curiosity. But two American psychologists, James Stigler and Harold Stevenson, have made it a new form of social criticism.

Disturbed by a host of studies that repeatedly showed Chinese and Japanese elementary students outperforming American kids in every math skill imaginable, the Americans visited hundreds of Asian classrooms to find the reasons for this disparity.

As long-time observers of Asian schools, the psychologists knew that certain cultural traits, including high esteem for learning, effort and work, partly accounted for the amazing numeracy skills of Asian students.

But when they saw how mathematical principles such as addition or fractions were actually taught in grade one and grade five classrooms in Beijing, Taipei and Sendai, their mouths fell open. They were both stunned by "the widespread excellence of Asian class lessons" and by "the high level of performance of the average teacher."

What angered the psychologists was the damning conclusion that the practice of primary teaching in Japan and China has achieved a uniform level of comparative excellence simply because Asian systems of education "encourage teaching excellence to develop and flourish," whereas our schools do not.

Perhaps the first important discovery that Stigler and Stevenson made was that Chinese and Japanese teachers present "coherent" lessons with beginnings, middles and ends. They also teach them in a thoughtful and non-authoritarian manner. Classes are not interrupted by rude intercom notices that send the teachers and students off track.

Contrary to North American perceptions, these lessons don't resemble army drills. Almost all start with real live problems and objects that demand the students to think, debate and investigate a variety of solutions.

A simple fractions lesson, for example, may begin with a related task such as figuring out the number of litres in a juice jar. Mistakes are not treated as damning failures but "as an index of what still needs to be learned." And seatwork, which always reinforces the skills being taught, is well paced in short bursts throughout the lesson. Asian teachers just don't give their kids the opportunity to develop sore bums or bored minds.

In schools they observed in Chicago and Minneapolis, the psychologists found a wildly different scenario. Lessons appeared out of nowhere with no beginnings or ends as students rushed off to band class or the sports field. Teachers, in turn, jumped from topic to topic (from addition to measurement, for example), all in one period. Questions, when the teacher asked them, elicited "Yes" or "No" answers rather than stimulating thought. In this "aura of disarray," nearly half of all seatwork had nothing to do with the lesson.

In contrast to the sustained and lively teacher–student banter that characterizes Asian schools, American classrooms hum with an appalling silence and inactivity. To their surprise the psychologists found that 51 percent of the time no one was leading instruction in America's grade one classrooms, while in Taiwan students worked rudderless for only 9 percent of their lessons.

This continental gap in time devoted to teaching math explains the gross innumeracy of North American kids. While our hapless teachers run around from desk to desk trying to provide individual instruction, they effectively reduce the amount of teaching time for the rest of the class, with predictable results.

Unlike North America's individualized approach to teaching, Chinese and Japanese teachers still focus on the whole class. They successfully address the educational differences among their students by varying their presentations and approaches to reach everyone. Thousands of years of experience have taught Asian teachers that instructional monopolies only cripple children and burn out teachers.

One of the key messages of this comparative research is that Americans and Canadians had better re-examine their long and sacred assumption that individualized learning automatically means "a higher-quality and more effective experience" than well-crafted group instruction.

Clearly, zen and the art of classroom maintenance have proven otherwise.

The psychologists also found that Asian teachers personified North American ideals of teacher effectiveness—they direct, test, challenge and involve all their students in a stimulating climate of problem-solving banter.

Stigler employs a useful metaphor to illustrate the continental divide: "The North American teacher is like a Maypole with strings out to every student. So it's no wonder the strings keep on getting tangled up. But in Japan or China there is only one string."

The researchers also noticed that Asian schools do everything possible to strengthen that string, whereas North American schools cut, tangle and snap theirs with dangerous regularity. Incredibly poor teacher training is responsible for this particular gap. Unlike Asian educators, North Americans naïvely assume that a staple diet of theoretical courses plus a month or two of practice teaching is all the preparation an elementary teacher ever needs.

As the two American researchers detail in *The Learning Gap: Why Our Schools are Failing and What We Can Learn from Japanese and Chinese Education* (Summit Books), Asian educators treat teacher training as a long apprenticeship that diligently proceeds under the guidance of master teachers. (Practice still makes perfect in the Orient.)

While beginning teachers in North America stumble through their first year with a full load, their Chinese cousins teach only one class for one hour a day. This humane schedule permits experienced colleagues to critique the novices' work and impart proven teaching methods. The Japanese demand that a new teacher receive twenty days of in-service training from the pros—a requirement foreign to Canadian schools.

In China the ongoing training of teachers also includes the sharing and refining of effective lesson plans. Dedicated Japanese and Chinese teachers even hold "teaching fairs" where their colleagues carefully grade the competitors.

This constant criticism and review does not exist in North American schools, where most teachers never observe another colleague in action. "We seem to think that to be a good teacher you have to constantly invent lessons on your own," says Stigler. "North American teachers place unrealistic expectations on themselves."

Because good teaching requires careful deliberation, Beijing teachers instruct no more than three hours a day, while their Japanese colleagues conduct classes only 60 percent of the school day. During the remaining time teachers assemble in a huge common room where they share ideas, correct papers and perfect lessons the way artisans polish stones. "They will take a couple of hours to determine the most effective way of asking a question to stimulate thought," says Stevenson.

In North America, elementary teachers, isolated in their rooms, teach hour after hour until the day ends. Most do their preparation at home, and when they do mingle with their peers, conversation understandably veers towards working conditions.

Now, Stigler and Stevenson are not suggesting that North American teachers turn Japanese or think Chinese. But they do want to alert North American educators to the behavioural and historical realities that make elementary Asian classrooms far superior to ours.

They also issue a radical challenge to the chaotic rule of individualized instruction: increase the number of students taught in each class and in exchange give elementary teachers two hours of preparation time to learn how to polish lessons that work for everyone.

In other words, give North America's overworked and undertrained teachers time to watch, critique and perfect their craft.

Astute readers will recognize the real message of this comparative research as a political and economic SOS. "We are not keeping up in the sciences and math," confides Stevenson, "and people are blind to the competition they are going to face." There is, concludes the iconoclastic researcher, nothing sacred about the West.

The Counterpoint

About four out of five educators don't care for these kinds of comparisons, and Gerald Bracey, a U. S. educational consultant, is one of them. Each year he prepares a report for *Phi Delta Kappan* magazine that says public education in North America is doing just fine, thank you very much. He says that Stevenson and other international researchers are comparing apples with oranges, or bananas with kiwis.

Bracey typically asks this kind of question: how can one compare the school performance of students in

Chicago—black or Hispanic children of poor, large and often fatherless families—with children in Beijing, where 50 percent of the homes have a grandparent at home and where most families, by law, have only one child? Stevenson typically replies that the learning gap is just as evident in Minneapolis among middle class kids in a mostly white population. And the results also show that Taipei has just as much of an advantage over North America as Beijing.

In reviewing other international studies Bracey also argues that the scores of the top 5 percent of students in all countries are identical. What he does not acknowledge is that economies rise and fall not so much on the performance of their élites but on the qualities and abilities of their workers, the 95 percent not performing as well.

Although Bracey's reports make public education in North America sound like the best thing on the market, he does add a caveat that oddly reflects the essence of Stevenson's research: the top third of our students are world class; the second third "are not in serious trouble"; but the bottom third "are in terrible shape."

Bracey is a public school booster, and so perhaps simplifies Stevenson's research. But his criticisms serve as a reminder that such studies should be reviewed carefully and from an educational viewpoint. That means educators should always ask "What can we learn from this study?"—whether they agree with the results or not.

The Endpoint
Stuffing the duck. Writing countless exams. Enduring long days.

That's how many new Canadian students enrolled in an English as a Second Language class at Earl Haig

Secondary School in the City of North York remember Asia's much-vaunted educational system. Their remarks were prompted by a reading of the iconoclastic research of Harold Stevenson and James Stigler.

Under the direction of their teachers, Sandra Katz and Marianne Glinski, the ESL class studied the Americans' comments and then wrote about the differences in teacher effectiveness and styles that they had personally experienced. Although the students readily agreed that Asian schools got better results, they noted that "polishing the stone" sometimes meant "stuffing the duck."

Their passionate descriptions suggest that Asia has as much to learn from our uncertain, post-industrial classrooms as North America does from Asia's no-nonsense, industry-fuelled schools.

Consider, for example, the thoughts of Helen Su. The sixteen-year-old emigrated from Taiwan a year and a half ago with "a very lasting memory" of its school system: "The education in my country was just like stuffing the duck—no thinking, you just do whatever teachers told and asked. Also, I thought the education in my country was dead. We studied many hours a day—from 6:00 a.m. to 7:00 p.m. and we also studied during weekends. We did not have many hours to sleep because we needed more time to study."

Shirley Tseng, another teenaged veteran of Taiwan's schools, conceded that Asian kids certainly learn more than North American kids, but then added this proviso: "In my country some teachers are very kind and work hard, but some are strict and savage. I bet you can't imagine it.... But in North America the teachers can be one of your friends because they want you to know that they are always caring for your feelings, sharing your secrets and helping you to solve problems. But in Asia teachers are teachers, they only care about marks, homework, tests but not the student.... I felt you wrote about the good, bright side to Asian education and didn't notice the bad, dark side...."

Eric Hong, twenty, unapologetically wrote that he preferred North American teachers to Asian ones. "First, I can freely show my opinion during the class time whereas I had to keep quiet while a[n Asian] teacher was lecturing in class. As a second reason, I would say the lack of creativity of Asian students due to one-way teaching. Passive, that is the word.... Human beings are supposed to be educated in the way of a human, not like a tool of industrial society. OK!!!!!!"

But Hong also noted that Orientals definitely had "a kind of passion for education" (it is the sole hope for their children, he explains)—a sentiment now fading in North American society. Hong disliked the endless distractions disrupting North American classrooms. "As I see it, a simple and unique timetable and tighter school hours are needed. The attention of students in North America is scattered in many ways."

Katherine Song, just ten months off the plane from Korea, found Canada's education system to be a bag of surprises. Her first big and "good" shock was sitting in a class of thirty kids instead of a crowd of fifty or fifty-five students. The second was the timetable: "School is open from 9:00 am to 3:15 here, but in Korea they open from 7:00 a.m. to 10:00 or 11:00 p.m. So I can feel more freedom and I can do something I want to as a hobby."

Song's third shock (freedom always has a price) was the number of students who had fallen "victim to drugs and other bad things." She says that she misses the moral tone of Korea's school system. And perhaps the last words should be hers:

"In Korea we were always educated about morality

from kindergarden to university. We always heard 'Be devoted to your parents, country and teachers.' But I've never heard that anywhere except in my church service. In Korea as the result of the education people have more relations with their parents, brothers and sisters, teachers.... They know what a real friend is.... How about here?"

Now here's Dr Stevenson's reply:

Dear Helen, Shirley, Eric and Katherine,

I read with interest your critical comments on our research on the effectiveness of Asian teachers, and assume that your remarks speak directly about the character of Asia's high schools.

As you well noted, Oriental high schools are often rigid, dogmatic and exam-driven. The popular Chinese cliché, "stuffing the duck," is not an inept description of how many Asian high schools work. In fact, I would argue that Asian teaching practices, in secondary schools as well as universities, are not something we want to emulate.

Although we are just now studying high schools, our research to date has focused solely on the effectiveness of teaching in the elementary grades, and little of what you have written applies to Asia's primary schools.

For starters Asia's elementary school teachers, unlike their high school colleagues, do not lecture. From observing classrooms in Japan, Taiwan and China I know that elementary teachers pose questions to whole classes to stimulate thought and discussion.

Unlike most North American primary teachers, Asian educators routinely direct students to evaluate the replies of classmates and to devise alternative solutions. When employing this inter-active approach Asia's primary teachers act and look more like intelligent guides than fact stuffers.

Asia's primary school educators also use manip-ulative materials such as tiles, clocks and rulers much more often and to greater effect than do their North American colleagues.

Our research found, for example, that a grade one math class in Taipei used attractive objects such as beads 50 percent of the lesson time while an average North American class (in this case Chicago's schools) employed these items less than 30 percent of the time.

This dramatic difference is all the more damn-ing when one realizes that most educators, regardless of their differing philosophies, agree that the use of concrete objects to teach abstract ideas to young children is a sign of good teach-ing.

Asia's elementary teachers are also adept at get-ting their students to attend to their well-polished and stimulating lessons. While 90 percent of grade one pupils in Taipei have no trouble focus-ing on their teacher's interesting presentations, only 60 percent of Chicago's students attend to their more lackluster instructors. Given such find-ings, I pose this question to North American edu-cators: how can we ever expect high levels of achievement here with such low levels of atten-tion?

Our research also found that Asia's elementary teachers revealingly declare their commitment to excellence in their choice of "the most important characteristic of a good teacher." While Chinese teachers elect "clarity," North American teachers predictably choose "sensitivity."

If you believe, as I do, that the goal of a school is to encourage learning and impart certain knowledge and skills, then clear teaching will fairly achieve that end much better than a roster of "sensitivity" lessons.

One of the signs of excellent teaching and high achievement, I might add, are happy students. Most of the hundreds of elementary school kids in Asia that we have studied freely admit that they like their teachers and their schools.

Unfortunately, this cheerful sentiment, as you have so well described, evaporates in high school. On a seven point scale of school enjoyment, Taiwanese students in grade five proudly award their schools a 5.2, while U. S. students give their schools a 4.7. But once these same Taiwanese pupils have entered high school, their enjoyment level plummets to 4.5. American high school students register no difference in their enjoyment.

In conclusion I agree with your critical comments about Asia's high schools. It has always mystified me how Asian educators can do so much so well in primary school but then fail so thoroughly to sustain that excellence in high school.

Sincerely,
Harold Stevenson

INVENTED SPELLING   Inventd speling. Chanzez ar, yuvff hrd abt it annd even mt peepl who do it. And chanzez ar, yuvff askt y in hll ar skools dooing it?

Invented spelling is really two things: a natural phase that prereaders and beginning readers experience when they first translate sounds into printed words, and a creative condition forced upon mature students in the absence of spelling instruction.

A curriculum document for the Metropolitan Separate School Board in Toronto generously defines invented spelling as children spelling words as they think best, "accepting the risk of misspelling a word," using ingenious means to spell correctly (can they find the right word on the blackboard?) and "using any given word because it is the best word for the situation."

According to Orin Cochrane, a whole language proponent, children will learn standard spelling if they write and read a great deal. He doesn't worry if some children spell by osmosis better than others, because "standard spelling is not valued and no attempt is being made to maintain standards."

Rebecca Treiman, one of the continent's foremost spelling researchers and a psychologist at Wayne State University of Detroit, doesn't subscribe to such extreme views. But she does agree that invented spellings are normal when students are learning how to read and write in kindergarten and grade one. This does not mean, however, that children should persist with invented spellings beyond grade one.

Treiman studied novice readers and writers in an extreme whole language classroom where the teacher never corrected spellings and never offered correct spellings, even when the students asked for them ("That was terrible," says Treiman). The psychologist found that the children's spelling progressively improved with exposure to correct spellings in books.

Although the research doesn't yet say what is best, common sense suggests that children should be learning conventional use by the end of grade one.

For starters, a child's ability to read well is directly tied to his ability to spell. "Everyone thinks that good readers [become] good spellers, but spelling directly feeds back into reading," says Treiman. Good spelling lessons give children new word-attack skills and language patterns to analyse. In other words, they reinforce and accelerate good reading. The emphasis that schools of old placed on spelling bees and drills was not entirely misguided.

Contrary to the belief of many whole language experts, any public document or letter is still judged by how well it communicates ideas and arguments clearly and accurately. Accurate spellings indicate that communication is reasoned, serious and thoughtful. Misspellings still don't impress employers. To postpone this lesson merely guarantees that more and more citizens will be disenfranchised.

Robert Dixon, the author of several good spelling programs such as Spelling Mastery and The Surefire Way to Better Spelling, says that "kids who misspell an awful lot of words are failures at spelling."

He argues that educators have used the sweet rhetoric of "invented spelling" (now, who wants to be against creating and inventing?) to hide some brilliant sophistry. If educators can sell "the notion of misspellings as a positive, desirable education outcome," then they can "sell any error, any misunderstanding, any misconception as a positive educational outcome."

Here are five precautions regarding this practice:

1. Invented spelling is not an approach suitable for every child. Students whose spellings are not logically phonetic but extremely arbitrary ("ys" for "was") should not be encouraged to spell inventively. "If the errors don't make sense, then that's something to worry about," says Treiman.
2. A great many children don't want to use approximations, misspellings or inventions, but insist on proper usage. "Some kids want to use the correct

spellings in grade one," says Treiman, and they shouldn't be denied because of the school's or a teacher's dogmatic commitment to misspellings.

3. Invented spelling has earned, and justifiably so, a dark reputation among parents because many schools don't know when to stop using it. Consider, for example, the "Standards for Student Success" set by North York's Board of Education. A student in grades seven to nine is expected to "use correct spelling for words he/she wants to use, including terms from different subject areas." Deborrah Howes, a Toronto reading consultant, wonders what the board means by the term "want": "How would a student experience it, as a desire, a need, a craving? Or would he be destitute? And, what if a student doesn't 'want' to spell words correctly but still needs to write words? What happens then—is this OK?" Apparently so.

   By the end of grade one or the beginning of grade two invented spelling reaches its logical limits, and formal spelling instruction should begin. Short drills and memorization that emphasize morphemes (*pre, re, de, ness*), word families and familiar spelling rules (i before e except after c) are both proper and necessary at this time. "The English writing system is so unwieldy and complex that the only way to learn how to spell many words is through memorization," notes Treiman. Good spelling programs or lessons, of course, always emphasize the application of correct spellings to written assignments across the school curriculum.

4. Almost all the research on invented spelling has taken place in whole language classrooms where direct instruction is often frowned upon. Linda Clarke, whose Ph.D. thesis studied the effects of invented spelling on Toronto students in whole lan-

guage programs, noted that the "invented spellers" wrote more than the children using correct spellings. But she thought these and other advantages would quickly disappear "if the reading program more effectively taught these skills." She also recommended invented spelling as a beginning approach for first graders that should immediately be "accompanied by instruction in letter-sound associations, lower case letter representation and sound sequencing."

5. Many teachers and parents readily buy the line that spelling doesn't matter because a thirty- or fifty-dollar computer spell-checker can take care of the mess. This is misleading information. Most spell-checkers don't work very well with bad spellers because they were designed for sophisticated spellers who make occasional and/or minor errors. Computers spell-checking a student's "himet" intended for "helmet" will often replace it with "hamlet." And so on. Children whose spelling skills are bad enough to warrant a placement in a special education program won't be able to use most spell checkers. There is no technological shortcut for good teaching.

See also Appendix 16.

K

KUMON MATH This popular made-in-Japan math program was developed by Toru Kumon more than thirty years ago. He developed the supplemental math program for his own son. Nearly 1.6 million Japanese students now study the Kumon Method (primarily to boost exam scores) while another 270,000 children around the world use Kumon as a complementary math program. The success of Kumon indicates to what degree basic math instruction has become a big business: in 1992 Kumon alone had sales of 47 billion yen.

In Canada, where Kumon has 250 after-school math centres, enrolment has jumped from fifteen hundred to sixteen thousand in the last five years. Tuition is $55 a month plus a one-time tuition fee of $30. Kumon insists that parents make a commitment to the program for at least a year.

Kumon Math offers nineteen levels of curricular difficulty, beginning with drawing lines and ending with differential calculus. The program is geared for children anywhere between the ages of four and fifteen. The well-paced program introduces concepts slowly and provides lots of practice. Kumon is designed not to replace a school math program but to enrich and enhance it.

Each level of difficulty consists of two hundred worksheets. "Individualized progress, repeated practice and standard completion times" highlight the method. According to the *Kumon Kronicles*, "every child has potential which can be expanded."

After taking a diagnostic test, students begin at a level that comfortably reflects what they know and can do. The Kumon classroom, usually located in a church or synagogue, is open two days each week. Each student arranges his or her own schedule for lessons.

In class, pupils hand in their homework, which is immediately marked, and then correct any mistakes. The pupil then completes another three or four worksheets, which are then corrected on the spot. The instructor, who has received four weeks of Kumon training, carefully notes how long it takes the student to progress. Based on the quality and speed of student work, the instructor then assigns more worksheets for homework.

This direct program can build self-confidence, improve study habits and often improve school grades. Kumon makes a difference for about 80 percent of students enrolled, provided their parents understand and remain committed to the program. For some students the program simply does not offer enough direct instruction or manipulative materials.

Parents tend to enrol their children in Kumon largely because they are concerned about the quality of basic math instruction at school or simply want to ensure that their children will be challenged.

Ed Barbeau, a professor of mathematics at the University of Toronto, evaluates Kumon deftly. Sending a child to Kumon and to school, he says, is like "sending a kid to two piano teachers—one for pieces and another for scales and arpeggios." He summarizes his evaluation this way:

1. Mastery of basic skills by a student is much to be desired.
2. It is unfortunate that the occasion of such mastery cannot be woven into the regular school curricu-

lum, especially since it seems evident from the
Kumon experience that when the tasks are sufficiently well paced, students are encouraged by a
feeling of accomplishment.
3. The danger with Kumon is that students may be
   deceived into feeling that all there is to mathematics is technical proficiency, and lose sight of the
   need for higher-order abilities and affective and
   judgmental approaches to the solution of mathematical problems.... To put the matter into context,
   there are two main types of students who flounder
   at university. The more prevalent type is the student
   who is not fluent with standard technical process;
   the second is the student who has had very strong
   rote teaching and can rehearse techniques on
   demand, but who has no "musical ear"; they cannot
   devise strategies, make judgments or obtain an intu-
   itive feel of the situation they are dealing with.

Given its success with math, which in some ways is a
reproach to the public schools' failure, Kumon has
now branched into English reading and grammar. For
more information call Kumon Math at 1-800-667-6284.

L

LEARNING DISABILITIES   Since I taught learning-disabled children in the 1980s, not much has changed in this grim field of education. A learning-disabled child, by the way, is merely a student who, for whatever physical, emotional or cognitive reason, will need better-than-average teaching and a better-than-average curriculum. Probably less than 15 percent of the population is truly learning disabled.

But the problems that parents with disabled children face in the schools are daunting. Few teachers have been adequately trained in effective teaching methods. Few administrators know what works, and even fewer care. The epidemic of identifying children as learning disabled who are really the unwitting victims of bad curriculum in regular classrooms continues unabated. (When many school boards list as many as 30 percent of their pupils as learning disabled, you know something has gone seriously wrong!) In addition, funding for learning-disabled children is generally the first to be cut. The push to dump more and more learning-disabled children into regular classrooms proceeds as thoughtlessly as ever.

Notes Barbara Bateman, one of the continent's foremost authorities on learning disabilities: "Special educators mainstream hundreds of thousands, if not millions, of children with learning disabilities, and other children, with no expectation that they perform at grade level and with nothing near the support that would be essential to increasing their chances of performing near that level."

Aside from fighting for the obvious, such as well-trained teachers and regular progress reports, parents also must pay attention to the curriculum. There is, says Bateman, "a serious mismatch between the commercial curricular materials so central to schools and the characteristics and needs of children who have learning disabilities. If teachers simply cannot do all the essential fixing of curriculum, it must fall to publishers to do it. But that will happen only when schools specify performance standards to be met by the children and adopt only the curricular materials that have demonstrated ability to get the job done."

The Learning Disabilities Association of Canada, which has chapters in every major city, recently concluded that the right to an education for the learning disabled should include the following:

1. The right to attend school.
2. The right of each student to an individualized education program based on identified need.
3. The right to early identification and education intervention through appropriate testing and evaluation.
4. The right to an education plan.
5. The right to placement in the least restrictive environment (the most enabling environment).
6. The right to ongoing review and reassessment.
7. The right of special needs students to have their interests represented through guaranteed due process.
8. The right of access to records and the right to confidentiality.
9. The right to "child-centred" legislation on special education that requires, when appropriate, that children be consulted about decisions affecting them.

10. The right to adequate funding for special needs and the guarantee that funds allocated will be used for their intended purpose.

These rights are explained in an informative handbook, entitled *Educational Justice For Special Needs Young Persons.* It contains many useful suggestions for parents on how to deal with reluctant schools and poor teaching methods. Copies can be obtained by writing the author: Yude M. Henteleff, Q.C., 2500–360 Main Street, Winnipeg, Manitoba R3C 4H6.

See also **ACCOUNTABILITY**, **INCLUSION**, **PARENT ADVOCACY** and **READING DISABILITIES**.

M

MONTESSORI

> A child's work is to create the man he will become. An adult works to perfect the environment but a child works to perfect himself.
>
> —Maria Montessori

Few educational voices speak as directly and urgently to the times as the legendary Maria Montessori.

She was among the first to invent furniture and didactic materials that fit the able hands and bodies of children; the first to use mixed-age classes effectively; the first to show that children between the ages of four and six can learn to read and write; and the first to develop an effective pedagogy for the poorest of the poor.

Yet like most prophets in education, Montessori and her ideas have been crassly ignored, routinely misunderstood or, as is the case in many public schools today, repeatedly taken out of context. In the process, a pedagogy designed for inner-city children has largely become the preserve of private schools for children with last names like Mulroney and Clinton.

The fiery iconoclast who looked at children "as a naturalist looks at bees" was born in the Italian province of Ancona in 1870. Daughter of an aristocratic father and pious mother, Maria, like many feminists of her day, was determined to be anything but a teacher. With the stubbornness and dedication that defined all of her efforts she defied male autocrats and became Italy's first woman doctor in 1896.

She first worked among "idiots" confined in Rome's insane asylums. Unlike her peers, she didn't believe that her naked and neglected charges were "extrasocial beings," but children who needed good teaching. For two years she studiously recopied and analysed the seminal works of two brillant French doctors (Édouard Sequin and Jean Itard, the grandfathers of special education) in search of suitable teaching methods. After completing her own self-styled degree in pedagogy she went to work. Within a year her so-called idiots were not only reading and writing but passing the public exam for normal children.

Determined to try her new methods—all marked by "brevity, simplicity and objectivity"—with normal children, Montessori entered the slums of San Lorenzo, Rome. To stop the rampages of sixty "little vandals" (ages three to six) in a crowded flat, a building authority offered the good doctor a big challenge and one room.

These children, like many public school pupils today, were poor, abandoned, hungry and listless. Their parents included the unemployed, prostitutes and former criminals. Given the needs of the children and the twelve-hour day they spent at Montessori's "Casa dei Bambini," the doctor clothed, fed and bathed them. But she also designed a "natural" classroom environment that gave the children the freedom to work with a selection of her special materials. And then Montessori sat back and watched with the eye of a biologist.

Several developments immediately "amazed" the doctor, and they continue to amaze visitors of good Montessori classrooms today. For starters she marvelled at the children's powers of concentration, their preference for work over play (toys in the room were neglected), their ability to make good choices, their appreciation of order and their fascination with writing before reading. (Montessori hadn't intended to teach reading to four- and five-year-olds but illiterate moms begged her to do so.)

To the shock of Rome's medical and teaching community, the children at the Casa performed as well on public exams as their middle class peers—or better. Foreign visitors flocked to the Casa, socialists praised the experiment, and soon Montessori had become an international figure. To validate her observations, she opened more schools for both the poor and the middle class.

Montessori spent the rest of her life refining her philosophy and training teachers. During World War II, when Italian and German fascists closed her schools, she spent several years in India, with the consequence that the Montessori movement, if it can be called that, is much stronger there than in Canada or the United States.

Although there is now a significant revival of interest in Montessori in the United States (fifty public school districts now offer Montessori education), Montessori remains a quiet though active force among Canadian private schools, especially in Ontario and British Columbia.

But as the good doctor noted before her death in 1952, the highest honour and deepest gratitude that anyone could pay her (and Montessori did possess a large ego) was "to turn your attention away from me in the direction in which I am pointing—The Child."

The Method

Fifty years ago Elsje de Boer, now a resident of Fauquier, British Columbia, attended a Montessori school in her native Holland. See Appendix 3.

She still remembers with great fondness the child-size sink for washing hands, the boxes of geometrical shapes and the determined engagement of her peers as they worked on mats in the middle of the room. During lunch the children invented secret languages and played cops and robbers, but during class the discipline of the Montessori "workplace" honed disciplined minds.

"In a Montessori classroom," recalls de Boer, "a child is not treated with amused indulgence nor with kindly condescension but with respect." It is this attitude, she adds, "which gives Montessori children the dignity, self-confidence and motivation for which today's schools strive so hard and with so little confidence."

If de Boer were to visit a Montessori classroom today, she would find its sparkling ingredients largely unchanged. There would be children performing meaningful work with a host of hands-on materials ranging from carrot peelers to colour tablets and two ever-observant teachers gently directing their development with the élan of symphony conductors.

"A lot of people think that Montessori is a room with a lot of things in it," notes Nancy Lowden, the energetic director of the Montessori Preschool of Calgary, "but it is an ethic and a reverence for children."

This ethic, once summed up by Montessori as "liberty in a prepared environment" is composed of four essential elements: a carefully structured classroom, the famous didactic materials, a well-trained teacher and a philosophy and pedagogy that respects the intelligence of children.

As one educator noted years ago, this method represents a dynamic if not unlikely synthesis of Jean Piaget and B. F. Skinner: "On the one hand Montessori accommodates the child's freedom and individualism;

on the other, she insures that the essential skills of the heritage will be accurately transmitted to the next generation."

To achieve this end, good Montessori classrooms have an almost monastic air of simplicity and beauty; they are welcoming rather than overwhelming.

Everything not only fits the child but is within his or her reach. As a consequence, children are responsible for returning materials to their proper place as well as cleaning up. "The environment is structured," notes Alison O'Dwyer, the director of the Montessori School—Calgary, "but the children have the freedom to choose what they want to do."

Montessori's didactic materials, which gave birth to North America's educational toy industry, are practical, well sequenced and generally self-correcting. Grammar, for instance, is taught with sentence-building exercises that use a black triangle (an immovable object) to represent nouns and a red circle (an active, rolling object) for verbs.

In addition to this special apparatus, a Montessori curriculum is rich in botany, biology and geography. Maria Montessori rightly observed that children have a passionate need "to understand, and appreciate the order, the harmony, and the beauty in Nature."

Montessori teachers, like good teachers everywhere, distinguish themselves with presentations that are clear, eloquent and precise. They typically receive rigorous training not only in the proper use of the materials but in child development.

Although the Montessori method is based on the belief that every child has a blueprint for his or her own outstanding education, the teacher is no passive observer. Notes Dhamitha Wirasinghe, a forty-three-year-old Montessorian: "Whenever a child is a little shy or needs some guidance, then we will help." Neither rudeness nor roughness is tolerated in a Montessori classroom.

Montessori pedagogy, then, goes way beyond the child-centred fads of many public schools. Both complex and wide-ranging, it recognizes that there are "sensitive periods" for learning how to read and write, and dramatically honours that reality. It also recognizes that the pursuit of truth by a child requires precision, order and discipline.

But given the incredible breadth of the Montessori method, it has always been vulnerable to piecemeal application, says Renilde Montessori. She is the sixty-four-year-old granddaughter of the great educator and director of the Foundation for Montessori Education in Toronto. "Montessori is a philosophy, pedagogy and an extremely practical program," says Montessori. "People pick up on only one of these, and then you get distortions."

The Controversy

The so-called Montessori controversy is really a complex of misconceptions, often fed by public educators who are either ignorant or dismissive of the method. Here then are seven wrong-headed ideas about Montessori that have effectively kept the method from being more widely implemented, especially in the nation's inner-city schools where it could do the most good.

"Montessori is only partly right!"

A great many Montessori ideas have been selectively looted by public education and then badly implemented. Multi-aging, the popular fad of grouping seven-, eight- and nine-year-olds all in the same class, is a perfect example. There are two validated approaches for this practice; John Goodland's non-graded classroom, which emphasizes the teaching of subjects to homogeneous groups, and Montessori's "prepared environment." But most public schools continue to choose the "open classroom" approach, where thirty to sixty children roam from one activity centre to another. Research on the open classroom has never been positive (See **OPEN CLASSROOM**).

Multi-aging works in Montessori classrooms because the didactic materials and curriculum are specifically designed for this kind of classroom organization. Moreover, Montessori teachers are specially trained to teach in such demanding environments. The lesson of multi-aging's disappointing performance in many public schools is simply this: you can't have Montessori without Montessori. (See **MULTI-AGED CLASSROOMS**.)

"Montessori is for the rich!"

Montessori schools in Canada are private schools only because public schools have taken no interest in the method. But in the United States, Europe, Ireland, Tanzania, Sri Lanka and India, Montessori schools are often public schools that touch the lives of many children, be they rich or poor, normal or disabled.

Montessori originally designed her program for children living in a Roman slum, and there are now a few good, long-time comparative studies on the effectiveness of the Montessori method for children of the poor. While direct instruction programs produce faster academic gains for disadvantaged children, one long-term study that compared the effects of four different preschool programs found that the Montessori method was "the most effective in producing long-term school success" and easily outshines the performance of traditional nursey schools on any scale.

The obvious question is this: why haven't public educators in Montreal's east end or Vancouver's east end developed Montessori preschool programs for their disadvantaged children?

"Montessori is outdated!"

Many educators have long argued that Maria Montessori was hopelessly out of date because she acknowledged the influence of many fine educators who preceded her. But Montessori was, in fact, ahead of her time, and it has taken early childhood education nearly a century to catch up, albeit imperfectly. Her program was based on universal human characteristics, and as Renilde Montessori sharply notes, "the human species has not mutated since these observations were first made a century ago." Unlike most pedagogical programs, the Montessori method appears to span time, technological advances and widely diverse cultures with the ease of a migrating bird.

The low-tech, hands-on materials designed by Montessori and other Montessorians directly challenge contemporary high-tech ways of accomplishing tasks to which we've become so accustomed. Montessori strongly believed that the graceful work of hands, not machines, built civilizations.

"Montessori is too structured! Montessori is too open!"

These contradictory criticisms partly reflect different interpretations of Montessori in North America. And even Montessorians agree that, in the wrong hands, the approach can be too strict and insensitive or too loose and directionless.

Different translations of Montessori stem partly from two competing schools in Canada: the Association Montessori Internationale and St Nicolas. AMI, which is headquartered in Holland, certifies schools and trains teachers in the classic tradition of Maria Montessori. In contrast, the St Nicolas program offers a more modern interpretation and trains many of its teachers by correspondence. Although St Nicolas teachers can be excellent in every regard, many do not have the same exposure to children and classrooms that AMI-trained teachers do. In my opinion, schools that are AMI approved or that employ many AMI teachers tend to avoid all the excesses, and do the best job for children.

Parents must also remember that there is no patent on the Montessori name. The directors of good Montessori schools pointedly tell parents "IT'S BUYER BEWARE!" So shopping for a good Montessori school is like shopping for any school: it can't be done without a thorough visit, a good talk with the director, phone calls to other parents and an hour-long classroom observation. The troubling lack of consistency and quality in Montessori schools mirrors the predicament of most public schools.

Regardless of the affiliation, the character of a true Montessori school should shine through clearly: eager and engaged children freely choosing purposive work in an environment designed to foster more and more independent learning. A good Montessori school also listens to its parents and makes parental communication a high priority.

"*Montessori is too individualistic!*"

This charge relates to the nature of the method, which encourages children to work individually at their own pace. However, there is a great deal of socialization among the children. Compared to other child-centred programs the interaction among Montessori children is simply more intellectual in content. Although it is not a staple of the program, group work ends or begins a Montessori day.

One interesting study of Montessori graduates found that they preferred more investigative jobs (botanist or computer programmer) than social jobs such as teaching or social work. And another study reported that Montessori graduates were "more guarded in response, more critical of others and less freely expressive" on the Children's Personality Questionnaire, but nothing beyond the norm. However, none of these studies suggests that Montessori graduates are any less community-minded than children schooled elsewhere.

"Montessori is just kindergarten stuff!"

Montessori wrote about a great many rather grown-up issues, from environmental studies to religious education. She also had a remarkable vision for educating adolescents that included a three-year work program in close contact with the earth. Such a placement, whether on a farm, ranch or hostel, would give adolescents a chance to participate, produce and preserve. This earthy curriculum not only respects the idealism and socialness of adolescents, but also marks their transition to adulthood.

Some thoughts from Maria Montessori:

The studies which have been made of early infancy leave no room for doubt: the first two years are important forever, because in that period, one passes from being nothing into being something....

Not in the service of any political or social creed should the teacher work, but in the service of a complete human being, able to exercise in freedom a self-disciplined will and judgment, unperverted by prejudice and undistorted by fear.

If education is to be an aid to civilization, it cannot be carried out by emptying the schools of knowledge, of character, of discipline, of social harmony, and above all, of freedom.

If we try to think back to the dim and distant past, so remote that not even bones remain, what is it that helps us to reconstruct those times, and to picture the lives of those who lived in them? It is their art. In some of these prehistoric ages there are signs of a primitive civilization based on physical strength. The monuments and artefacts are formed from huge blocks of stone, and we ask in amazement how they came to be set up. Elsewhere, more refined art shows an indisputably higher level of civilization. So we may say that man's hand has followed his intellect, his spiritual life and his emotions and the marks it has left betray his presence. But even without the psychological view of things, we can see that all the changes in man's environment are brought about by his hands. Really, it might seem as if the whole business of intelligence is to guide their work. For if men had only used speech to communicate their thought, if their wisdom had been expressed in words alone, no traces would remain of past generations. It is thanks to the hand, the companion of the mind, that civilization has arisen. The hand has been the organ of this great gift that we inherit.

Montessori Resources

Maria Montessori. *The Montessori Method.* New York: Schocken Books, 1967.

John Chattin-McNichols. *The Montessori Controversy.* Albany N.Y.: Delmar Publishers, 1992.

Paula Polk Lillard. *Montessori: A Modern Approach.* New York: Schocken Books, 1972.

R. C. Orem. *Montessori and the Special Child.* New York: G. P. Putnam's Sons, 1969.

E. M. Standing. *Maria Montessori: Her Life and Work.* New York: Mentor, 1962.

Foundation for Montessori Education, 2444 Bloor

Street West, Toronto, Ontario M6S 1R2. Telephone:
416-769-7457.

See also Appendix 9.

MULTI-AGED CLASSROOMS   This fashionable idea
comes with many names: mixed-ages, family grouping,
split-grade and multi-grade classrooms. Such an
arrangement means grouping children of different
ages (two or more consecutive grades) in one room.
One in five Canadian children now attend a multi-aged
class on the basis of philosophy or administrative convenience. The concept, of course, is not new. The one-
room schoolhouse was multi-aged and never made a
big deal about it. But it got good results because of the
school's small scale: twenty to forty kids, well-sequenced
instruction and subject-based teaching. Many small
rural school boards still practise these principles.

Another successful multi-aged model was developed
by Maria Montessori, the great Italian educator, nearly
a hundred years ago. She based it upon the classic
observation that older children are good motivators
and teachers of younger children. She noted that children "do not help one another as we do.... They
respect one another's efforts, and give help only when
necessary. This is very illuminating because it means
they respect intuitively the essential need of childhood
which is not to be helped unnecessarily."

As a consequence, Montessori schools group children in three cycles (three to five, six to eight and
nine to twelve). Her mixed groupings have achieved
good results because the Montessori curriculum is
sequential, strongly academic and offers didactic materials for all ages. Montessori teachers are also specifically trained in this approach. (Eighty percent of all
public teachers in multi-aged classes have received no

special training.) The Montessori method also impos-
es strong controls on the practice. Multi-aged
Montessori classrooms, for example, typically have two
trained teachers for no more than twenty-four to twen-
ty-eight children. And the class will usually take no
more than two special-needs children into such a setting. In contrast, some multi-aged classes in public
schools have as many as sixty students, with no limit on
the placement of needy or handicapped children—a
clear case of academic child abuse.

In my own observation of Montessori classrooms in
which kids aged three to five are working together, the
older students sometimes appear bored and restless
because they aren't being challenged enough. This is
not to say that the three- and four-year-olds don't relish
their attention and learn from them. They do. It's just
that the older students are ready to learn more. Some
Montessori preschools compensate for this fact by giving their five-year-olds more opportunities to work
together in a special afternoon program.

Although many teachers dread the idea of working
in a multi-aged classroom, some absolutely relish the
challenge. Successful experiences are usually based on
the tried and true: highly structured classrooms and
subject-based instruction with different teachers handling math, reading and social sciences. In such classes the students are grouped according to performance, not age, and constantly regrouped based on
their achievement. Good teachers who have taught in
such programs, which are largely based on the John
Goodland model for a non-graded classroom, admit
that few schools accept or recognize the preconditions
for successful multi-aging.

This observation is borne out by British studies on
mixed-age classrooms. They found the greater the
mixing, the more stressed the teacher, with the result

that a third of the students—the slowest and the quickest—didn't receive enough teaching.

Parents with children in multi-aged classrooms have made similar comments. Notes Valerie LeBaron, a Calgary mother of three: "Give me the statistics that show that multi-aging works best on all kids. So far I've seen grade one kids bowled over by the chaos; grade two kids lost and uninterested in the grade one lessons being taught; and grade three kids giving up because they aren't half as smart as the grade fours in their class....

"In talking with other parents it has become very obvious that there is a wide discrepancy in teacher expectations even within the same grade. This includes the emphasis placed on drills and basic academics. Some teachers feel it is strongly required, others not at all. And yet we received a notice stating we shall not be allowed to require specific teachers for our children? I know my children and I deserve the right to make an informed decision. If most parents choose one teacher over another in a specific grade, maybe that should tell Administration something about our teachers and your system!"

The Canadian Education Association produced the only national review of multi-aging in 1991. It reproduces a strict set of criteria established by the Montreal Teachers' Association for selecting children for this kind of class: "average or above-average school achievement, autonomous learners with no behavioural or emotional difficulties." It also notes that parents prefer to be given the choice of having their children placed in such a class; in other words, *consent* is important. Lengthy in-service training with experienced teachers is essential, as is a low teacher–pupil ratio and full-time classroom aides. Clearly, this is an expensive model for a limited audience that would seem to favour white upper middle class neighbourhoods unless a Montessori program is being provided.

In sum, schools should approach the idea of multi-aged classes cautiously. They should not do so without parental consent or without appropriate resources. They should keep their plan simple and be required to demonstrate the effectiveness of the new organization within six months. Failing that, they should revert to conventional practice.

See also **OPEN CLASSROOM** and **NON-GRADED CLASSROOM**.

N

NEW AGE EDUCATION   Perhaps the most popular proponent of New Age educational practices is Jack Canfield. He is the author of *100 Ways to Enhance Self-Concept in the Classroom* (Prentice-Hall) and numerous articles with titles such as "The Inner Classroom: Teaching with Guided Imagery."

Canfield's specialty is the shaping of children's imagination. He makes a living by advising teachers to practice "a new paradigm of learning" with Sufi dances, "warm fuzzy stories," "dreamwork," "psychodrama" and something called "meditation/centering." This practice involves asking children the following questions: "What's this thing called 'the Force' in *Star Wars*? How does Luke communicate with it?... Would you like to have this kind of experience?"

The object of all this is to imbue a child's mind with the message that "the self is sufficient unto itself." Canfield admonishes teachers to have their students repeat mantras like this: "May I be well, happy and peaceful. May all beings in this room be well, happy and peaceful...."

Canfield and a host of other New Age educators regard children as noble and blissful innocents who have the answers to all of the world's problems inside them. Notes William Kilpatrick, a professor of education at Boston College: "If this sounds more than vaguely familiar, its because what Canfield offers is a back-to-the-future model of educaton. It is values clarification with a mystical twist. Any answer is as good as any other, as long as it feels right and as long as you first check it out with your inner spirit guide."

Dreamwork and meditation teaching is popular in some Ontario classrooms as well as in British Columbia. Because New Age's idyllic mysticism is really a pseudo-religion, no child should be forced to participate in such programs without full parental consent.

See **VALUES CLARIFICATION** and **CHARACTER EDUCATION**.

NON-GRADED CLASSROOM   Throughout the continent, school administrators are trying to sell an old idea from the sixties and seventies, the non-graded classroom, and in so doing prove that educational reform, like remarriage in Samuel Johnson's definition, is often a "triumph of hope over experience."

Although a good argument can be made for reorganizing classes flexibly on the basis of what students can or can't do (the Canadian-born educator John Goodland certainly made one in 1963), the new advocates of non-graded classes generally promote a whole series of new fangled ideas under the rubric "developmentally appropriate practice." (See **DAP**.)

The DAP model for a non-graded classroom defines teachers as mere facilitators, children as playful constructors of their own learning, and knowledge as something best discovered in an integrated context, unhindered by "artificial subject-matter distinctions." DAP's theoretical premises are highly controversial and often contradicted by scientific research.

In an attempt to sort out opinion from fact, Bonnie Grossen, the editor of *Effective School Practises*, a quarterly American education journal, recently contrasted what the research says about non-graded classrooms and what DAP's proponents say, using a question and answer format. Here is my condensed version of her findings:

Should a primary school move to a non-graded organization?

DAP: Yes. Non-graded classrooms avoid the thorny problems of retaining, failing or socially promoting students from grade to grade.

Research: Certain models of non-graded primaries that respect distinct subject matter and offer direct instruction to whole groups of children attain better achievement scores than many traditional classrooms. However, non-graded classrooms that offer individualized instruction with activity centres or learning stations make little or no difference in achievement, because they reduce the amount of teaching delivered at the student's precise instructional level. (This is the model being promoted in Canada.) Study inconsistencies on the overall effects of non-graded classes show that there are many other factors more important for learning than simply not grouping by age. They include the quality of teaching and the content of the curriculum.

If children are not grouped according to age, how should they be grouped?

DAP: Mix children up regardless of age or skill level and group the young and old, disabled and normal, the calm and the frenzied all together like one utopian family. DAP promoters claim that "multi-age grouping is one strategy to promote social interaction among individual children and their more capable peers, an effective way of enhancing language competence and generally assisting children's progress to the next level of development and understanding."

Research: Place children at similar skill levels in similar groups for specific subjects such as reading, writing and mathematics. Schools that use the flexibility of

mixed-age classes to group students at the same learning level in order to give them the direct teaching they
need to progress report the greatest learning gains.
Schools that follow DAP guidelines and provide individualized instruction have much lower gains. Parents
should remember that DAP's free market classroom
model (pupils of all ages choosing activities and materials from an integrated curriculum) has never been
evaluated as part of a non-graded model. Two educational researchers, Robert Slavin and Roberto
Gutierrez, recently concluded in an excellent study on
non-graded classrooms (*Review of Educational Research*,
Winter 1992) that "the effectiveness of the non-graded
school organization plan may become confounded
with innovative instructional methods (DAP).
Whether these instructional methods will have positive
or negative effects on ultimate achievement is currently unknown."

*Should instruction follow the intent of the teacher or the
intent of the child?*

DAP: The child knows best. Instruction designed by
the teacher is inappropriate and may become "a
source of stress for young children."

Research: Follow the intent of the teacher. The
teacher should lead the class towards the desired goal,
constantly adjusting instruction based on the student's
responses to the lesson. Ample opportunity should be
provided for students to integrate and apply the
knowledge they have acquired in group or individual
projects.

Pedagogy that treats students like informed consumers of educational merchandise discriminates
against children who do not come from white, upper
middle class homes. In 1975 a group of British
researchers concluded that so-called progressive or
child-centred schools had unprogressive outcomes

and merely maintained existing class structures: "We are suggesting," wrote the researchers, "that modern child-centred education is an aspect of romantic radical conservatism."

Can problem solving be improved by acquiring more knowledge?

DAP: No. Process matters more than product. It's not what a student learns, it's how he or she learns it.

Research: Yes. The main difference between expert problem solvers and poor problem solvers is a well-organized knowledge base in the subject that is relevant to the problem. Whenever children have been taught general problem-solving strategies in isolation or without meaningful content, the teaching has been for naught.

Should students invent their own learning, or should the teacher communicate knowledge?

DAP: Students should invent their own learning. The U. S.-based National Association for the Education of Young Children, the founding fathers of DAP, theorizes that "knowledge is constructed as a result of dynamic interactions between the individual and the physical and social environments. The child's active experimentation is analogous to spontaneous research; in a sense, the child discovers knowledge."

Research: The teacher should communicate knowledge, primarily key ideas and strategies, in a lively environment of give and take, question and answer, banter and laughter. Students also need regular practice in applying and transferring this knowledge.

Should instruction be divided into specific subjects such as reading, mathematics and history?

DAP: No. Teach reading holistically and present a progression of authentic problem-solving activities in math.

A curriculum built on themes and topics should

provide "for long blocks of time to bring naturally related subjects together," and should not "require minimal time allotments for instruction in discrete subject matter." Some DAP supporters regard science or history merely "as material to mess around with."

Research: Yes. Erasing traditional subject boundaries for holistic treatment of themes is like taking away the frame of a house. Several studies now show that "thematic teaching" has negative effects on learning because it thwarts the active development of a meaningful intellectual discipline (such as history). The research also shows that learning written language holistically is a discriminatory practice, particularly with children from language-poor homes.

Should there be common standards for measuring progress?

DAP: No. Standards imply the same expectations for all learners. Fixed expectations do not appropriately respect individual diversity.

Research: This is not a question that science can answer. But folk wisdom and traditions of public schooling have always maintained that proficiency in the rudiments (reading, writing, math, history and the arts) is necessary for participation in democratic life. Clear standards should be based on the attainment of these basics. Using measuring tools derived from these standards, schools can evaluate the effectiveness of the instructional programs they use and the quality of service they provide to the community.

A last word: A strong case can be made for nongraded classrooms provided two simple principles are respected: flexibility in pupil grouping with frequent monitoring of progress at every level; and increased amounts of teaching time for whole class or small group instruction. If your school is going for a nongraded model make sure that it picks one with a proven track record. DAP is nowhere close to this camp.

See also **DEVELOPMENTALLY APPROPRIATE PRACTICE** and **MULTI-AGED CLASSROOMS**.

NUMERACY A few years ago a Toronto high school teacher, Lou D'Amore, became worried about the number of students he encountered who couldn't make change from a five-dollar bill. To determine the extent of such innumeracy he decided to conduct a simple study. It finally took the shape of a ten-question arithmetic test that he adapted from a grade three course of study in the 1932 Ontario school text *The Opportunity Plan.*

Numeracy, of course, means more than the mastery of grade three math skills, no matter how high the standards might have been in 1932. But in a populist sense numeracy is really nothing more than the ability to conceptualize simple mathematical ideas and to perform the key computations. The American biologist Garrett Hardin summed it up best when he wrote that "the numerate temperament is one that habitually looks for approximate dimensions, ratios, proportions, and rates of change in trying to grasp what is going on in the world. Given effective education—a rare commodity, of course—a numerate orientation is probably within the reach of most normal people."

To D'Amore's dismay he found that many of his grade nine science students had been denied a solid grasp of the numerate temperament. Their poor performance prompted him to challenge other teachers to give the test. Soon a total of twenty-three schools across Canada and seven in the United States were participating in the impromptu study. In the end, 2,436 pupils from grade five to twelve tried their hand at multiplying 92 by 34 and solving elementary word problems like this one: "Jane had $2.75. Mary had 95 cents more than Jane. How much did Jane and Mary have together?"

The results were not good. Less than 30 percent of the Canadian high school students (grades nine to twelve) could score a perfect 10 on a test of grade three computational skills: they managed a median of 84 percent. Students in grades five and seven scored an average of 76 percent correct.

More than any other question, the Jane and Mary problem flummoxed students. Fifty percent of the pupils in grade five either couldn't read the problem or couldn't add decimals with any degree of accuracy. General students in grade nine didn't fare any better and earned a 44 percent failure rate.

D'Amore's inexpensive yet elegant study heralded, if not predicted, the findings of a 1993 national math achievement test. Designed by the Council of Ministers of Education, the test found that more than one-third of the thirteen-year-olds couldn't work with numbers, algebra and statistics. Nearly 40 percent of the sixteen-year-olds bombed out as well.

The national study also illuminated stark provincial differences. Students in Quebec, Alberta and British Columbia, Canada's most numerate provinces, fared much better than their peers in Ontario, Saskatchewan and Manitoba. The worst number crunchers attended schools in the Maritimes or the territories. A prestigious 1991 international assessment ranked provincial performance the same way, with one glaring exception: Ontario, the nation's battered industrial heartland, came last.

These assessments don't really tell the whole story about eroding math standards. University and college teachers typically report that the general level of preparation of first-year students has declined substantially in the last five years. It's not that excellent students aren't graduating from high schools, says University of Toronto math professor Ed Barbeau. "It's just that there is a disturbing trend that sees them coming from a smaller group of schools." The business community has made similar observations, notes Peter Casquinha, the senior deputy director for the Institute of Canadian Bankers: "There is a perception that, in terms of basic skills, a grade nine education two decades ago stood an individual in better stead than a grade twelve diploma today."

The federal government has also amassed its own telling statistics, the kind that help explain why consumers must check and recheck their bills and receipts these days. According to the National Literacy Secretariat, 38 percent of the population can't use numbers to perform simple day-to-day tasks. That's a sizable underclass, many of whom are struggling bravely with the word as well.

What these tests and other indicators suggest is that Canadians are becoming less fluent with numbers just as an increasingly technological society demands they be more knowledgeable of the uses and abuses of figures. Despite happy assertions from many educators that electronic calculators will fill the learning gap, such claims miss the point, says Barbeau, a long-time crusader for better math instruction in the elementary grades. Numeracy, says the professor, gives the numerate two gifts: "personal autonomy and a conceptual overview of the importance of numbers in the scheme of everyday life."

A person who can't balance a chequebook or compute a mortgage becomes dependent on others—a relationship that ultimately dims vigilance and fosters corruption. Given the importance of numbers in financial, political and environmental dealings, an innumerate public is an uninformed public. To be blind to numbers, then, is be disenfranchised.

The silent and insidious erosion of numeracy didn't happen overnight. There aren't many places in the world where elementary teachers will brag about their hatred of math or where it is socially acceptable to confess a fear of numbers. But Canada and the United States are such places, and proudly so.

Although these attitudes have tainted our schools, they are seriously compounded by bad classroom practices. Perhaps one of the most odious culprits of innumeracy is the aptly named "spiral curriculum." Entrenched in North American schools for nearly twenty years, this curriculum trots out nearly the same army of math topics and marches it back again on the double, year after year. The well-intended theory behind such repetition posits that children can't deepen an understanding of an idea without revisiting it again and again.

Alberta's grade seven math program, for instance, introduces 163 concepts, and all but 7 are repeated in grade eight. What pupils eventually learn from such boring repetition is that it is not worth the trouble to learn concepts now because they will pop up again next year. The consequence of all of this spiralling is that the same familiar goals linger like ghosts, never taking any definite shape in children's minds. "For students, it's just awful," explains Charles Ledger, an award-winning math teacher and consultant with the North York Board of Education. "They find it frustrating and there is nothing ever to get excited about."

Neither Europe nor Asia has bought into this queer pedagogy. The Germans and the Japanese, for instance, have stuck with the tried principles of direct instruction: teach in depth, test, and review in a cumulative sequence. Build from the known to the unknown. And where practice and drill are necessary, do them with flair and vigour.

But if spiralling numbers turns many Canadian children off math, their teachers often fail to turn them back on again for lack of good training. Ontario's provincial auditor recently noted that 60 percent of the province's grade six and grade eight math teachers had no university-level math credits. The situation among elementary teachers is even worse: most have never looked at a math text after grade ten, which means that many experience, on average, an eight-year hiatus from numeracy before entering the teaching trade. "You just can't engage students or kindle their enthusiasm with that weak basis," argues David Hogg, a former math teacher and adviser to the popular school-reform group Organization for Quality Education.

This is not a situation tolerated by other countries. Of fifteen nations participating in a 1991 math test, Canada predictably ranked fourteenth in teacher specialization. Korea, Taiwan, Switzerland, the Soviet Union, Hungary and France reported better-prepared teachers and, not surprisingly, higher test scores (Canada stood ninth in correct answers). It seems that the secret of Quebec's success in topping both national and international math assessments boils down to a simple requirement that its grade seven teachers know some math.

The teacher training crisis is often exacerbated by poor methodology or none at all. Math teachers graduating from faculties of education now usually come armed with one model of instruction: activity centres. This discovery approach offers students different math tasks at kiosk-like centres. The method works much the same way as a supermarket presents food: if you know what you need, you can find it. Without any direct teacher instruction such a model inevitably leads to children with a weak mastery of the basic skills that can and should be learned by the end of grade four. "Teacher training has to look at both process and content," says Ledger. "As it stands now, many teachers are reluctant to do math in depth because they feel that they will be over their heads."

Technology and television have also played a subversive role in the numeracy débâcle. The image has not only triumphed over the word in public discourse (most people get their news from TV instead of print), but it has also debased the number. While part-time workers now punch pictograms on cash registers at fast-food restaurants, math consultants eagerly pass out calculators the way some sex educators dispense condoms.

Such practices pose two dangers. What you don't use on a regular basis, you are apt to lose. And what you don't know you can't do or correct. Giving children calculators before they have mastered basic math facts and the thinking processes behind them not only impairs their cognitive development but also their independence. A calculator can be a useful tool, but it should be earned. Ledger, whose dislike of calculators is not shared by many of his peers, always set a standard of proficiency and fluency in basics that his grade seven classes had to pass as a group before he pulled out the calculators.

The hardy enemies of numeracy, including the spiral curriculum, nonexistent standards and poor teacher training have been known to educators for a long time. With some thought they can also be corrected. Requiring that math teachers know more of their subject and introducing a well-paced curriculum that tackles exciting mathematical ideas in a connected and sequential manner are eminently achievable goals. In fact, most schools in the developed world teach math this way.

But in Canada, with the exception of a few schools and a growing band of concerned teachers, ministries of education just don't seem capable or willing to add up all this information into a coherent long-term reform.

The basic truths are almost as clear-cut as two plus two equals four. "It's important that an elementary student's mastery of basic math be automatic and confident," says Barbeau with a sense of weariness. "But that is the reality that is missing in the current direction of public education."

A clear illustration of how Canadian educators have rejected such common sense was when Bernadette Kelly, an American math teacher, came to town.

Classroom Practice

When Bernadette Kelly, an American authority on math instruction, recently gave several Ontario workshops on "reforming the math curriculum," the thirty-three-year-old learned a rude lesson in subtraction.

During two of the sessions (in Toronto and Sudbury), more than half of the participants walked out at lunch time. Now, to forfeit a $150 tuition charge, an educator either has to have very grand lunch plans or, as in this case, be very angry.

One of the disgruntled departees, Jeff Martin, president of the Ontario Mathematics Co-ordinators Association, wrote Kelly that he was "uncomfortable and upset."

He criticized her talk about mastering fractions and "dull, drill-like arithmetic" and her follow-up workshop for its absence of "real problem-solving, geometry and reasoning." Martin then spelled out a common

set of questions and beliefs that probably motivated
most of the premature departures:

> Who does the child's learning for them? Is it the
> national curriculum? Is it the teacher, the super-
> visor? Is it Dr Kelly? No, the child does his/her
> own learning for themselves. If we want to know
> how kids learn then we need to watch them, ask
> them thought-provoking questions, involve them
> collaboratively in the discovery. Mathematics is all
> about children making discoveries about patterns
> and structures and using these discoveries to dis-
> cover more mathematics.

What drove Martin to such child-centred eloquence
was Kelly's indelicate challenge to the "let them discover math" fraternity and the flawed design of math curricula that recently earned Ontario, Newfoundland
and Nova Scotia failing marks in a twenty-nation survey.

Kelly typically begins her workshops with the simple
(and apparently outrageous) assumption that knowledge is transferable and that teachers can do a lot of
direct things to ensure that this transfer is efficient,
accurate and democratic.

Sending kids, Columbus-like, off to discover
Pythagoras might be appropriate for 5 percent of the
population, notes Kelly, but most children need good
systematic math teaching to succeed. "The purpose of
math instruction is not to have kids reinvent the wheel
but to learn its applications."

According to Kelly, the "discovery math" approach,
when combined with spirally designed textbooks,
places most North American kids "at risk."

"Kids will work on decimals or geometry for several
weeks and then drop it and go on to a new topic,"

explains Kelly. "What they learn is that nothing is really important because it disappears."

The International Association for the Evaluation of Educational Achievement highlighted the weakness of the spiral curriculum in 1987 when it reported that only 40 percent of U. S. kids could add $2/5 + 1/8$ at the beginning of grade eight even though they had pursued fractions spirally throughout elementary school. Predictably, more spiral fraction teaching increased the percentage of fractions achievers at the end of grade eight by only 19 percent. In other words, only one in five kids benefited from more spiral teaching of fractions.

In contrast, only 5 percent of French students—who aren't served a math smorgasbord in elementary school—could answer the problem at the beginning of grade eight. But after intense and thorough coverage of the subject, 73 percent of the students, more than two-thirds of the class, had learned the concept by year's end.

According to Kelly, most breakfast cereals are more rigorously scrutinized than school texts. "There just isn't the basic assumption that if the kids aren't learning ... something should be done to make the texts better."

The research now being ignored by most publishers and school boards is that a "strand" textbook design works best. That means taking several topics (say, fractions, geometry and problem-solving) and developing them cumulatively and concurrently over time. "You teach a continuous progression of skills and every concept fits together like a jigsaw," says Kelly. "You keep skills alive by discriminately applying them in ever more difficult situations instead of dropping one topic after another."

One of the few Ontario teachers who appreciates

this avant-garde message and who did not walk out on Kelly's workshops is Charles Ledger. By developing a strand curriculum at Zion Heights High School, he has helped rank his students as the nation's top math achievers.

A Good Math Teacher

No one from Ontario's ministry of education has beaten a path to Charles Ledger's classroom yet, but the conscientious fifty-nine-year-old master teacher is patiently waiting. For in a province with a consistently bad math curriculum (Ontario's thirteen-year-olds multiply and divide below the national average), Ledger's math classes have become an enduring beacon of numeracy.

The evidence of Ledger's success is awesome: for five of the last seven years, students at Zion Heights Junior High School in the City of North York have taken first place in the prestigious Pascal Contest of the Canadian Mathematics Competition. The Pascal is a tough three-part exam (chock-full of intricate problems) that is run by the University of Waterloo and written annually by 35,000 students in grade nine.

No other Canadian school, not even asylums for the privileged such as Toronto's Upper Canada College or St Michael's University School in Victoria, can claim such a remarkable string of achievements as Zion. Nor has any other Canadian school put 121 students (an average of 10 percent of Zion's graduates a year) on the contest's honour roll since 1985. (The nearest competitor, St Michael's, has managed only forty-three honorees.)

Despite this outstanding national record, Ontario's educators haven't bothered to ask Ledger ("Mr L" to his devoted students) what in the name of rational integers is going on at Zion. "We even asked for someone to study our program so that we'd know what we are doing right," confesses Ledger, a former Anglican missionary in Uganda. "But nothing has ever happened."

As an innovator and trend bucker, Ledger is both mystified and disappointed by this uninterest because he sees no reason why more Ontario schools can't get the same satisfying results as have his students. The very ordinary and reproducible key to Zion's math fame, he adds, is a school-made math program that outperforms every other math text on the market. "The work we do simply isn't in those books," says Ledger.

Instead of cruising from one topic to another, as does an Addison-Wesley or Ryerson math book, Zion's program (developed and revised by Ledger, Fraser Simpson and Lou Stewart over the last decade) presents students with a logical and sequential or strand approach to skill development. The program also demands that students regularly practise and apply what they learn, the same way a hockey player uses his stickhandling skills to play a creative game.

That means daily (and popular) ten-minute drills in long division or multiplication to develop number fluency and basic skills. A grade nine student will do as many as a thousand word problems a year.

In contrast to most schools, Ledger's students don't use pocket calculators until the class achieves an overall average of 70 percent in its drills (students graph both individual and class performance every day). "We build up their number skills first."

Like the world's very best math classrooms in Korea or Switzerland, Zion's students also do a lot of group work. They check homework in teams and often analyse word problems in groups. (This is co-operative learning at its best!)

Zion's program also emphasizes the enjoyment of math as a pure science. "It should have value in its own right and not just because it's useful," explains Ledger. "Perhaps standard textbooks concentrate too much on math's usefulness."

Not suprisingly, students uniformly love Zion's math program, drills and all. Even kids who would normally dread the idea of meeting an absolute equation attend Ledger's classes without fear, reports sixteen-year-old Zion graduate Lee Andersen. "No one ever felt they couldn't learn there. When Mr Ledger taught something, he didn't teach it as a skill but how it could be used to solve a problem," adds Andersen. And thanks to Zion's superior program, she is now a grade eleven student studying a grade twelve honours math course.

Ledger developed his uniquely Canadian curriculum by examining techniques and materials that worked in private and public schools across the country. He ignored many U.S. math experts because they often championed ideas unproven in classrooms with real kids of varying abilities.

The source of Ontario's math woes, argues Ledger, lies primarily with administrators who frequently make decisions about how math should be taught without ever having taught prime factoring, much less formal logic. "I don't know how you can create a math program if you're not working with kids."

The solution would require identifying schools that teach math well, defining the characteristics that make a difference, and then applying them to the general school population, much as Ledger did at Zion.

"But I don't think there is any interest in doing that," he says wistfully. "As a teacher you just can't get very far."

Update: Charles Ledger retired recently and is now a math consultant for the North York Board of Education. But the math curriculum developed by Ledger and Fraser Simpson is now available for classroom use or home-schooling. Designed for students in grades seven to nine, Spirit of Math costs about $150 for six units (that's one year's worth of work). For more information call Irwin Publishing, 905-660-0676, or fax 905-660-0676. Outside of Toronto call 1-800-263-7824. Parents or teachers interested in corresponding with Charles Ledger should write: Spirit of Math, Suite 180, Unit 12A, 4981 Hwy. 7 East, Markham, Ontario L3R 1N1.

John Saxon, another maverick math educator, has also produced a math series far superior to the graphic-laden texts peddled by most big publishers. Saxon's textbooks, which are hot property in the education underground, emphasize ten minutes of direct teaching, review of previous problems and cartoonless exercises with short explanations. The series has been particularly successful with inner-city schoolchildren in the United States. Copies can be ordered from most educational bookstores in Canada, including The Bookman: 1-800-461-TEXT.

O

OUTCOMES-BASED EDUCATION (OBE)   Many Ontario school boards have been attacked by a bad case of outcomes fever, a neurological ailment that appears to be provoked by the oncoming millennium.

An outcome, by the way, is straight edubabble for what "students should know, be able to do and value in order to be successful in the twenty-first century."

The Grey County School Board, for example, proudly lists "effective communicators, responsible global citizens, lifelong learners and quality contributors" as its essential school "outcomes."

The Waterloo County Board of Education glowingly tops these outcomes with a mixed bag of adjectives and nouns: "global, work, culture, learning, relationships, citizenship and personal." The board's "personal" outcome promises a utopian citizen: "A happy, wise and caring individual who: applies critical, flexible and creative thinking; uses ethical values throughout one's life; takes responsibility for one's personal well-being and sets realistic goals and strives to achieve one's personal best."

The Toronto Board recently tried to develop its own "graduation outcomes" for something called "spheres of living." The spheres included learning ("life-long"), relationships ("our relationship to others") and spirituality ("personal practices of meditation, prayer ... not religion per se"). Its helpful albeit inarticulate definition of the environment sphere read like this: "Our habitat: the planet; quality of water, air, earth, ozone layer; food production; population; species of animals."

The father of outcomes-based education is William Spady, an American sociologist who bills himself as a sort of "future-oriented visionary" and "paradigm pioneer." Spady is also an outcome of the Ontario Institute for Studies in Education, where he worked from 1969 to 1973. He is now the director of the International Center on Outcome-Based Restructuring in Eagle, Colorado.

Like many American education reformers, Spady is a genuine school restructurer. As such he believes that schools have to be set on their heads if public education is to survive "the flood of internal and external economic, social and political problems making daily headlines." He defines restructuring as a "collaborative, flexible, transdisciplinary, outcomes-based, open system, empowerment-oriented approach to schooling." (Neither brevity nor clarity seems to be an essential OBE outcome.)

When a school board gets a case of outcomes fever, its bureaucrats do some amazing things. For starters, they form strategic design teams to examine, critique and synthesize the "best available information about the conditions of life students are likely to encounter in their future." The bureaucrats then decide what attributes a successful school graduate should have and then design a school program accordingly.

In this process, subject matter such as history, English, geography and science conveniently disappear. That's because the purpose of OBE, says Spady, "is to adapt content to the explicit development of the higher-order competencies and orientations in the exit outcomes, rather than to foster subject knowledge in isolation."

Another prominent feature of OBE is the absence of deadlines. It posits that students should move at their own pace and be granted multiple opportunities

to pass tests that demonstrate mastery of some outcome. (As one teacher recently noted, OBE programs
offer students all the time they need to become irre-
sponsible.)

Most of OBE's concepts were anticipated by Carl
Rogers, the father of the human potential movement,
in 1968. At the time he predicted that future education models, such as OBE, would replace teachers with
facilitators, push aside subject matter, eliminate deadlines in favour of self-pacing behaviour, promote feelings of exploration in the classroom and uphold the
principles of life-long learning. Wrote Rogers:
"Learning will not be confined to the ancient intellectual concepts and specializations. It will not be a
preparation for living. It will be, in itself, an experience in living. Feelings of inadequacy, hatred, a desire
for power, feelings of love and awe and respect, feelings of fear and dread, unhappiness with parents or
with other children—all these will be an open part of
the curriculum, as worthy of exploration as history or
mathematics." (See **CHARACTER EDUCATION**.)

Spady categorizes fierce parental opposition to OBE
in Minnesota, Virginia, Pennsylvania, Iowa and Ohio
as a "clash of world views." He is right. As community-
based enterprises, schools have traditionally had one
foot in the past and one in the present, with their eyes
on the horizon. Spady, the futurologist, says that's an
outdated notion. He wants schools and children to
jump into the future with both feet. To his credit, he
doesn't think that "implementing authentic OBE"
should be mandated; it's an "evolutionary process," he
says.

If one transported Spady's brand of social engineering to Chiapas, Mexico, a strategic design team might
read the entrails of laissez-faire capitalism and conclude
that the future has no place for the Mayan language,

corn and the spirit of Jacinto Canek, the eighteenth-century freedom fighter. Such folksy, conservative stuff would give way to the global outcome of "informed world citizens" who "evaluate and respond to social, economic and political issues in an ever-changing world" or the "work outcome" of "quality-conscious, productive workers" who "adapt to change in positive, innovative ways."

Like the peasants of Chiapas, American parents have wrung their hands over such thinking. In Colorado, they have laboured through OBE report cards with 95 grading categories listing "intellectual curiosity," "self-esteem" and "creative expression," vainly looking for a section on reading or math. And in Pennsylvania, they have questioned the sanity of 545 outcomes (later condensed to 55) that can't be measured objectively. Try this one: "All students apply the fundamentals of consumer behavior to managing available resources to provide for personal and family needs."

What has upset parents most about OBE is its blatant endorsement of a feel-good curriculum. Most parents intuitively know that assessing a student's competence in "personal well-being and accomplishment" or "cultural and creative endeavours" will at best be difficult and at worst purely subjective.

Peg Luksik, a former teacher in Pennsylvania, notes that most of the outcomes set by OBE are poorly defined and silly. When schools mandate outcomes like "tolerance of differences," Luksik asks some pointed questions: "So could you please tell me how you test tolerance? If this is a graduation requirement, how much tolerance is enough tolerance? And how do you remediate? And if a particular student doesn't work well with others, should he or she be denied a diploma?"

Canadian school administrators have no shame (or immunity for that matter) when it comes to catching

American fevers but they should at least have the good sense to ask two questions: Is there any good empirical research supporting this epidemic of outcomes? And do Canadians really want their public schools to be rootless laboratories for the future?

If your school board or school is embracing OBE, make sure the following qualifiers are all properly addressed. Given the hostility and public outcry that OBE eventually engenders, educational experts now recommend four major changes:

1. Be clear about stating desired results. Mushy-worded outcomes undermine what is good in OBE: the idea that all children can reach fairly high competencies in a variety of skills and subjects.
2. State outcomes in terms of specific content area. That's what parents value, that's what is fairly assessable and that's ultimately what matters. Students can't integrate disciplines they don't know.
3. Don't state outcomes that can't be fairly measured. It makes sense to suggest that displaying ethical conduct is a worthy outcome. But to award a diploma conditional on its attainment is, as one educator recently noted, "to cross a big line."
4. Give parents the choice to opt out of an OBE program. In other words, don't commit an entire school system to an unproven and poorly studied fad that parents have trashed in more than five American states.

Transitional OBE

William Spady outlines a number of stages that a school may go through before it achieves "Transformational OBE." One of the intermediate stages is "Transitional OBE"; this much-simplified version of Spady's millennial goals is actually content-based, eminently workable, highly successful and parent friendly. A shining example of its success can be found in the math program of Alberta's Fort McMurray schools.

In the oil sands capital of Canada the Fort McMurray Catholic Schools Board has decided that all children can learn and all teachers can teach with Transitional OBE. "It's a process with a good product," says Phyllis Geddert, the project's consultant.

Predictably, the need for Transitional OBE started with a math disaster. Four years ago superintendent Jerry Heck took a look at the chronically below-average scores of his students on Alberta's math tests, and decided he didn't like the results. Fishing for effective ideas, he encountered OBE in a Colorado workshop run by William Spady.

After much deliberation and in-service training, Fort McMurray introduced an OBE math and science program in 1989 at two pilot schools where Heck finally saw results he liked. Before OBE only 49 percent of grade three students achieved a "standard of excellence" in math or a mark of 80 or above. But after OBE the success rate grew to include 70 percent of the class. In grade ten, the math results were even more dramatic, as the number of achievers climbed from 15 to 89 percent of the class.

"We have set our target achievement level at 80 percent for all students," notes Geddert. "And our experience tells us that with high expectations and the other key principles of OBE, this is achievable."

The principles of Transitional OBE combine the old and new. They include "a clear focus on what is important for the student to learn," well-defined criteria for success, more than one chance to learn, and "continuous instructional improvement based on the results."

In the classroom, these principles pointedly highlight the differences between "mystery learning" (the

norm in most schools) and the historic goal of education: mastery learning. With the mystery approach
students do a lot of guesswork in educational environments that provide few goals and even less feedback.
But in a Transitional OBE classroom a student should
know where he is coming from, where he is going and
how he's going to get there. "There is much more
clarity," explains Geddert.

Transitional OBE requires teachers to review the
research on effective teaching practices and to reflect
on their own beliefs and experiences. More important,
the program also expects a phenomenal amount of
Asian-style teamwork to ensure the continuity of subject matter from grade to grade, as well as the attainment of shared goals.

To date, most reviews of the experiment have been
positive. While teachers report that they "have never
felt so focused before," students admit that the program encourages them to work harder and "learn
faster." Parents also say that it builds confidence in
their kids, and reinforces "the importance of working
steadily towards a goal."

OPEN CLASSROOM   The open classroom was an
untested fad that swept through North American
schools in the 1970s. It promised "a style of teaching
involving flexibility of space, integration of curriculum
areas, and more individual or small-group than large-
group instruction." In practice, children were allowed
to do what they wanted at their own pace in the company of thirty to sixty children in one big noisy room.
Learning was supposed to be more creative and
human this way.

Administrators loved the concept—an offshoot of
affective (feel-good) education—and tore down class-

room walls at great expense without having any data to support their frenzied activity. A decade later most of the walls went back up, because two hundred empirical studies reached one overwhelming conclusion: that "the record of effectiveness of programs of open education does not inspire confidence about this approach."

The studies revealed that white middle class children in the open classroom didn't do as well in basic skills and did only marginally better in creative thinking than their peers in traditional classrooms. For immigrant, inner-city, and learning-disabled children the open classroom was a nuclear bomb, because it placed responsibility for learning on children who needed first to be taught the fundamentals. In this way the open classroom openly discriminated against children who needed more instruction or better instruction in order to succeed in school.

In spite of the research (educators have no memories), the open classroom has recently made a comeback as part of "developmentally appropriate practice" or DAP—a theoretical set of child-centred guidelines for schooling. If your child is in such a class, check to see if the teacher keeps detailed records on the academic achievement of each child. The records should clearly show where each child is and where he or she ought to be. Lack of records indicates a sloppy program; withdraw your child immediately.

Good schools recognize that certain children will do well in open classrooms and others won't. As a consequence, they offer parents real choices and provide alternatives such as traditional classrooms. A black American principal noted several years ago that "if you're part of the Third World, you can't afford the luxury of a child of yours going through that kind of thing [the open classroom] and not getting enough out of it." Most Canadian working and middle class families would agree with him.

See also **DEVELOPMENTALLY APPROPRIATE PRACTICE** and **"INNOVATIONS" vs. "REFORMS."**

P

PARENT ADVOCACY   When I taught children with special needs in Winnipeg and Toronto, parents often asked me how they could make their school work better for their learning-disabled or teaching-disabled kids.

My basic reply was that a parent's role as an advocate is a natural but difficult one. Ensuring that a child receives exactly the kind of teaching that child needs to succeed means investing time and energy in the community school.

Here is the five-step program I offered to parents on how to make the schools work for their kids. It's derived partly from Siegfried Engelmann's book *Your Child Can Succeed* as well as from my own experiences in dealing with scores of parents, teachers and principals.

Step 1: Know your school.

Visit the school and keep track of school developments. Meet your child's teacher and principal in person. If possible, work as a school volunteer or aide. Join the Home and School Association or PTA. Principals and teachers listen to familiar voices, and good schools welcome parental involvement. And the more you express a daily interest in what goes on in the school the more your child will consider school an important place.

Step 2: Make the most out of the teacher interview.

Ninety-nine percent of all problems can be solved

with a teacher interview. So go in prepared. Talk to your child and identify the specific problem. Write down your questions. Establish a goal and a purpose for the meeting. If possible, bring in proof of concern (spelling or math samples). Never go into a meeting angry.

A teacher interview should yield answers to the following questions:

1. What is the problem?
2. What can the teacher do about it?
3. Why will the agreed upon solution work?
4. How can the parent help?

Be polite and self-assured. State your expectations clearly and strongly. Acknowledge any positive things your child has mentioned about the teacher or class.

Do not accept evasive or vague replies to your questions. Take notes. Have the teacher clarify anything you don't understand. If appropriate, arrange for a follow-up meeting. Don't expect immediate results. Be understanding. But trust your instincts: every family has its own curriculum and every parent is a teacher too.

Step 3: Visit the classroom and observe.

If you still have doubts about the quality of instruction your child is receiving, arrange to observe the classroom. This can be done through the principal and teacher. Make sure you observe the specific lesson (reading or math) that has become a problem for your child.

The purpose of a classroom observation (and I did many as a teacher) is to document whether your child is receiving good teaching. You can do this with a tape recorder or notepad. Sit quietly in one place and watch for the following:

1. Extreme management problems (are the kids hanging from the ceiling?);
2. Tasks students don't understand after instruction;
3. Tasks students are asked to perform that are not related to the subject being taught;
4. Clear and cohesive teaching with evidence of students sticking to the work at hand and applying the lesson.

Step 4: Interview the principal.

The research says that principals set the academic tone of a school. So a laissez-faire teacher with low academic expectations might merely reflect the attitudes of a principal who likes to clip his nails all day. But always be prepared and civil.

Present your documents or tapes that show that your child is not receiving good teaching. Take note of the principal's familiarity with the problem. Request that your child's teacher change his or her teaching methods to meet your child's needs. If necessary, ask that your child be assigned to an experienced teacher who can do the job. And ask the following questions:

1. Is this teacher a competent professional?
2. Can I see the test results on student performance in this teacher's class?
3. How many children failed in this class or were still below grade level at the end of the year?

Step 5: Go to the top.

If you still haven't got answers to your questions, or a satisfactory response to the problem, arrange to meet the following people in this order: school superintendent, school trustee and your local MLA. Explain

to each your child's academic history and produce
your evidence of educational malpractise. This is the
end of the line, and if you don't get satisfaction here,
it's time to hunt for a good school in a neighbouring
school board.

Generally, when parents run into deep educational
holes and find themselves exhausted and angry at
STEP 5, it's either a sign that the principal is a total
jerk or evidence that the community itself is not functioning as a community. Schools, after all, often mirror the lives of their neighbourhoods. Although
schools should be accountable to taxpayers, they don't
work very well without responsible ongoing parental
involvement and support. The best schools are always
the ones in which the principal, teachers, parents and
kids are all accountable partners.

Every time parents treat a school as a glorified babysitting service (and I hear this from teachers all the
time) or neglect their role in the school partnership,
they weaken an already unbalanced system and, ultimately, get the schools they deserve.

See also **EFFECTIVE SCHOOLS**, **ACCOUNTABILITY**,
LEARNING DISABILITIES, and Appendix 6.

PERRY PRESCHOOL PROJECT   This is the preschool
model most often cited to defend the expansion of federal or state-sponsored daycare. The project, carried
out in Ypsilanti, Michigan, followed 123 poor black
children over a twenty-year period. Unlike most daycare centres, the Perry Preschool project was well funded, well staffed and elicited a high degree of parental
support and involvement. Children who spent one or
two years in the program remained in school longer
and managed to avoid the poverty traps of teenage
pregnancy and crime much better than the control

group. The Perry kids' ability to earn a decent wage also seemed to improve. A cost-benefit study of the project concluded that society gets back three dollars for every dollar it spends on early childhood education.

But the study has a number of flaws. It has been heavily criticized for differences between the control and project groups and the project's failure to assign students to the two groups randomly. The methodology of the cost-benefit analysis has also been questioned. More disturbingly, the model seems to have been more effective for girls than boys. A Ph.D. student at the University of Michigan found that the differences in long-term outcomes between the control and treatment groups were significant for girls but negligible for boys. This finding strongly suggests that intervention for high-risk boys after the age of three is probably too late; the damage has already been done.

Last but not least, the Perry Preschool project is not representative of the generally uneven quality of daycare offered in Canada or the United States.

See also **DAYCARE** and **PROJECT FOLLOW-THROUGH**.

PHONICS   Few aspects of reading are as controversial as the teaching of phonics.

But the facts are these: English, like German, Finnish and Spanish, is written in an alphabetic script. This means that each letter of our alphabet represents a single speech sound most of the time. Since the Golden Age of Greece, parents have taught their children how the speech sounds and letters match in order to read, write and spell. Approximately fifty-five letter-sound matches decode 80 percent of the language. This body of information is called "phonics," while the study of such sound patterns is known as "phonetics."

If taught at all in primary school, phonics is usually presented in one of two ways: directly or indirectly. In a direct approach a teacher might write *s* on the blackboard and say: "This sound is *sss*. What sound?" In an indirect approach a teacher might write *soap* on the blackboard and ask students: "What letter does the word *soap* begin with?"

Hundreds of research studies say that reading programs that include direct phonics instruction produce more able readers than the indirect approach. Rudolf Flesch, Jeanne Chall and Marilyn Adams have written extensively about these studies. Noted Adams in her monumental study, *Beginning To Read*: "Approaches in which systematic code [phonics] instruction is included along with the reading of meaningful connected text result in superior reading achievement overall, for both low-readiness and better prepared students."

In most countries phonics instruction takes place in kindergarten and grade one alongside other reading activities. Thereafter the program focuses purely on reading for meaning, vocabulary development and spelling patterns. A school that continues phonics instruction into grades three or four is probably a school with a bad reading program.

The most effective phonics programs are well-sequenced and multi-sensory in which students trace and draw the sounds on sandpaper. Anywhere between a third and a quarter of all middle class students will need systematic phonics instruction in order to learn how to read fluently.

Teaching phonics, of course, does not mean that one ignores reading comprehension, writing or spelling. Nor does it mean that phonics or sounding becomes the be-all or end-all of a reading program. Jeanne Chall, a Harvard educator who reviewed the research on phonics for her classic study, *The Great*

Debate, notes that "teaching only phonics—and in isolation—was not a recommendation" of her work. Like many whole language advocates she also recommends "that library books, rather than workbooks, be used by children not working with the teacher and that writing be incorporated into the teaching of reading." Chall admits that "some teachers may inadvertently overdo the teaching of phonics, leaving little time for the reading of stories and other connected texts."

There are many bad phonics programs on the market. Perhaps the most infamous example is "Hooked On Phonics," a $300 tape program produced by Gateway Educational Products in California. Gateway sells nearly two thousand copies a day of this untested but well-advertised "educational program."

"Hooked On Phonics" consists of eight cassette tapes, nine decks of flashcards and word lists. That's all. The program is not only badly sequenced, but it provides no meaningful context for using the sounds it has allegedly taught. Chall, who reviewed the program, concluded that it fails to define what it promises—"a super reader"—or even to identify what a person might be able to read after completing the program. Adds Chall: "The claim that it is appropriate for all ages, from preschool to adult, seems highly unlikely.... It is hard to imagine an older poor reader who would have the patience and motivation to read through page after page of unrelated words, not knowing if she/he is decoding them accurately or not." (For information on tested phonics programs see **READING**.)

Good schools will not be hooked on phonics but will teach sound–letter matches early, systematically and directly as part of a comprehensive reading program. However, less than one-third of Canada's elementary schools now do this.

If your school is not teaching phonics directly, and

your child is struggling with reading in grade one, act quickly. Either purchase a good program or hire a tutor. Don't waste valuable time fighting the school or its anti-phonics dogma. Save that battle for later. Your first priority is to help your child learn how to read so that they can read to learn.

Parents interested in learning more about phonics and reforming reading practices in the schools should subscribe to a journal published by the Reading and Literacy Institute (*RALI*). It examines all aspects of the Great Debate and is published four times a year. For a subscription, mail $10 to *RALI*, 68 Akins Drive, St Albert, Alberta T8N 2Y7.

See also **WHOLE LANGUAGE**, **READING** and **PHONEMIC AWARENESS**.

PHONEMIC AWARENESS   Phonemic, phonological and auditory awareness are big academic terms that simply refer to a child's ability to make sense of sound sequences in the language and to use them to read and spell. It is a kind of pre-phonics skill and one of the most important predictors of a child's ability to read.

A great many children who bog down in reading (about a third of all beginning readers) do so not for lack of teaching in sounding out or meaning, but for lack of specific instruction in how to identify and make specific sounds smaller than a syllable.

For example, a child with poor phonemic awareness cannot answer the following questions: What word would be left if the /k/ sound were taken away from *cat*? What is the first sound in *rose*? How many sounds do you hear in the word *cake*? What word starts with a different sound: *bag, nine, beach, bike*? And so on. In other words, a simple seven-minute test administered in kindergarten can tell a teacher who needs good phonemic awareness training and who doesn't.

The research on the need for such teaching is one of the most important breakthroughs in reading research in the last twenty years. A seminal study by two British researchers found that struggling readers couldn't make sense of rhyme or alliteration. They took two groups of five- to six-year-old children, both having trouble matching and manipulating sounds, and gave one group forty sessions of training in categorizing sounds and the other (the control group) standard context exercises. The kids who got the phonemic training made a four-month gain over the control group in reading ability, which jumped to an eight-month gain by the age of eight.

A long-term Danish study reported similar findings in 1988. Researchers took a group of kindergarten students who were three times as deficient as the control group in making sense of sounds. With good phonemic training they had these children outperforming the control group. The resulting gains in reading and spelling continued until grade two and ended their school's history of inferior reading instruction.

Two of North America's pioneers in auditory or phonemic awareness are Pat and Charles Lindamond from San Luis Obispo, California. Over a twenty-year period they have developed a highly structured, scripted program that develops oral and phonological awareness—the Auditory Discrimination in Depth Program. Sylvia Hannah, a director of the Edmonton Literacy Centre, one of two Alberta clinics that use the ADD Program, describes the essence of their work this way:

> One of the essential components of successful speech therapy is that clients be made aware of the correct functioning of the articulatory apparatus:

tongue, teeth, lips, air. Through language, clients are directed to an awareness of what they need to do to form sounds accurately and consistently. When people become self-monitoring then they are able to produce speech sounds accurately in conversation. They need to become self-monitoring and self-correcting.

Pat, a speech therapist, thought that if students could become aware of the articulatory features of English sounds, then they could monitor and correct their own responses to print by feeling and thinking about what they need to do to match speech to print.... Pat and Charles have found that the kinaesthetic, or feeling, component of speech sounds is the link to the auditory and visual information required by the reader and speller so that accuracy can be achieved.

Individuals are first taught the articulatory components of all English speech sounds. Then they practise feeling, monitoring and altering sound sequences. The more they practise sound sequences and sound changes, the more accurate their responses become. The goal is automatic and accurate judgment about sound sequences. The articulatory knowledge gives students the tools to make their own judgments about their reading and spelling responses. They become independent and successful readers, spellers and writers.

The message of such reading research is dramatic. "Identify early, remedy early and focus on phonological awareness," says Canadian reading researcher Keith Stanovich. But several obstacles stand in the way of common sense. Few teachers have been trained in phonemic awareness, most whole language theories ignore it and an incredible number of administrators have no idea what phonemic awareness is, let alone how to teach it. But if schools paid attention to this issue they could probably reduce membership in their special education programs by more than 50 percent.

Parents can help draw attention to the issue of phonemic awareness by pressing for several reforms at the school board level. First, demand that all kindergarten children be screened for phonemic awareness. There are several good, economical tests on the market: the Lindamond Auditory Conceptualization Test, the Test of Phonological Awareness and Jerome Rosner's Auditory Analysis.

Second, request that all kindergarten teachers receive in-service training in phonemic awareness. Good kindergarten teachers make sure their pupils do a lot of fun and engaging work with nursery rhymes, rhyme, alliteration, segmentation and sound/symbol relationships.

Finally, recommend that the board use reading programs that directly develop phonemic awareness such as *Open Court* or *Sing, Spell, Read and Write.* Whole language schools might want to try "The Phonological Zoo," a language awareness training program developed for group instruction with groups of twenty-five children. Systematic in scope and sequence, the program suggests two lessons per week that can be integrated into the existing curriculum. Its author, Linda Ayres, can be reached at 313-644-2713 in Michigan.

Parents might also present their teachers, principals and trustees with copies of Marilyn Jager Adams's excellent book, *Beginning to Read: Thinking and Learning about Print.* It says a great deal about phonemic awareness in clear prose. For information on how to order *Beginning to Read,* or a summary of the book, phone the Center for the Study of Reading in Illinois: 217-244-4083.

See also **PHONICS, WHOLE LANGUAGE** and **READING**.

PIAGET   If the great Swiss psychologist Jean Piaget were alive today, he'd be amazed—if not frightened—by how his ideas have been abused by modern education. Although pedagogues religiously cite Piaget as the author of elementary curricula devoted to play, sandboxes and "activity-centred learning," the researcher never claimed to be an educator or, for that matter, a sandbox salesman.

This systematic distortion of Piaget's experimental theories by "child-centred" dogmatists has long irked York University's Dr Margarete Wolfram, because she studied and worked with "the old man" for four and a half years in the early 1960s. "His primary interest in children was a source for his studies on intelligence," says the fifty-four-year-old educational psychologist and mother of three.

Yet Piaget, who popularized the good notion that human knowledge proceeds in stages, has been rudely appropriated by modern educators to justify pedagogical whims that have invited "a lot of underachievement and pseudo-retardation in the modern school system."

According to Wolfram, the real corruption of Piaget began in the 1960s, when "learning theory" or the mechanistic drill and rote approach to education came under well-deserved attack from a new wave of humanist and cognitive psychologists. Sensing that learning theory had nowhere to go but down, educators abandoned ship and looked for new transportation.

Not surprisingly, most educators rushed as far away as they could from learning theory's singular emphasis on the role of the environment in a child's learning and towards Piaget's charming evocations of natural maturation and self-learning.

Piaget's theories, however, encompassed both camps. "He believed there was an interaction between genetic disposition and maturation on one hand and the environment on the other," says Wolfram. "But North Americans only took over one side of Piaget and created an educational system as one-sided as the one before it."

Educators tend to favour simple theories over complex ones, which explains in part their embrace of half a theory. To be fair, however, Piaget had a tendency to satisfy the biases of his audiences, and so emphasized maturation in North America and environment in Europe. Consequently, North Americans took the idea that knowledge develops on the basis of pre-established innate patterns and came up with the wild conclusion that all learning is self-discovery and exploration.

In the process, educators compounded their errors by transforming Piaget's research style ("He followed kids around in an unobtrusive fashion to see where it would lead," reflects Wolfram) into a kind of self-serving teaching method that involved no teaching at all.

"Learning theory had the teacher out front doing all the talking, which was not good," adds Wolfram, "but to turn it upside down and have the teacher follow the children around waiting for learning to take place is just hopeless." It is also the basis of much of Ontario's elementary school curriculum.

Yet most parents know, as does Reuven Feuerstein (one of Piaget's top students), that children need to be guided, prompted and focused by adults if real intellectual growth is to occur. Too often this kind of rigorous interaction directed by a teacher with a clear set of goals has been rejected by many of our schools—in the name of Piaget.

Because Piaget did a lot of concrete activities with kids, North American educators also deduced wrongly that the children should noisily play with an army of concrete objects. But unlike his interpreters, Piaget recognized that even most two-year-olds have already moved beyond the concrete world to become mental abstractors as well as playful doers.

Yet, notes Wolfram, many modern classrooms with their frantic devotion to play no longer provide the time or peace for concentrated thought and deliberation. "That's very hard to do in a noisy classroom."

Another unfortunate misreading of Piaget has been the permissive celebration of "readiness." In schools across the country teachers often hide their inability to teach by saying that Johnny can't read or Sally can't write because the kids just aren't ready.

Piaget, who raised three children, knew that kids acquire the ability to understand certain tasks at vastly different ages and argued that these differences are directly related to the amount of environmental stimulation the child receives. His famous readiness ages of seven and eight years, which are still applied today, are outrageously late. The subjects of his fifty-year-old studies received much less stimulation at home than today's children.

But in the hands of modern educators, notes Wolfram, the whole concept of readiness has ultimately become a sorry excuse to wait and withhold teaching, particularly in reading: "Just give Johnny time and he'll figure it out himself." This withholding of teaching compounds "the intellectual neglect of an underprivileged child already suffering from a lack of instruction."

The disembodied spirit of Piaget also resides in most provincial curriculum guides. Such guides routinely speak of play or boast that education, like digestion, is "a personal metabolic matter": parents and teachers may create conditions for learning but "the actual learning experience is intimate and subjective, for each human being reaches out to the world in his own idiosyncratic way." (Ontario's Common Curriculum says that it is up to kids to "construct their own meaning.")

When applied to the daily life of a classroom this child-centred credo has often meant letting kids forage for themselves in jungles of "active learning"—an outright misreading of Piaget's core theory.

Wolfram, who does not tolerate these misinterpretations of her mentor quietly, knows that Piaget had a complex definition of play and it didn't mean "a laissez faire, anything-goes attitude." In studying intelligence Piaget noted that children learned about the world by engaging in a sort of "shuttle service" between two polar but complementary aspects of behaviour: assimilation and accommodation.

With the former ("the purest form of play") children transform the ordinary tools of life, such as spoons, sticks or stones, into imaginary and fanciful explorations. And with the latter they modify their responses to the real world by spontaneously imitating language and other social skills. The two complement each other. Without the earthiness of accommodation, assimilative play raises Me Generations, and without the imaginative wonder of assimilation, accommodation merely begets obedient robots.

Not surprisingly, modern educators ignored the importance of balance and largely adopted the principle of assimilation with its exaltation of individual creativity. This selective halving of Piaget's ideas, says Wolfram, is alarming. Kids need spontaneity the way a car needs a motor, but they also need, as do cars, "a well-functioning brake system" as an inhibition on excessive spontaneity, and "a map" to reach worthy intellectual goals.

As an educational vehicle, the inadequacy of play alone became clear in a little-publicized 1978 study by the Etobicoke Board of Education. Originally designed by Mary Ann Evans and Brian Usher, two Ontario researchers, to show the superiority of play, the study compared ten child-centred, play-based experimental projects from grades one to three with ten "traditional," teacher-directed classrooms.

To the dismay of play's disciples, the study's 168-page report found that formal classrooms fostered achievement in reading and mathematics "to a greater extent" than the experimental classes, where some teachers "did not yet get around to teaching reading."

It also concluded that sandboxes, water tables and fantasy props could have beneficial effects, but to make a difference they required structured interventions and direction from highly skilled teachers, "which was not the case in the classrooms observed.... When children played, the teacher was seldom involved."

Although the top performers in both programs differed little in achievement (indicating either that parents might have taken over where play failed or that top performers learn no matter what you throw at them), the lower performers tell a horrifyingly different story.

Here the results showed that the average performance in reading and math of the kids bombing out in the play program was much lower than that of the kids struggling in the traditional program. This means that a steady diet of play actually made the poor kids academically poorer and conditioned them for a life of poverty.

Wolfram finds such results (now corroborated by a host of studies) exceedingly cruel, given that the public school system was explicitly created 160 years ago to reduce inequalities of class. Yet "activity learning" remains the norm in many Ontario classrooms because educators ignore studies that challenge their ill-conceived experiments with kids.

Although she has no antidote to the progressivists' corruption of Piaget or its dismaying effects other than strong parent organizations, Wolfram recognizes that the school cult of play has signalled a significant shift in the purpose of education.

"The goal of the public school was to prepare the next generation," says Wolfram, "but now its only purpose seems to be to create employment for the present generation, and that's terrible."

Wedded to child-centred nostrums and "metabolic" curriculums, elementary teachers have pressed for smaller classes (and more teachers) in the name of "quality education." Is it as rewarding to watch eighteen students frolic in a sandbox as it is to direct thirty kids to high achievement?

Piaget, who sent his own children to Montessori schools, often wondered where so much mindless school play would lead. The answer now appears to be a massive squandering of intelligence.

See also **CONSTRUCTIVISM** and **YEAR 2000**.

PRINCIPALS If there is one remaining truism left in public education, it's that principals can make schools sing or croak. Since the 1970s, American and Canadian educational studies have consistently declared that the most reliable sign of an effective school is a principal who has established an ethos of high achievement.

In contrast, a bad principal usually establishes an arrogant "I'm-only-going-to-be-here-for-three-years-

and-don't-give-a-damn" tone. He or she might have an open-door policy, but usually has a closed mind. Parents know one when they meet one, because bad principals never give straight answers, rarely take responsibility and never solve academic or behavioural problems economically or immediately.

A good principal stands out like a spruce on the prairie. First and foremost he or she is an instructional leader. Effective principals are never content with just pushing paper or managing a building. Nor does he or she hide behind the three B's: the board, the budget and the bull. Unlike administrators hell-bent on survival, the good principal spends more than half the day in the hall and in classrooms directly engaging kids and teachers. He or she often begins the day by greeting each child by name with a handshake.

Effective principals make a point of putting the academic achievement and happiness of their students first and foremost. They do so by carefully selecting their teachers and by actively monitoring their performance. With strong backgrounds in reading or science (as opposed to physical education—a common background), effective principals know how to evaluate teaching in ways that make a difference. "They discover problems and then demonstrate that they can be solved," once noted the U. S. Council for Basic Education.

Not surprisingly, the principal who does his or her job well has little tolerance for bad teachers. Conversely, he or she recongizes good teaching with meaningful awards and additional responsibilities. And an effective principal works very hard at making struggling or inexperienced teachers "good enough" by modelling the skills and commitment that can get them there. If a teacher needs training, he or she will make sure that it is offered.

James Enochs, an innovative California educator and school superintendent, once described three different types of principals. There are the "thoroughbreds" who keep running and jumping no matter how high the bureaucratic obstacles; the "plowhorses" who stay in the field and on track until five o'clock, as long as they are faced in the right direction; and the "donkeys" who bray and shift their load even when being pushed and prodded.

Principal humour: A wry view from the frontlines

H.S.S.B. PRINCIPAL circa 1993

MINI-VULTURES
-waiting to pick the bones clean.

POOR VISION
-caused by trying to read all the memos, bulletins, notes, acts, regs, directives and computer printouts.

DENTAL PROBLEMS
-teeth ruined due to constant grinding and gnashing 24 hours a day.

INCIPIENT ULCER
-due to insane efforts at juggling curriculum demands, budget, staff relationships, bus routes, interest groups, disintegrating family life, etc., etc., etc.

LONG ROPE
-used to hold up pants and may be used as a noose on "dark days."

FRICTION FINGER
-caused by unceasing attempts to dial the transportation dep't.

ROOPING SOCKS
caused by weight loss which stems from poor eating habits.

TORN, WORN OUT SNEAKERS
-just no time available to replace those cross-trainers.

EXTENSIVE HAIR LOSS
-accompaniment to loss of nerve which occurred some time ago.

FURROWED FOREHEAD
-caused by constant brow-beating from parents, media, superiors, trustees and mother.

HEARING AID
-necessitated by abuse of hearing through excessive phone use because of voice mail.
-also allows principal to tune out when necessary.

WORN OUT JACKET
-graduation suit jacket considered by principal to be the height of fashion.
-displays no taste at all.

HAND AMPUTATED
-it got mangled during an attempt to break up a fight in the staff room.
-when prosthesis is ready, he will be known as Capt. Hook.

BULGING POCKETS
-key rings and bottles of pills for various ills cause lumpy clothes.

WEIRD TROUSERS
-if he's treated like a clown, he might as well dress like one.

ADVANCED AGE
-actually, he is 38 years old but has aged visibly, dramatically since being promoted.

Percy Ciurluini

Both American and Canadian surveys have found that there are more donkeys running schools than thoroughbreds. The average principal is a white, middle-aged male who takes few risks and believes that everything and everybody is "above average" at his school. A Canadian analysis of how "chief education officers" including principals, spend their time found that they devote less than 10 percent of their day to the nuts and bolts of instructional leadership. In terms of priorities, these same white, middle-aged males ranked program delivery as their fourth concern, below political, communication and management issues.

Being a good principal can be hazardous to your health. In the late 1960s Seymour Gang took an altogether "disadvantaged" school in Harlem and brought its students' performance to new heights. When the Council for Basic Education cited the school's success and praised Gang's leadership abilities, he "was shelved by promotion and ultimately speeded out of the city system," reports Jacques Barzun in *Begin Here.* "Excellence is for sloganeering exclusively." His performance embarrassed the system because it showed what good leadership could achieve even in the most hellish schools.

Educational appointments are often a matter of politics. The qualification and certification of principals doesn't always bear much relation to the characteristic that really matters: instructional leadership. Notes University of Western Ontario professor Derek Allison in a recent discussion paper on the training of principals in Ontario: "The overall certification process appears more akin to a randomly distributed set of hurdles than a coherent continuum." It's also quite possible for "impeccably prepared principals to be subject to the authority of superintendents who do not possess the qualifications necessary for appointment to the principalship." And so on.

Several years ago the New York journalist Nat Hentoff suggested that principals be selected the way reporters research a complex story, by "extensive interviews with students and faculty in the schools where the applicant worked, and a careful canvassing of the surrounding communities.... Was he a clock-watcher, or the kind of educator who stayed as long as each day's crises and conundrums required? And, of course, how well did the kids he taught or supervised do after they left his school?"

School reformers could achieve much good and help a great many teachers by ensuring that school systems select and retain principals on the basis of their essential role: instructional leadership. Demanding that boards evaluate principals, if not all educational leaders, in terms of their students' achievement would also make a big difference for kids.

See also **EFFECTIVE SCHOOLS** and Appendix 1.

PROJECT FOLLOW-THROUGH   In 1967 the United States government launched Project Follow-Through, one of the largest and least-publicized experiments in the history of public schooling.

The project's initial purpose was to sustain the social gains made by inner-city children in Head Start—a preschool program that offered hot lunches and free health care. But financial constraints transformed the new federal initiative into a concerted search for teaching programs that worked with black, Hispanic and Indian students.

At its peak, the ten-year study compared the academic and attitudinal effects of thirteen different teaching approaches for poor children from kindergarten to grade three.

Of the thirteen educational approaches studied in the project, nine yielded comprehensive information on student achievement. And of these nine, three focused on basic skills while the other six focused on fostering self-concept or thinking skills. The nine methods were as follows:

Direct Instruction: This method maintains that all children can learn with carefully sequenced lessons and that disadvantaged kids must be taught at a faster rate than normal if they are to catch up with middle class peers. Group instruction, scripted lessons and lots of teacher supervision characterize this approach.

Cognitive-Oriented Curriculum: This method, based on the developmental theories of Swiss psychologist Jean Piaget, encourages individual children to make their own choices about what to learn.

Bank Street College Model: Incorporating the philosophies of John Dewey, Sigmund Freud and Jean Piaget, this progressive model uses a "language experience" reading program in which students write and read their own stories.

The remaining models were Behavioural Analysis (a Skinnerian way of tackling the basics), Language Development (bilingual teaching in Spanish), Responsive Education and Southwest Lab (more self-confidence building), the Florida Parents Education Model (let the parents do the teaching) and TEEM, the Tucson Early Education Model (another child-centred approach).

Of the nine approaches yielding comprehensive data only one, Direct Instruction, showed consistent

The results of Project Follow-Through.

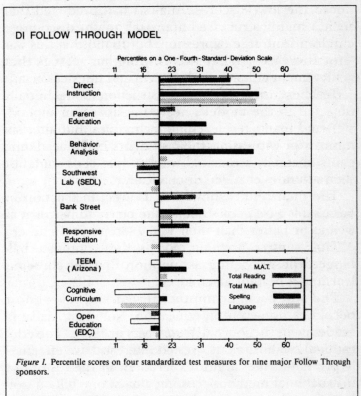

DI FOLLOW THROUGH MODEL

Figure 1. Percentile scores on four standardized test measures for nine major Follow Through sponsors.

gains in reading, writing, math, spelling and language as well as thinking skills.

In contrast, the progressive approaches, which highlighted discovery, activity and good feelings, consistently racked up negative scores. In fact, the results indicated that these indirect approaches often exaggerated the educational deficits of disadvantaged children by making the intellectually poor, poorer.

To everyone's surprise, Direct Instruction also yielded the highest scores in children's self-esteem, whereas the approaches that emphasized good feelings produced the lowest scores. Analysts had predicted that such a highly structured approach might discourage children from free expression, but found that this was "not the case." What this finding suggests is that achievement enhances self-esteem and not vice versa.

Teachers using the Direct Instruction model initially objected to the model's heavy in-class room supervision and mandated teaching techniques. But after six months of witnessing their students make academic gains normally associated with middle class students, their attitudes changed dramatically.

The final results showed that direct instruction in basic skills gave poor students the power to perform as well as or better than their well-to-do peers. In an era of child-centred learning models, these findings challenged the prevailing assumption that self-directed learning is best for all children.

The study was promptly shelved and has almost become a non-event in education. Noted an Alabama academic in the journal *Youth Policy* in 1988: "The educational establishment's vested interests have effectively prevented the largest experiment in the history of instructional methods (costing almost one billion dollars) from having the impact on daily classroom practice that its results clearly warranted."

In the end, Project Follow-Through proved in a very quiet but dramatic way that middle class beliefs about learning often penalize economically disadvantaged students. It also demonstrated that the direct teaching of basic skills to children of the poor requires different attitudes and skills among teachers and administrators than these professionals now receive in training.

In a few inner-city schools where Direct Instruction is still used (often in violation of progressive sanctions) so-called disadvantaged children typically read

Homer in grade four and *Macbeth* in grade five.

"Students from low income families do not need to fail in schools," recently concluded the authors of the Direct Instruction model. "They can be taught."

See also **DIRECT INSTRUCTION**.

R

RACISM AND MULTICULTURALISM In 1993, two very different reports, one from the commons and one from the powers that be, appeared in the North American press. Each responded to unsettling summer riots and each championed school reforms as one means to prevent further disorder. But here the similarities end.

The élite report, by Canada's former UN ambassador Stephen Lewis, reviewed the troubled state of race relations in Toronto, Canada's capital of commerce, after two days of window-breaking and looting. The street report, written by two notorious street gangs, the Bloods and the Crips, made a series of proposals for rebuilding the smoldering ruins of inner Los Angeles.

Each report came with a different mandate. In Toronto's case, Ontario premier Bob Rae had invited his colleague, the well-spoken Lewis, to advise him on race relations. The prolix politician's foray into race and education garnered the usual media fanfare.

In Los Angeles, no one asked the Bloods or the Crips how they thought their city could be rebuilt, but the gangs produced an agenda anyway. Aside from an article in the alternative magazine *Z*, their work went unnoticed. *Z*'s editors expressed admiration for the two gangs, "unencumbered by years of conforming education and bureaucratic regimentation," for producing such a strong vision.

During his brief investigation, Lewis found an "intractable dilemma around race relations in contemporary education" in Ontario's schools, and then asked: "How do you get the best of policies and programs into the individual classrooms?"

His tentative answer was a call for more "multiculturalism and anti-racism in the schools," the hiring of more minority teachers, a broadening of the curriculum, the elimination of streaming, and lots of meetings with principals, superintendents and community groups.

Aside from a few throw-away lines on the streaming of minority students, Lewis's terse and highly personal report makes no mention of upgrading standards for the poor and disadvantaged. Instead, he regards as "vital" the implementation of more policies on multiculturalism and anti-racism.

The Bloods and Crips, with no progressive legacy to uphold, addressed the issue more boldly. They called for a maximization of "education standards in low income areas," the upgrading of textbooks and computer supplies, and higher salaries for teachers in order "to give them an incentive to educate in our districts."

They recommended programs for accelerated learning, aggressive teaching methods and mandatory after-school tutoring for all students with "sub-level grades." They also proposed that high-achieving students be awarded federally funded bonus bonds to buy more education after high school.

The gangs then called for the removal of all teachers "who have not proven to have a passionate concern for the students ... they serve." They also asked that all teachers be given a standard competency test to verify that they are up to date on their subjects and modern teaching methods.

Last but not least, the gangs proposed a basic, limited no-nonsense curriculum inundated with "advanced sciences and additional applied math, English and writing skills." Their report makes no mention of multiculturalism policies.

With such starkly different priorities, the two documents sharply illustrate an ever-widening gulf in educational thinking. It seems that what well-meaning and well-educated liberals think is right for working people and the poor often bears little relationship to what these same people value: a powerful grounding in the rudiments of learning.

Although Lewis evoked the spirit of equal educational opportunity by calling for more resources to be delivered into the hands of professional groups that organize multiculturalism programs, the street gangs demanded the very inverse of the equality doctrine. Spend money directly and spend more of it, said the gang report, on those youngsters whose abilities are such that they are least likely to develop their minds in our schools. And spend these funds, not on policies, but on developing the highest standards of teaching and learning for *all* students.

Several years ago the populist historian Christopher Lasch concluded that sweet-sounding rhetoric in education often led to unforeseen and unwanted ends. It doesn't matter to the victims, he wrote, whether bad teaching justifies itself on the grounds that the poor cannot master the intricacies of math or English or whether, on the other hand, "pseudoradicals condemn academic standards as part of the apparatus of white cultural control...." In either case, progressive reformers effectively preserve the most insidious form of élitism, which holds, in one guise or another, that the poor white, Indian or black is "incapable of intellectual exertion."

Racism takes many forms, but the most insidious is the refusal of many Canadian schools to acknowledge that many immigrant cultures value directness. Child-centred education doesn't have much of a reputation in Caribbean, Asian, Iranian or Nigerian school systems because of its indirectness. Yet Canadian educators expect people of colour to flourish in unstructured environments where adults veil their authority with an egalitarian niceness. And when these children don't flourish, the educators quickly blame the children.

Lisa Delpit is the only educator I've ever encountered who recognizes that the black community and many immigrant cultures "expect authority to be earned by personal effort and exhibited by personal characteristics." They expect this authority to be direct and not necessarily nice. And they would view the typical progressive response to immigrant children (a suspension of standards and a corresponding elevation of warmth and concern) as not only paternalistic but blatantly racist.

According to Delpit, the characteristics of direct teaching may vary across cultures, "but in the black community they tend to cluster around several abilities. The authoritative teacher can control the class through exhibition of personal power; establishes meaningful interpersonal relationships that garner student respect; exhibits a strong belief that all students can learn; establishes a standard of achievement and 'pushes' the students to achieve that standard; and holds the attention of the students by incorporating interactional features of black communicative style in his or her teaching."

Rather than get bogged down on endless committees devoted to racism or multiculturalism, parents and particularly immigrant parents should demand what matters: high standards, authoritative not authoritarian teachers and effective schools.

See also **EFFECTIVE SCHOOLS**.

READING   Learning how to read is a complex neuro-logical task that some children master effortlessly and with which others must struggle. The lucky minority that, abracadabra, just take to print like fish to water usually have been exposed to many books and have been read to consistently since the age of two.

But anywhere between a third and half of all middle class readers, no matter how many good books adorn their bedrooms and schools, need something more than exposure and luck: they need sound instruction.

If this good teaching doesn't take place in kinder-garten or grade one (or at home) and include some form of phonemic awareness (such as phonics instruc-tion), then the school is not doing its job. A parent can quickly tell this by checking on the number of stu-dents in special education classes. A school with an epidemic of "learning-disabled" students and over-worked resource teachers or a board with 30 percent of its children labelled "special education" signals inef-fective reading programs.

Most educators know but rarely tell parents that the probability of a student being a poor reader in grade four is largely determined by how well or how badly he or she is reading at the end of grade one. If the job isn't done right in grade one, few schools, it seems, take the time or effort to correct what could well be shoddy instruction.

The central excuse most schools provide when near-ly a half or a third of their grade one students can't read is that Johnny or Mary is just not ready. This is usually a lie and a very big one. Most children are ready to read between the ages of four and six. Getting kids ready for reading is just as much a matter of well-organized instruction as it is teaching them the sounds of letters. Either the school prizes reading or it does not. And most schools prize how children *feel about* books as opposed to how well they can *read* them.

So a good kindergarten program, in addition to giving children lots of time to do things with their hands, should build a strong letter knowledge and book awareness (looking from left to right) that grade one can transform into fluent reading and writing. Students who need good sequential instruction in phonics (and that may well be half the class) should get it at this time. If your school is not prepared to build upon foundations laid in kindergarten or to offer systematic phonics instruction in grade one to those students who need it, then find a school that is prepared. Don't waste time fighting ill-trained educators who put theory ahead of the needs of children.

Once students have become fluent readers and writers, a good primary program logically focuses on excellent literature: fables, fairy tales, myths (Greek, Roman, African and First Nations) as well as some of the great classics: *Black Beauty, The Hobbit, The Secret Garden, The Lion, the Witch and the Wardrobe, Robinson Crusoe, The Once and Future King, The Red Badge of Courage, Treasure Island, The Jungle Book, The Little Prince, Huckleberry Finn, Julius Caesar, The Iliad, Martin Fierro* and *Great Expectations*...

In addition to good novels and short stories, students should also be reading time-honoured selections from science, history and geography in order to broaden their vocabularies and introduce them to the wonderful world of non-fiction. Too few schools now use original accounts of the exploration of Canada, for example, whether they be *The Jesuit Narratives* of life and death among the Huron or William Butler's marvellous 1870s ode to the prairies, *The Great Lone Land*.

Every good primary reading program gives students opportunities to study and read books of their own selection. But a program totally devoted to a child's predilections guarantees unequal results, with some children making better and more literate choices than others. Such a school is indeed an Animal Farm. If the public school doesn't demand that students jointly study some of the world's great literature, which is really to explore the qualities of being human, then who will?

Schools with good reading programs also tend to group children homogeneously for instruction. Students learn better and faster if they are grouped according to what they already know regardless of their age. Known as the Joplin Plan, this practice is supported by a great body of research.

Now, here's a sample of some beginning reading programs that have proven track records with disadvantaged, teaching-disabled or ordinary children. Most of these programs teach reading, writing and spelling together, because they logically reinforce each other. Good schools, which are few and far between, use these approaches either to supplement their whole language programs or to ensure that all of their children are reading by the end of grade one.

The Writing Road to Reading

Romalda Spalding, an experienced elementary school teacher, designed this program in 1962. She observed that the Dick and Jane look-say approach to reading fostered guessing and bad study habits; much research proved her right. Her method emphasizes the teaching of sounds and basic rules of spelling, and demands that children spell and write before they do much reading. It is very similar to the Montessori Method and has a good track record as a home-school or remedial program. The Riggs Institute has adapted supplementary materials for the approach. For details write 4185 S.W. 102nd Ave., Beaverton, Oregon 97005; phone 503-646-9459 or fax 503-644-5191.

Open Court

Long a favourite of inner-city school teachers, this is the most effective phonics-based reading series on the market. Backed by three years of solid classroom testing, Open Court integrates writing, spelling and reading in a series of kindergarten-to-grade-six readers. Phonics is heavily emphasized until the end of grade one, and thereafter students tackle extremely good literature from around the world, including interesting scientific and historical selections. Fast paced and well organized, Open Court produces superior readers and writers. No province has yet put this reading series on its approved reading list for the elementary grades.

See also **EFFECTIVE SCHOOLS**: St Francis of Assisi.

Orton-Gillingham

Samuel Orton, an American physician, spent much of his life studying dyslexia, and Anna Gillingham, an extraordinary teacher, spent much of her life applying his ideas to teaching dyslexics. Their program stresses auditory discrimination (listening to and accurately reproducing sounds) as well as kinaesthetic and tactile learning (tracing letters, writing letters in the air, and so on). It is a well-sequenced phonics program that makes good use of tracing, copying and dictation. For getting dyslexics started on the road to reading, few programs can match its organization and attention to detail.

See also **READING DISABILITIES**.

DISTAR

DISTAR is the most highly structured phonics program on the market. Siegfried Engelmann, a brilliant instructional designer, fashioned this direct-instruction program for hard-to-teach children in the inner city. Although consistently validated in many classrooms with children from the poorest of neighbourhoods, teachers and school boards were loath to adopt DISTAR because they didn't like the repetition or the drills. Students rarely complained about such activities because they were learning how to read. As a consequence, DISTAR is now used in a few Canadian schools as a remedial program for at-risk children. But it has had spectacular success with black children at Wesley Elementary School in Houston, Texas.

Sing, Spell, Read and Write

This kindergarten-to-grade-three program is designed to lay a solid foundation fast. It is multi-sensory (music plays a key role in this program) and well sequenced. It has been validated in classrooms with high-risk and normal children. Home-schoolers also report success with this program. Wise Choice Learning Systems markets the program in Canada; phone 705-726-5971.

Success for All

Robert Slavin, a well-respected educator at the Center for Research on Effective Schooling for Disadvantaged Students (Johns Hopkins University) developed this tutorial program to prove that even ordinary schools with unexceptional staff can get much better results in reading with poor children than they normally do.

Key principles include well-trained reading tutors, one-on-one tutoring combined with small, homogeneous group instruction, and direct instruction in the development of basic language skills and sound and letter recognition skills. Intervention begins in kindergarten and grade one to get the job done right the first time around. Teachers receive detailed manuals and students are assessed every eight weeks.

Success For All has lived up to its name by helping children in the poorest neighbourhoods to read at par with their middle class peers. It has been tested and validated in seventy schools. To date, no Canadian school has participated in Slavin's no-nonsense program.

See also **PHONICS, PHONEMIC AWARENESS, WHOLE LANGUAGE** and **READING DISABILITIES**.

READING DISABILITIES (DYSLEXIA)

The existing school system is irrational, ineffectual, authoritarian, inept, smug, defensive and undereducated. I suspect that ineffective teaching and poor methodology cause about 90 percent of the reading disabilities in our schools.

—Dr Carl Kline

Among its many distinctions, Vancouver is probably the only North American city to have three schools for dyslexic children: Kenneth Gordon, James Cameron and the Fraser Academy. And this remarkable educational novelty is largely due to the pioneering work of child psychiatrist Dr Carl Kline.

For more than thirty-five years now, Kline has had a powerful interest in children's learning problems. It started with his first practice in Milwaukee, Wisconsin, where he routinely encountered youngsters with "puzzling psychiatric symptoms" that included sleeplessness, anxiety and depression. "All of the children had trouble reading or spelling," recalls the seventy-seven-year-old.

After much detective work, Kline discovered the little-known work of Knud Hermann (the Danish scientist who first described dyslexia as a form of "word blindness") and Dr Samuel Orton, an American neurologist who helped design an effective phonics program for teaching dyslexics how to read. These pivotal findings led Kline to conclude that some of the sad and angry children in his practice did indeed suffer from what doctors now define as a neurological language disability that is genetically passed on from parent to child. The non-medical remedy, of course, is lots of good teaching at an early age.

When Kline moved his family to Vancouver in 1967 (his vocal opposition to the Vietnam War unsettled Milwaukee's medical establishment), the psychiatrist quickly earned a reputation for his interest in reading problems and was soon flooded with referrals. Notes Kline, who is now a professor emeritus of the University of British Columbia: "Reading problems are the leading cause of emotional difficulties among children and adolescents in North America." The specialist supports this sober observation by candidly noting that 69 percent of all prisoners, 85 percent of all unwed mothers, 79 percent of all welfare dependents and 85 percent of all school dropouts typically suffer from a poverty of basic skills such as reading.

At his Vancouver practice Kline soon found that the bulk of his referrals were not frustrated dyslexics but frazzled students disabled by poor reading instruction. In other words, their varied emotional problems, all stemming from or exacerbated by losing battles with the written word, arose from substandard teaching or no teaching at all.

Kline now calculates that no more than 10 percent of the school population that can't read or write well are true dyslexics; the majority of struggling readers, he contends, are the products of whole language reading approaches that have neglected to include the structured and sequential teaching of multi-sensory phonics.

"I am not criticizing teachers," adds Kline quickly. "Most want to do well. But they have not been trained well by faculties of education."

Given the paucity of good phonetic instruction in Vancouver's public schools, Kline and his wife Carolyn eventually trained hundreds of tutors and parents, often at the Klines' expense, in an effective reading method: Orton-Gillingham. Since 1967 the Klines have also encouraged parents, betrayed by the public school system, to establish three schools with reading programs dedicated to producing able readers.

For Kline, separating the teaching disabled from the dyslexic was a relatively easy task. With intensive phonics instruction, the teaching disabled quickly shed their emotional problems and learned how to read. In contrast, the dyslexics required "intensive one-on-one help at least an hour a day five days a week. It's a long haul." But many of his former patients are now well-read doctors, engineers and lawyers.

Based on four thousand detailed case histories and the experiences of other countries, Kline is now convinced that good, intensive phonics instruction could save a lot of children much emotional grief. Czechoslovakia, he says, has only a 2 percent incidence of reading disabilities because its schools teach reading phonetically. Japan also has a 99 percent literacy rate, not only because the genetic factor associated with dyslexia is absent, but because its schools also use phonics to teach the katagana script.

To Kline, the lesson for North American educators, who now lord it over a sorry illiteracy rate anywhere between 25 and 35 percent, should be obvious: schools can and should be in the business of preventing rather than abetting reading failure.

READING RECOVERY   Developed in the 1980s by the New Zealand reading expert and whole language proponent Marie Clay, Reading Recovery targets six-year-old children who are fumbling with words after a year in school.

The program works like this: specially trained teachers test a child at risk before providing one-on-one instruction for thirty to forty minutes each day. Tutoring ends after the child achieves an independent reading level at or above class level. The whole process usually takes twelve to twenty weeks, or in some cases as long as a year.

Reading Recovery has become something of an international phenomenon in education. The Americans are gung-ho; the British are doing it; and now Canadian educators have jumped aboard. Early intervention to prevent reading failure is, of course, a sound idea; kids who are not brought up to grade level within their first three years of school rarely catch up. But parents and teachers might want to consider if Reading Recovery is really the best vehicle for the job.

For starters, New Zealand's schools, where Reading Recovery was developed and first practised, use whole language exclusively for reading instruction. They have done so for nearly two decades. Espoused by reading theorist Ken Goodman, whole language theorizes that all children can glean meaning from text by guessing or using context cues.

Contrary to Goodman's predictions, this approach has not made New Zealand a literate paradise. A 1991 study by the International Association for the Evaluation of Educational Achievement found that in reading ability, New Zealand nine-year-olds ranked in the top ten but behind those in Finland, the United States, France and Italy. The country's Adult Reading and Learning Assistance Federation recently reported that "between 20 and 22 percent of the New Zealand workforce are not coping well with the literacy demands of employment." And according to a study by the country's Otago Medical School, 35 percent of the general population have literacy deficiencies.

And then there's the reality that whole language routinely fails 25 percent of New Zealand's beginning readers. They enter Reading Recovery programs at the end of grade one at an expense of $10.4 million U. S. a year. If the program extended to more than just 61 percent of the nation's schools, the percentage of children needing remedial help might top 40 percent.

Such facts prompted Auckland University lecturer in education and Reading Recovery critic Tom Nicholson to spell out the obvious: "New Zealand is keeping a top place in international [reading] surveys but only by having a huge ambulance at the bottom of the cliff in the form of Reading Recovery."

Now, research shows that the effectiveness of Reading Recovery is not earth-shaking. Children with poor word-recognition skills tend to make more gains during the program than those with higher-level skills—a very modest finding, given all the one-on-one tutoring. One American study by the Johns Hopkins researcher Robert Slavin even found that 80 percent of the initial gains made by inner-city kids simply evaporated by grade three. Not much of a recovery there.

To determine why so much effort produces such modest rewards, two New Zealand researchers, Sandra Iversen and William Tunmer (*Journal of Educational Psychology* 1993), asked a key question: Are RR's specific teaching methods more effective than other remedial approaches?

The researchers speculated that children in Reading Recovery might learn how to read much faster and better if their tutors chose a methodology that applied elements missing from Reading Recovery's approach. Rather than emphasizing the shape or context of words, the researchers decided to focus on "the interrelatedness of the visual patterns and sounds shared by different words." But given Marie Clay's aversion to the direct teaching of phonics, instead of using a skill-drill phonics approach, they smartly chose a training method that emphasized word families such as *light, fight, might* and *light*, which share "-ight."

Then they formed three carefully matched groups of thirty-two children each, using their modified approach, the standard Reading Recovery and another intervention. The results were stunning. The modified program sent its independent readers back to the classroom after forty-one lessons, while the standard version took fifty-seven lessons. In other words, Clay's Reading Recovery was 37 percent less efficient than the modified approach.

The conclusion was elementary. "Children selected for Reading Recovery learned to read much more quickly when they were given systematic instruction that was designed to make them aware of the correspondences between elements of written and spoken language," wrote the researchers.

So Reading Recovery can work, but it works much better with word-attack skills than with guessing. It also makes one wonder how necessary such programs would be if educators simply plugged the holes in whole language in the first place.

See also **WHOLE LANGUAGE**, **PHONICS** and **READING**.

REPORT CARDS   This is the story of Peter Marsan, an elementary school student with reading problems, as told by his primary progress report cards over a two-year period (1991–1993).

It is also a cautionary tale about dishonesty in public education and the failure of British Columbia's reporting system to inform parents clearly and simply of school results.

The fourteen-inch-long documents written about Peter, a tall, skinny six-and-a-half-year-old first grade student, are euphemistically called "anecdotal reports." They contain no letter grades or even Satisfactories, Goods or Very Goods.

Developed as a means to provide more individualized and accurate descriptions of student performance, these documents look and read like personal letters. They are now under review by the government because of public concerns about their content.

Composing "Dear Peter" reports often takes a teacher an hour or two per student. But with the aid of a word processor, an enterprising teacher can simply write one report and then customize it by changing the student's name. One B. C. parent with twin daughters recently noted that the wording of their report cards was identical.

In many British Columbia schools, the effort required to compose such documents has become so laborious that supply teachers are hired to teach for a day while full-time teachers retire to the staff room to collect anecdotes. Before the reports leave school they are routinely edited, checked and signed by the principal. Anything that might offend a parent or indicate a serious problem is changed or omitted. Schools don't want problems and certainly don't want to imperil anyone's self-esteem. This bureaucratic practice is routine in many other provinces.

As originally conceived nearly a decade ago, the province's anecdotal reports were to tell parents five

things: what their child can do, how these achievements compare to those of children the same age (late
or early), what the child can't do, what the school is
doing about it, and what the parents can do to help.
But, as finally implemented in the school system,
British Columbia's anecdotal reports eschewed directness and results. As Peter's case illustrates, they serve
as condescending and vague advertisements for children's positive doings, attitudes and interests.

Peter's first report card, dated Nov. 1991, began
with the usual clichés ("Peter is a bright boy who
appears happy in our classroom") and then entertains
some inanities: "Peter is able to work independently,
although he prefers to work alongside others. I feel
Peter benefits from interacting with the other students, as children learn much from one another, as
well as from adults," says his teacher.

No attempt was made to explain what Peter could
do in math; it was simply noted that Peter "participates
actively." Peter also did a lot of participating in "reading activity times." Added his teacher: "This is an
encouraging sign, as attitude is half the battle as children move towards becoming readers. Peter is able to
memorize small predictable books, knows all but a few
of the letters of the alphabet, knows some letter sound
symbol relationships. For example, when prompted,
he wrote 'Ms' for monster and 'bom' for bottom."

The progress report then went on enthusiastically
about one of Peter's basic strategies for expressing
ideas: "Talking is certainly one of Peter's strengths, so
it is not surprising that he relies on it heavily. As learners, children, and Peter is no exception, choose to do
things at which they feel successful." The report added
that Peter had begun one-on-one sessions with the
Learning Resource Teacher with the expectation that
it would benefit Peter "as he continues the process of

learning to read."

There was no mention that Peter couldn't read and was making no progress. Peter's mother, Karen, made inquiries and was told that his reading problems were all due to a slight articulation difficulty.

Peter's next progress report began with this therapeutic novelty: "This term, Peter has certainly experienced one of the key ingredients of modern day life—change! A significant friendship was tested and retested with the end result being a renewal of that key relationship, along with the establishment of several new friendships. Change can lead to progress! As one of the adults watching these shifts, I found myself concerned about Peter's hurt feelings. However, Peter's youth (the young are so much more adaptable!) and supportive family helped see him through this interesting time."

The report didn't mention any progress on the reading front but did note that Peter was now "interacting" with a different resource teacher due to "the need for financial restraint."

His mother observed no reading progress at home.

True to form, Peter's final report for 1992, dated June, actually began "Dear Peter." His teacher told the seven-year-old that she would like to share "some of the ways that I believe you have grown in your learning this year at school.... You have a great curiosity about how things work. I expect that someday you will be an inventor, engineer or builder. You were able to figure out how some of the construction materials worked better than most anyone else in the classroom, including me!... It is wonderful to see you putting that great mind of yours into breaking the reading puzzle!... You have continued to be a fine 'math thinker.'... Your latest journal and book are works of art!... I hope your summer is a safe and happy one."

After all this Peter's teacher privately informed Peter's mother, Karen, that she thought Peter might have a learning disability, was uneducable and "might spend his life on welfare." The school principal added that it would cost $500 to test Peter and that the money was just not available. At home Peter had started to sleepwalk and complain of headaches. At this point, Ms Marsan no more trusted his school reports than she did the headlines in the *National Enquirer.*

After summer break, Peter began Year 3 (that's grade two in British Columbia) with great unease. He now told his mother that he hated school and didn't want to go. His persistent lack of progress in reading, however, simply got a new definition in his November report card: "Peter continues to develop as an early reader. When encouraged, he will participate during group or buddy reading activities.... Peter is developing picture cue and word decoding strategies to help him accomplish his reading tasks. Good thinking Peter!"

At home, his mother tried to teach Peter how to sound out words, but at school this strategy was discouraged. Peter's sleepwalking and headaches persisted. One day he confessed to his mother that his teacher no longer spoke the truth: "She keeps telling me I'm doing so good but I can't read. She's lying."

Meanwhile, the clichés and lies continued to appear in Peter's anecdotal reports. His March card noted that the boy "has shown an interest in learning to read and write and has participated in all our Language activities. Peter has done very well with the reading of the book 'A Duck is a Duck.' We will encourage Peter to become familiar with another book this next term."

Rather than wait for more false praise and insignicant observations, Marsan transferred Peter to a Seventh Day Adventist School. It offered Peter something he needed, basic instruction in phonics. Within two months he was reading at grade level. His new teacher said, "If Peter deserves a label, it's that he's a gifted child."

When the private school report card awarded Peter an A average for hard work well done in math, handwriting, science and reading (categories that don't exist in anecdotal reporting), the boy "glowed." His headaches disappeared and so too did the sleepwalking. "You were right, Mommy," he said, "I'm not stupid." Eight-year-old Peter began to look forward to going to school.

Marsan, of course, knows that simple letter grades are not the most complete reporting mechanism. But they do tell a few basic truths economically, such as what Peter is doing well or not doing well. As for the inflated praise and therapeutic language now polluting anecdotal report cards, she says that most parents just "laugh at it." This partly explains why the British Columbia government recently introduced a new, structured reporting system in which "a clear, complete description of a student's progress will be provided to parents."

In order to restore confidence in the public school system, the new report cards should ban New Age lingo. They should tell parents what Johnny or Mary can or can't do in specific subjects, and do so in common English.

Marsan, for example, would have been gratified with clarity and directness: "Peter can read a short story containing both sight and phonetic words at a grade one level." Or "Peter can't yet read at a grade one level and here's what we are doing about it and how you can help!" A sample of written work from the beginning and end of the year would also be a nice touch.

That there are now thousands of Peter Marsans and reams of feel-good reports about such students is a tragedy that has sullied the reputation of public schools. Educators can either ignore this dangerous loss of faith or restore the creed. To accomplish the latter means giving parents and students what they really deserve: clear-eyed measures of achievement as opposed to a surfeit of cheap feelings.

See Appendix 9 for a sample of good and bad report cards.

RITALIN   Ritalin is the brand name for methylphenidate, the most widely prescribed drug for hyperactive children. The high-powered stimulant is related to morphine and barbiturates.

Its positive effects are limited: a child on Ritalin will be better able to sit still, perform repetitive tasks and concentrate for longer periods of time. That's it.

Now for the bad news. Ritalin has absolutely no effect on 25 to 40 percent of all hyperactive children. For many hyperactives, placebos (sugar pills) are as calming as Ritalin. Nor is the stimulant a cure; it only suppresses the fidgeting and selective listening that characterize so many hyperactive children. Last but not least, Ritalin will not improve academic achievement. Only good teaching and a sequential curriculum can do that.

Every drug has side-effects, and Ritalin is no exception. It may temporarily stunt growth, impede a child's memory and impair a child's ability to think.

No parent should ever put a child on Ritalin without seriously examining and changing the style of classroom and teaching that the child has been exposed to. Matching the child with the right teacher will, in most cases, make medication unnecessary. If the school is unco-operative (and many don't know how to teach hyperactive children effectively), change schools. Home-schooling is another option parents should consider.

See also **ATTENTION DEFICIT DISORDER.**

RURAL SCHOOLS   Wendell Berry, one of the continent's true remaining social critics, has long argued that North America's spiritual and cultural renewal will begin in back-country towns. Rural communities that have successfully resisted the advances of destructive economies and thoughtless governments, he notes, have probably held fast to a sense of place, memory and neighbourliness. And to Berry, these values are essential moral ingredients for rebuilding a society both mindful of children and homelands.

This same bold observation also applies to the continent's battered school system. If there is any hope for revival of this institution, it, too, rests in the country, not because of any virtue that rural educators might possess, but because of the nurturing environment a rural community can provide for its school. As educational researchers have recently discovered, good schools, whether urban or rural, thrive on high common standards, parental involvement, accountable leadership and a shared work ethic. In the heartland these values are not only easier to marshal but are more likely to be a community priority. As well, the hinterland can foster these ideals with a minimum of intervention from the educational bureaucracy.

Consider, for example, the singular case of Youngstown, a small community of three hundred, located deep in the heart of cattle country, 165 miles northeast of Calgary. Its local school has a dozen hard-working teachers who, unlike their urban peers, all live where they work, and therefore have a strong commitment to place. The school's authoritative principal, Stuart Ian Wachowicz, came for one year and stayed for seventeen. He has taken full advantage of the school's remotenesss from urban tribulations to help the school's 120 grade one to grade twelve students perform consistently "above average."

By any pedagogical yardstick the school spells success. Eighty percent of Youngstown's grade twelve graduates go on to receive advanced diplomas. Compared to Alberta's provincial dropout rate of 30 percent, the school boasts an enviable rate of 1.5 percent. And in the academic TV show, *Reach for the Top*, Youngstown students routinely beat their Calgary counterparts who purportedly come from schools with better resources. "When you expect excellence, you achieve excellence," says forty-five-year-old Wachowicz.

The values of the school, as one would expect in a ranching community, are profoundly conservative in the best sense of the word. The school emphasizes both diligence and structure. Its totally unconventional though telling motto reads "All Hard Work Yields A Profit," and profit in beef country has a broad Biblical meaning as opposed to a strictly commercial one. "There is a general agreement between teachers and parents that we want to operate like a big family," says Wachowicz. "There is great strength in that unity." Agreement on goals and principles, however, does not mean a mute Parent–Teachers Association. "Parents are not reticent about expressing their views, and that's absolutely obligatory," says Wachowicz.

Youngstown has achieved distinction, not by copying urban trends, but by mixing the tried and true with skilful innovation. "Don't throw out the old pail until you know that the new one holds water," says the principal. So instead of employing officially sanctioned techniques like whole language or "discovery learning," Youngstown sticks to an "old-fashioned program." That means phonics, spelling, geography, history, grammar and intensive writing in all subject areas. It also means an art as history program and a novel agricultural class that emphasizes soil science and Israeli irrigation techniques.

The school's commitment to the welfare of its community extends even to homework: in grades seven to twelve students take home two to three hours of work each night. The point of so much hard work, adds Wachowicz, is the duty to prepare students, particularly those who elect to stay and strengthen their community's heritage, to make a difference. "Why can't a rancher tend his cattle and come home at night and listen to Mozart?" asks the unorthodox principal. "We need a well-educated farming community.... And I don't think people should be embarrassed to say that they enjoy reading, even if the beer commercials say they should be enjoying other things."

But Youngstown has achieved these very human ends, results that very few other schools in Canada can muster, by saying "No" to bureaucracy and "Yes" to Youngstown. "I won't bring my school down to the provincial average," says Wachowicz. The school's effectiveness is a unique testament both to the advantages of remoteness and to the power of local decision-making.

The unheralded success of Youngstown demonstrates that rural communities that care about education can forge powerful schools. They can produce citizens who want to contribute to society at large and, better still, make Youngstown a good place to live. It also proves that good rural schools can outperform their urban cousins by actually ignoring pedagogical fads.

And it shows, as Berry has long argued, that good schools cannot exist without "a love of a place and community."

See also **EFFECTIVE SCHOOLS**.

S

SCHOOL CHOICE   Creating schools of high quality that don't all look and sound alike is the central agenda of every school reform group in the country. And there are more recipes than you can shake a stick at.

Like much of the literature about changing the structure of schools, *Thinking for a Living*, a book by Ray Marshall and Marc Tucker, identifies the dour influence of Frederick Winslow Taylor as the key obstacle to choice. Taylor, the father of the modern industrial workplace, believed that tasks should be broken down into simple bits easily performed by people without much schooling. He believed that thinking was the preserve of managers, and "machine-like efficiency" the proper domain of obedient workers.

As Taylor's precepts changed the nature of North American workplaces in the 1920s and 1930s, the central aim of schooling shifted from real intellectual mastery to the process of "adjusting" men and women to vocational roles in the industrial economy. The authors of *Thinking for a Living*, argue that while the spirit of Taylor has long since left many workplaces, it still shackles our schools.

To "de-Talyorize" the schools the authors call for a massive change in how they are governed, staffed and managed. Their reform recipe (and there is more than one) reads like part common sense, part Total Quality Management and part business hokum:

It begins with clarity about goals for the students: what the community expects students to know and be able to do when they leave high school. It requires the development of measures of student performance and a new curriculum that accurately reflects those goals. It assumes that many decisions now made by the state ... about how to get the job done will be devolved upon the principal and the teachers, and that much of the intervening bureaucracy will go. It entails a major effort to get the highest possible quality of staff in the schools, and to support that staff by giving it the information and skills it needs to do the job. It requires development of a whole new set of incentives and accountability measures that provide real rewards for school staff whose students make real progress and real consequences for those whose students make little progress.

But even if many good schools observed these precepts (and many have, without referring to the participants as "clients" or "customers," as Marshall and Tucker do) there would still remain the problems of choice and differences in educational beliefs. As Leif Stolee wisely observed in a speech before a group of Alberta school trustees, two ideological groups are now actively competing for the soul of our schools.

On one side stand the "little schoolers"—parents and teachers who believe that schools should stress achievement, accountability, knowledge, skill, discipline and personal responsibility. On the other side sit the "big schoolers"—those who consider the acquisition of knowledge almost as a pastime, and self-fulfilment, leisure and self-esteem the true concerns of modern schooling.

Given these startling differences, Stolee proposes a reasonable solution: an Edmonton public school system with a central authority that has a three-tiered delivery system. Parents would have the choice of sending their children to "little schools" (the traditional model), "big schools" (the progressive beat) and maybe a religious system "based on broad Protestant principles." After a plebiscite to determine popular support for each system, the city's 240 schools would be apportioned accordingly. Funding would follow the student, and provincial and city-wide testing would be mandatory and its results made public. Teachers and principals would be given the choice of deciding where they wanted to work.

Concludes Stolee: "The results would be competition rather than monopoly, choice rather than compulsion, flexibility rather than force, and public contentment rather than protest." But he then adds that "this proposal is far too sane and sensible for our sclerotic, moribund establishment."

Perhaps the most extreme proposal for choice is the voucher system. This deregulation and privatization scheme, first proposed by the Chicago economist Milton Friedman, means giving parents public money to send their children to private or public schools of their choice. It is based on the theory that, given the marvels of an unfettered school market, choice will encourage competition, weed out bad schools and expand good ones.

As in most school debates the political rhetoric on school choice runs far ahead of practical evidence supporting its merits. Despite various experiments in the United States and England there is little research that says that allowing parents to choose their children's school actually improves a school's effectiveness or a student's learning.

A recent review of parental choice in England, in fact, directly refutes the assumption that more choice leads to higher standards or better schools. Geoffrey

Walford discovered that parents selected schools, as they do cereals, on a broad range of criteria including good discipline, single-sex intake (a big issue in England) and proximity to home. Academic excellence often came at the bottom of the list. "There is little evidence for equating 'popular' with 'good' in terms of parental choices," concludes Walford. "Additionally, the child's wishes have been shown to be of great importance to many parents, and some parents appear to delegate the decision of choice of school entirely to their child. This concern with the wishes of the child may mean that she or he has a happier time at secondary school (which is not insignificant!), but there is even less evidence that the choices of 10-year-old children are likely to be primarily related to the academic effectiveness of the schools, and it is highly unlikely that the sum of many such choices will automatically lead to higher educational standards for all."

Although limited forms of choice may ultimately help parents and educators solve some very difficult school problems, it would be wise for policy makers and avid school reformers to consider these four warnings: choice alone cannot improve schools or guarantee high standards; choice that is poorly planned and delivered as another consumer good will fail; choice without better information on student performance will merely lead to more subjective evaluation of schools; and current choice experiments bear careful scrutiny before being heralded as useful instruments for school reform.

SCHOOL DISTRICTS/BOARDS   The advent of consumerism helped create the durable myth that only money and lots of it could secure good schooling. Peter Coleman and Linda Larocque, however, found that the truth is vastly different. They published their findings in a slim, unpopular book called *Struggling To Be Good Enough* (Falmer Press). Coleman is a fifty-nine-year-old professor in the field of educational research at Simon Fraser Univeristy and Larocque is a forty-two-year-old associate professor in educational administration at the University of Alberta.

In *Struggling To Be Good Enough*, the two researchers report that good school districts or school boards achieve good results with a "productive ethos" and not by spending more money or hiring more teachers—a message that has yet to find a welcome home in Canadian schooling.

"It's just not good news for a lot of administrators," says Coleman, a former high school teacher. "The book challenges the basic assumptions that people have that good schools are the result of spending lots of money." (That's now a $50 billion belief in Canada.)

Like most of the world's growing community of researchers on school effectiveness, Coleman and Larocque didn't find any meaningful links between high spending and high student achievement. What they did find, though, was that high-spending districts are rarely those that achieve good student performance, because bad districts treat quality as a commodity that can be purchased. Bad districts try to solve their problems by weighing down their schools with more bureaucrats or non-teaching staff, whereas good districts use their teachers wisely and motivate everyone with a "productive ethos."

The good districts studied, dubbed Jointure, Reussir and Benevolent in the book, paid a great deal of attention to helping their teachers make a difference in the classroom. The bad districts, humorously nicknamed Moribund and Halfheart, paid little attention to training or curriculum improvement.

Concluded the professors: "High performing districts are those which create, through training, shared norms and working knowledge. We found little evidence of concern for assessing effectiveness and making changes to improve in schools in districts which had failed to develop such norms and knowledge."

Like most educational goals, the values and beliefs that define the running of good districts are hard to achieve but easy to define. In excellent boards, administrators simply try to do the following six things with some consistency:

1. They focus on instruction.
2. They encourage the monitoring of progress with informal or formal tests on a regular basis.
3. They change specific practices when they don't get the results that teachers, parents and students expect.
4. They help shape and direct a commonly shared commitment to excellence among all staff.
5. They report their results to parents on a regular basis.
6. They actively seek parental feedback and input.

Coleman and Larocque sum up the soul of a good school district as a shared commitment to excellence. According to Coleman, this sharing doesn't exist in districts like Moribund or Halfheart, where teachers aren't aware they are part of anything.

The superintendents who foster this common and moral purpose don't lord it over their schools. But they do model energy, efficiency and a heartfelt concern with accountability. Last but not least, they also encourage principals and teachers to do their jobs better. They are always struggling to be "good enough."

Although Larocque has found teachers and principals highly receptive to the productive school district ethos ("The world we are describing is the one teachers and principals want to work in"), many superintendents have not yet warmed to the idea of spending less money and working harder.

See also **EFFECTIVE SCHOOLS** and **"INNOVATIONS" vs. "REFORMS."**

SCHOOL VIOLENCE   There are no national statistics on violence affecting Canadian schools, but parents, police and teachers all agree that there is more mayhem, bullying and incivility in schools and their communities than ever before. Notes one principal: "It used to be that kids would have a scuffle, shake hands and then it would be over. But now they'll get their friends together and go at it again, and then there'll be a knifing or a shooting. The rules have changed and that's what is scary."

A recent report by the British Columbia Teachers' Federation aptly sums up the new rules:

* Children as young as five are biting, kicking and punching their peers and teachers.
* The traditional one-on-one fight has been replaced by more group attacks, often involving different ethnic groups. The violence is generally more severe, with attacks continuing even after the victim is down.
* More and more weapons are appearing at school, ranging from machetes to guns. A 1993 survey of Calgary high school students, for instance, found that one in five carried "some sort of weapon," including knives and brass knuckles, because they didn't feel safe in school. In Metro Toronto the number of school-based violent incidents, including weapon assaults and armed robberies, rose from

1,181 to 1,882 from 1990 to 1993.
* More and more adolescent girls are bullying and assaulting other students.
* There is a growing lack of respect for teachers and principals, and a corresponding lack of fear about the consequences of incivility.

The causes of violence in the schools are complex. The problem has its roots both in the schools and the larger community. Although many principals would be reluctant to admit it, schools can actively support or unwittingly generate a climate of fear and violence in six ways:

1. Allowing reading problems to continue. There has always been a strong correlation between illiteracy and violence in schools. Schools have traditionally diagnosed reading disabilities in grade three (which is much too late), with the consequence that grade five turns into a frustrating placement for many angry students. According to Dr Carl Kline, a Vancouver psychiatrist, reading disabilities are still the major cause of emotional problems in children and adolescents. An elementary school that doesn't teach reading early and effectively will graduate depressed students or budding juvenile delinquents.
2. Disregarding the effects of scale. The proper size for an effective high school is about twelve hundred students, and for an elementary school, about four hundred. Yet many cities have schools with twice that number of pupils. And the greater the school population the more impersonal and anonymous the relationships in the school. Big schools, like big cities, have trouble establishing a sense of community. As a consequence, the mayhem affecting large schools is simply a reflection of their alienating size.

3. Refusing to set limits. Schools that don't have a code of conduct are inviting trouble. And schools that don't enforce the code fairly and consistently are their own worst enemies. Notes Calgary principal Larry McIntosh: "Kids want limits, and they want to feel safe coming to school."

4. Failing to give students a sense of ownership. Schools that don't actively encourage and expect their students to be responsible participants reap vandalism and discord. Schools that give students the responsiblity to paint murals, to govern programs, to plant gardens and to debate issues of governance usually don't have a problem with graffiti or property damage. The owners—the students—just won't tolerate any defacement of their special place.

5. Failing to make learning matter. The potential for violence in schools is inversely proportionate to the demand for academic performance. Elsje de Boer, a British Columbia parent, has noted that schools located in the worst neighbourhoods and operating under some of the worst conditions have turned things around by re-instituting discipline, a dress code, respect and an emphasis on academic achievement. "These schools give their students precisely the sense of belonging and the values with which to establish a pecking order that they might otherwise have sought in a youth gang, a cult or neo-Nazi group." De Boer's lesson is simple: if students aren't engaged in meaningful school work, they will find other employment.

6. Not realizing that physical education is good for the soul. A school that doesn't provide its students with a meaningful sports program is not only neglecting the welfare of its charges but will find its students letting off steam in other ways.

Cultural Sources

The primary cause of aggressive and unruly children is poor or inadequate parenting. Several Quebec studies by the social scientist Richard Tremblay recently found that between 10 and 20 percent of the children currently entering kindergarten arrive there with such aggressive and anti-social behaviours that they are labelled "stable high fighters." These are not bullies but kickers, biters and fighters. Male children who suffer neglect at an early age tend to develop more testosterone than those cared for. Not surprisingly, these same children, tracked over time, become Quebec's school dropouts.

Products of poor nurturing and little stimulation at home, these children come from neighbourhoods where drug and alcohol abuse is epidemic and where the unemployment rate is 25 percent. Observes Fraser Mustard of the Canadian Institute for Advanced Research: "This is a very deep problem that schools traditionally aren't trained to handle."

The media, and television in particular, have no respect for childhood. Most children will have witnessed eight thousand murders and more than a hundred thousand acts of violence by the time they enter elementary school. Although studies trying to link television-viewing with aggressive behaviours in children are inconsistent and contradictory, they do suggest that effects exist. While TV violence portrayed as being justified or rewarded is often imitated; random violence tends to make people anxious. Even so, the bottom line here is not so much the number of violent acts watched by children, but the number of homes where television has become a substitute for parental guidance and authority. (See **TELEVISION**.)

Aggressive children are also a symptom of laissez-faire or narcissistic parents. Maybe a third of middle class parents now fit this role by accident, complacency or sheer overwork. As the American historian Christopher Lasch has boldly written, children have paid "a heavy price for the new freedom enjoyed by adults.... They spend too much time watching television, since adults use the televison set as a baby-sitter.... They spend too many of their days in child-care centers, most of which offer the most perfunctory kind of care. They eat junk food, listen to junk music, read junk comics, and spend endless hours playing video games, because their parents are too busy or too harried to offer them proper nourishment for their minds and bodies. They attend third-rate schools and get third-rate moral advice from their elders. Many parents and educators, having absorbed a therapeutic morality and a misplaced idea of egalitarianism, hesitate to 'impose' their moral standards on the young or to appear overly 'judgmental.'" And so what parents sow, the schools unfortunately reap.

Society's new sexual precocity has also contributed to the lack of respect for authority. Under the misguided pretext of "spreading a scientifically based sexual enlightenment" in the schools, educators have exposed children to sexual themes with complete disregard for their ability to make sense of them. To present children with ideas and information they are not emotionally prepared to absorb ultimately compromises children's faith in adults. According to the famous child psychologist Bruno Bettelheim, the consequences are painful: "The child comes to feel that he and they live in different spiritual worlds."

School Responses

For the violence spawned by broken homes and poverty, no school response will ever be adequate. Only broad public policy can address the causes of broken

families and community collapse. But in the interim
many Canadian schools have chosen one or a combination of three key strategies and programs.

Perhaps the most popular is a technocratic
American import called "conflict resolution." Nearly
every urban school board in the country has now
adopted one or more programs with names like
Peacemakers, Problem Solvers or Peer Mediators. All
of these U. S.-based programs encourage kids to
express their feelings without blame while listening to
the other side of the story. The idea is to get embat-
tled and angry kids to suggest peaceful solutions. But
very few of these conflict resolution programs come
with any hard research demonstrating their effectiveness. Their fragmented approach to the issue, an
amorphous blend of "empathic skills, anger management and impulse control," treats violent children as
simply a management problem.

Although some schools believe these programs have
temporarily decreased scuffles on the playground,
many critics question the appropriateness of turning
children into policemen. Notes Fred Mathews, the
director of Central Toronto Youth Services: "I fear that
some of these programs are an abdication of responsibility on [the part of] adults and parents." In a few
American schools, high school students charged with
the responsibility of being peer mediators have committed suicide because they could no longer take the stress.

Another popular approach to school violence is the
"zero tolerance" policy, with its Orwellian name. Both
the Scarborough and Calgary school boards have
established fixed and firm rules for expelling students
whose behaviour endangers others or deprives them
of their right to learn in a safe environment.

Scarborough recently told its students that individuals caught carrying guns or knives, or attacking other

students, will be recommended for expulsion. Calgary has also made it clear that students suspended for violent acts won't be readmitted to schools unless they and their families have gone for counselling.

Although every board should clearly define for students what's acceptable and unacceptable behaviour, many parents feel "zero tolerance" is too little, too late. "There is nothing in it to prevent bad habits," charges Diane Malott, the founder of an Ontario group for the victims of school violence. In other words, "zero tolerance," like conflict resolution, manages the problem without tackling the root causes of violent behaviour.

In contrast to these half-measures, many safe schools concentrate on character education. This is not a technocratic program like conflict resolution but a philosophy about what matters in schools. It posits that certain values, such as honesty, responsibility, courage and diligence, are universally respected and should be modelled by all school staff at all times. True character development requires students not only to actively practise these values in school but to apply them in their community. History and English teachers often inculcate many of these values in studies of heroic men and women. Schools that focus on character education not only have fewer discipline problems but fewer conflicts to resolve.

Perhaps the most novel approach to dealing with school violence was adopted by George McKenna, superintendent of Inglewood Unified School District in California. Faced with an epidemic of guns and shootings, he recruited grandmothers and parents to patrol his schools. (He gambled that even the most unruly students would be reluctant to shoot their grandmothers!) Soon the violence dropped off and civility returned. As an offshoot, community–school relationships also blossomed.

Safe schools, then, are community-minded places that teach values by their conduct and only set fair rules and provide logical consequences for children. They are models of civility, where children are progressively given more and more responsibilities and where adults set the limits. But such measures must begin at the top with a principal, staff and parents committed to the same moral vision.

This is exactly the approach taken by Larry McIntosh, the balding, straight-talking principal of Woodman Junior High in Calgary. When he arrived at the school in 1991, the kids were scrapping, fighting and smoking at the front doors. During his first week, twenty-six parents appeared in his office, demanding transfers for their kids. The school's notoriety stemmed from students who bullied their peers, intimidated teachers and coolly collected "red cards" (a notice system to send unruly students to the principal) as badges of honour.

Then McIntosh went to work. He established a few hard-and-fast rules. "Students caught with drugs, knives or guns are history," he said. But that was just the beginning. He also abolished red cards. Aggressive students now went directly to his office. "I ripped their lips off and brought them back to class. We simply concentrated on getting the problem solved." He supported his teachers, walked the halls and got to know every student. He created a new slogan for the school: "A Great Place to Learn." He invited parents back into the school.

Now Woodman's reputation has changed dramatically. Parents line up to get their children into the school because Woodman emphasizes quality teaching, student responsibility and hard work, with rewards such as "student appreciation days." More than two-thirds of the students are on the honour roll and there is no violence. Says McIntosh, who proudly wears outrageous ties: "Kids want limits. And they want to feel safe coming to school. Hey, they want to be in an environment where they can find happiness and be kids."

Would that other schools learn from Woodman's example.

See also **EFFECTIVE SCHOOLS**, **BULLYING** and Appendix 14.

Note: Parents whose sons or daughters have been the victims of school violence would be well advised to contact a parents' group. In Ontario call OVER (Outlaw Violence in Education Right Now): in west Metro phone 416-237-1142; in east Metro phone 416-724-8089. In Alberta call FOCUS (For Our Children's Unconditional Safety), Maureen Gosling, Vice-President: 403-934-4499.

SELF-ESTEEM   Self-esteem is the "Mom and apple pie" of education. While no one would oppose building such a strength in any child, many schools consider it their first priority.

Recognizing that children who think poorly of themselves carry an albatross around their necks, educators have sought to parcel out self-esteem like candy. If children are shy, self-critical and emotionally wounded from the slings and arrows of outrageous parents, educators reason, then surely our goal should be to build their esteem and make them feel good about themselves.

Ever since the 1970s, self-esteem has been a major educational enterprise. Some American states have set up "Bureaus of Self-Esteem," while many schools have adopted a host of self-esteem programs with names like "Pumsy in Pursuit of Excellence," "Developing

Understanding of Self and Others," and "Quest."
(Pumsy, a preadolescent dragon with an inferiority
complex and a posse of bullies after him, encourages
children to chant "I am me and I am OK.") Thanks to
self-esteem consultants, self-esteem books, international conferences and loads of rhetoric, a majority of primary teachers now think that their primary job is to
build self-esteem in their charges.

In the process of adding self-esteem to the curriculum many educators decided that standards, grading
and competition were inimical. Such practices, they
argued, entail hard work or intellectual endeavours,
which might make some children feel bad because
they can't do them well at first. They made a similar
argument about failure. Thus the pursuit of "feeling
good about yourself as a reader" has supplanted "reading well" in many classrooms.

Educators in California, the first home of such
thinking, regard self-esteem as the social vaccine "that
empowers us to live responsibly and that inoculates us
against the lures of crime, violence, substance abuse,
teen pregnancy, child abuse, chronic welfare depen-
dency, and educational failure." Concludes the 1990
Task Force to Promote Self-esteem: "The lack of self-
esteem is central to most personal and social ills plagu-
ing our state and nation as we approach the end of the
20th century."

Thus, self-esteem is a commodity with no links to
family or community; if a child doesn't have enough,
then it's simply a matter of picking a program and getting him some more.

Research, however, suggests that what has been
robbed from or never nurtured in children can't be
returned or restored so easily. Nor is there much evidence to suggest that spoon-feeding children with self-
esteem will make them more confident learners.

Berkeley sociologist Neil Smelser sums up the case well when he explains that scientific efforts to establish links between self-esteem and academic achievement or other social markers are slim and elusive.

In fact, the opposite may be closer to the truth. Two Australian educators recently noted that research on child development clearly warns that "expressing warmth and sympathy towards students when they fail to succeed on school tasks serves to reduce further the students' beliefs in their own capabilities. Add the researchers: "Expecting children to 'discover' new knowledge by themselves and being sympathetic when they fail to do so would seem to be entirely at variance with the goals of education and social equity."

Self-esteem is due more to the acknowledgment of good work in math and reading than to mantra-chanting sessions that take up math and reading periods. Jacques Barzun, a long-time critic of modern schooling, has no doubt that bureaucracies devoted to self-esteem will produce more educational bureaucrats championing the creation of more bureaus devoted to self-esteem. But true self-esteem, he adds, "comes from work done, from new power over difficulty, which in school means knowing more and more and coping easily with serious tasks."

Effective teaching is perhaps the most effective way to build self-esteem in children. Pupils feel good about themselves when they have learned something, struggled towards a goal and participated in serious structured work, no matter what chaos might await them outside the school. Most parents intuitively know that a hundred and one lessons with "Pumsy" and other therapeutic creatures cannot take the place of the achievement, competence and self-worth that are engendered in a challenging and caring classroom.

See also **REPORT CARDS** and **CHARACTER EDUCA-TION**.

SEXUALITY AND SEX EDUCATION   Few issues are as contentious as sex education. What initially began as an attempt to explain certain principles of biology and the difficulties of love, however, has blossomed into a full-scale industry obsessed with condoms, AIDS, anal sex, oral sex and so-called "alternative lifestyles." Consider, for example, the controversy over the Toronto Board of Education's sexual orientation curriculum: "Homosexuality, Lesbianism and Homophobia." The curriculum was developed partly in response to the 1986 murder of Kenneth Zeller, a highly respected school librarian and gay man, by five Toronto teenagers. Yet, despite its noble intentions, it neither honours the dead nor speaks to the heart of the matter.

According to John Campey, a gay Toronto school trustee and a supporter of the guide (with some qualifications), the purpose of the curriculum is to let students know that there might be gays studying or teaching in the school, that homosexuality does not mean the end of the world and that gay people can lead satisfying lives and should be treated with the same respect accorded others.

Although most parents may not object to this agenda, what they may read in the draft curriculum is a loaded political tract that engages in some heterosexual-bashing.

"I'd be happy with a discussion of homosexuality in the classroom," says Sue Careless, one the curriculum's critics and a mother of four teenagers. "But I want balance, not gay activist gospel."

Drafted by a committee that included the gay community but no parent representatives, the document presents a gay perspective with a political vocabulary that is probably foreign to most teachers and students. For instance, the 291-page report, defines as blatantly sexist or "heterosexist" the view that heterosexuality is the norm, and adds that the social attitudes of straight people towards homosexuality cause "more unhappiness than sexual tendencies" alone. The report adds that if there is an attitude problem it doesn't lie with homosexuality and lesbianism, "but with homophobia and heterosexism."

The document also accepts Alfred Kinsey's dated and contested statistic that 10 percent of North America's population is gay (scientists now suggest 5 percent or less) as the final word. While the document roundly debunks conventional psychoanalytic theories about homosexuality, counselling abilities of eighty-eight listed Toronto gay and lesbian organizations, including a sadomasochist club, are well advertised.

What is most striking about the draft is its one-sidedness—something gays have had to contend with for a long time in heterosexual culture. One passage, for example, notes that "there is clear evidence that the traditional heterosexual nuclear family is a dangerous place for women and children—a place where the prevalence of physical and sexual abuse/assault is disturbingly high." Yet there is no parallel acknowledgment of the health problems of gays or lesbians, such as high incidences of alcoholism and drug abuse.

There are some surprising omissions. The guide ignores the fact that many gay and lesbian youths in Toronto are hustling on the street because they were rejected by their parents. Although there are several pages on the merits of "coming out," the advice of some gay activists that young people shouldn't "come out" before they finish school or get a job is absent.

In an attempt to be correct and positive and to provide answers where there sometimes are no answers, the document ultimately misses the point: that a teacher's or student's moral goodness has nothing to do with sexual orientation.

Perhaps the real danger of the resource guide, as it is now written, is that high school students will see through the proselytizing, and ask why they are being treated like Sunday school children, rather than as adults with a right to hear all sides of a very human story.

Campey, of course, does not want to come out with a document perceived as discriminatory or unbalanced, but his primary concerns fall elsewhere. He says the document is too long, outdated and even "homophobic." He also reports that he has heard very few concerns from parents in his ward. But Sue Careless doubts that many parents have read the document, let alone heard about it.

Although the school board recently defeated a motion to postpone the guide's implementation for a year to allow more public input, parents and gays can only hope that this curriculum will be revised to sharpen its message that it matters not one whit whether a student or teacher is gay and that there are more perspectives on homosexuality than those articulated by gay activists.

Political correctness honours no one—least of all, the dead.

Update: The Toronto board re-drafted its curriculum but did not balance its content. Nor did the board give parents any voice in the re-drafting. As a consequence the curriculum's central weaknesses remain: it discourages intellectual honesty and legitimate disagreement; it mocks and ridicules therapy; it glosses over the health dangers of promiscuous homosexuals, and it trivializes religious concerns and matters of conscience.

If you don't want your children exposed to sexual education programs written by special-interest groups, make your point of view well known to your school board. If you have doubts about the content of the sex ed courses in your schools, sit in on them. And if you don't like the message, withdraw your child. It is your right.

For more information on these issues contact Citizens United For Responsible Education (CURE). Although the acronym may sound ominous, CURE is not interested in curing anyone. It is, however, a broadly based multiracial group of parents and taxpayers concerned about balance and choice in sexual education matters. Phone 416-693-CURE or fax 416-237-1721.

SINGLE PARENTS   A two-parent family makes what the American social critic Amitai Etzioni calls "a two-piston engine of effective education." While one parent offers support ("I know you tried your best!"), the other goads the child to achieve ("Did you study for your test today?"). In this way a "mutually supportive educational coalition" comforts when simple assurance is needed and challenges when a kick in the pants is required. Some single parents can fufil both roles very well, but they are more the exception than the rule.

A divorce, followed by new partners, remarriage and another divorce, has consequences for both the child and the community. These changes in role models represent a breach in the two-parent educational coalition and a serious disruption in the child's education. Here are some of the effects that teachers observe on a daily basis as recorded by a 1991 American study for the National Center for Health

Statistics (Canadian data, which are not as complete or tidy, echo the American findings):

1. Children living in single-parent families and step-families are more likely to fail in school. They are also more likely to need treatment for emotional or behavioural problems.
2. Of children who need to repeat a grade, 12 percent come from intact families, 22 percent come from step-families, and 30 percent live with single moms who never married.
3. Of children suspended from school, 4 percent come from intact families, 9 percent from step-families, 11 percent live with divorced moms, and 15 percent live with unmarried moms.

When the divorce rate was only 15 percent, the community could cope with a broken marriage and its consequences. But when it hits 40 percent (or much higher in some Canadian communities), the educational fallout becomes too much for the school to sustain.

The message here for single parents is simply this: after a divorce or separation try to re-establish that important educational partnership with a grandparent, teacher, friend or new partner as soon as possible. It will make a big difference for your child and your school.

Single parents, particularly moms, would be well advised to seek out schools with male teachers in the elementary grades. Most young boys need strong male role models. Schools that are structured and consistent in their academic expectations for children also have a much better track record with kids from broken or fatherless homes than schools with no sense of purpose or mission.

STANDARDIZED TESTING There are few issues in public schooling as contentious as when to test whom with what. While parents tend to have an inordinate faith in the ability of testing to correct bad schooling, educators tend to have an unreasoned belief that testing is irrelevant to schooling altogether.

Sooner or later, most of the confusion and controversy boils down to the use of one assessment: the standardized achievement test.

It uses a multiple-choice format and is normed, which means it has been taken by a large population of pupils to establish ranges of achievement. As such it can compare an individual's performance with that of his grade or age group. One of the most popular such instruments, aside from provincially made tests, is Nelson's Canadian Test Of Basic Skills.

Educators, most of whom know little about the purpose and value of assessment, either shun these tests, use them inappropriately or give them without ever reporting the results. An achievement test, for example, should never be used to evaluate teacher or student performance, but it has much merit for evaluating the quality of a school's programs or curriculum.

As a general rule achievement tests have no individual or diagnostic value (a child's ability to fill in squares does not reliably or consistently measure what he or she knows and doesn't know). Nor do they gauge with accuracy the relationship between what has been taught and what is being tested. Nations that submit their schools to one battery of achievement tests after another tend to produce multiple-choice curricula that are trivial and fragmented.

The arguments that standardized tests foster mindless memorization, stress out children, create idiot curricula and inevitably force teachers to teach to the test are true if standardized tests are misused or become the only assessment tool a school or board ever gives. The absence of such testing, however, does not mean that schools are doing a good job. For these tests remain, in spite of their shortcomings, an effective and cost-effective way to monitor and track the performance of programs and curricula over time. If two schools with comparable student populations take the same achievement test and one bombs out in math while the other excels, adminstrators should start overhauling the math program in the failing school pretty quickly.

A criterion-referenced test offers much more useful information than achievement batteries. It is not concerned with norms but rather with a student's ability to perform specific tasks outlined in the curriculum. Instead of offering students multiple choices it expects them to put their figuring or writing on paper. Schools concerned about quality use criterion-referenced tests because they test what has been certifiably taught.

Therefore, they are very useful at identifying what students have not learned and what teachers have trouble teaching. They provide detailed diagnostic information that suggests coherent instructional solutions to immediate problems. They can pinpoint exactly where a school should change specific exercises in writing, boost particular teaching skills in math, or develop a new reading program for at-risk students. The national reading, math and science tests that have been developed as part of the School Achievement Indicators Program (SAIP) by the Council of Education Ministers are all criterion referenced.

Margarete Wolfram, an educational psychologist at York University and a former student of Jean Piaget, recently discussed parental concerns about testing in this unpublished essay:

Feedback is necessary for the development and functioning of any adaptive system and the safeguarding of standards. Students need feedback, so do teachers, so does the board and the ministry. The only way this can be achieved is through the use of standardized tests.

It is true that some types of tests require nothing more than mindless memorization, but there is no reason to use those types of tests. It is also true that assessments can have a traumatizing effect and can stifle learning as many such tests did in the past. But there is no reason why it has to be that way.

Assessments are made for two different purposes: selection and diagnosis. Tests that are given for the purpose of selection have all the characteristics of a final judgment. Either one passes or fails. And for those of us who have not always come out on the side of the winners, these tests are naturally anxiety arousing. Even though such tests have been and still are used in the schools, they are really quite inappropriate for that purpose.

The tests that should be used are the diagnostic type. These tests aim for a particular product. Good testing provides information as to how the current state of affairs compares with the results one wants to obtain and what corrective action needs to be taken to assure the desired outcome.

It is the sort of test we use when we taste a meal that we are preparing for an important occasion. The question we ask is not whether we should keep the stew or throw it away, but rather what can we do to make it a big success. Nobody in his or her right mind would avoid tasting the dish during the cooking for fear that the results may be too traumatizing. And if one did delay the testing until late in the process one would indeed run the risk of ending up with something that is unfit for the party, especially if using recipes which are as poorly tested as the methods presently used in education.

Here's an example of a school board with a comprehensive and well-balanced approach to assessment. Justine Hare, the learning and behavioural consultant with the Haldimand-Norfolk Roman Catholic Separate School Board, uses a variety of tests, including standardized ones, to assess individual children and to determine the effectiveness of specific programs and curricula. Here's her description of how Haldimand wisely uses these tests:

In evaluating the progress of individual children, primary emphasis is placed upon teacher analysis of the day-to-day performance of the child within the classroom setting. Ongoing observation, conferencing and analysis of work samples afford the teachers a balanced perspective on the child's development over time in a natural setting; therefore, they are likely to provide the most accurate information. Group standardized testing is conducted yearly in grades three, five and seven. Both nationally standardized measures [such as the Canadian Test of Basic Skills] and provincial tests are utilized for this purpose. As system personnel were cognizant that commercial standardized tests assess only a limited number of skills and may not totally reflect system curricula, all teachers at the grade three, five and seven levels were asked to review the tests to determine if the content was appropriate. Although the limited nature of the skills assessed was confirmed, context was deemed sufficiently appropriate to allow these measures to be used as screening devices to identify the need for further in-depth analysis. While no decisions regarding formal identification, placement or program change are made based upon these results, they have served to alert school personnel to the presence of previously undetected skill deficiencies, enabling them to provide the necessary intervention and remediation.

Due to the small size of the system [approximately 2,900 students] it was felt that locally developed and normed measures would not provide a broad enough context in which to evaluate children's progress. As the system does not as yet have a high school, our students currently attend as many as seventeen high schools in six counties. It is imperative that our system have some assurance that the children are progressing appropriately within a provincial and Canadian context in order that they may be able to compete successfully in divergent educational environments. Other methods of evaluation, such as obtaining feedback regarding student progress at the high school level, are also used to evaluate preparation.

Where standardized tests are used to evaluate system progress, once again they serve only as screens to indicate possible areas of curriculum weakness. Only when trends have been established over a period of three years or more are system personnel asked to review curriculum in depth to determine possible need for change.... While every effort must be made to avoid the excessive and inappropriate use of standardized tests, which has occurred in the United States and Great Britain, judicious use of these screening devices can provide information that is highly useful in preparing our students to succeed academically in environments beyond our system.

A Case Study

For many years, Ontario's London School Board has had the jaunty motto "Success for Every Student." But in the spring of 1994 school trustee Robin Ainslie blew a gaping hole in that image by releasing school rankings on city-wide achievement tests in reading and mathematics.

Her controversial act angered a great many educators, created an enormous debate in the staid western Ontario city and raised some damning issues concerning social class and public schooling.

Ainslie, a manager with Bell Canada, obtained the information through the Freedom of Information Act after first making two requests to the board. Darrell Skidmore, the director of education, says the board had every intention of honouring Ainslie's request, but "when she didn't get a response when she expected it" she went her own way.

Once she had received the test data, Ainslie analysed the results with a group of parents and ranked the performance of sixty-two elementary schools. The assessments included an American standardized reading test (Degrees of Reading Power), which merely pinpoints reading levels, and a criterion referenced math test based on the board's school curriculum. Until this year the board did not share test results with schools, parents or pupils. Trustees had been presented with summary data in February, but the local paper didn't report them.

So Ainslie called a press conference and highlighted the key trends: a system-wide decline in reading comprehension over five years and a growing gap in school performance between the city's middle class west end and its working class neighbourhoods in the east. On reading tests, Ainslie found that "the poorest-performing school is doing almost half as well as the performance of the best school." The lowest-ranked school predictably had a high number of Vietnamese immigrants, who find English notoriously hard to learn.

More alarmingly, the number of "at-risk readers" had grown from 5 percent of the grade four population in 1985 to more than 20 percent of the grade three population. "There is a strong correlation," says Ainslie, between the board's introduction of whole language in 1987 and the growing number of children, particularly in the east side, struggling with print.

A lot of educators, including all of her fellow trustees, reacted to Ainslie's rankings with consternation. They accused her of "stigmatizing" certain schools.

Ranking schools is a problematic exercise because it disguises differences between the highest- and lowest-ranked schools. For example, the top school in reading might have a 72 percent average while the bottom school has 68 percent, 50 percent or 10 percent. But averages also make the rankings misleading, says Derek Allison, an education professor at the University of Western Ontario. "A few outstanding students in a school with a low average, for example, could well have higher scores than many of the students in a school with a relatively high average score."

But people schooled in the east end said they didn't feel stigmatized or cruelly fingered by the test rankings. "I would remind everyone that the stigma is already in place," wrote an angry citizen to *The London Free Press*, who pointed out that it was time the board took a serious look at "the long-term consequences for students who are stigmatized not by statistics but by their early experiences in education."

The point this graduate of admittedly "lousy school-ing" made quite effectively was that there shouldn't be a correlation between income and class. In fact, all the research on effective schools screams loud and clear that a school's commitment to achievement, engaged learning time, discipline and instructional leadership is fifteen times more powerful than a student's social class in predicting school achievement. You can have good schools in any part of town if you have the will and know-how.

Skidmore, who has committed the board to full dis-closure of all test results (minus the rankings), agreed. He admitted that even increases in the number of spe-cial education or foreign-language students can't account for the board's troubling reading perfor-mance. He noted that the board had been planning a "compensatory program" for low-performing schools that would focus on literacy, numeracy, the arts and higher thinking skills.

He also admitted that whole language may work bet-ter in some communities than others and that the board needed to reintroduce "more structure" to the teaching of the language without sacrificing whole lan-guage's altogether healthy emphasis on writing and good literature. "We are trying to swing the pendulum back to the middle."

Skidmore's vision of "compensatory education" would have London's schools employing a diversity of explicit reading methods in different neighbour-hoods, squarely based on the needs of children. East-end schools might find that they can't level the playing field with west-end programs. And educators just might come to the conclusion that Sue Dickson's Sing, Spell, Read and Write, Robert Slavin's Success for All, Marie Clay's Reading Recovery (with a strong phonet-ic component), Siegfried Engelmann's Direct

Instruction or even elegant phonemic awareness training in kindergarten respects the needs of east-end children much more than the "emancipatory" dogma of whole language.

Ainslie says she released the information because of the number of parents who had long complained that their children didn't have the language skills they thought they should. "The test scores prove that the parents were right all along."

See also **WHOLE LANGUAGE** and **EFFECTIVE SCHOOLS**.

STANDARDS   Many parents and educators often confuse standards with standardized testing. The two are not the same. A standard simply states what everybody in grade three math or grade seven English is expected to master. In contrast, a standardized test is a multiple-choice exam that may or may not measure how effectively standards are being upheld.

Standards are essentially goals in common that the community has recognized as important, valuable and essential. Without them, we can't distinguish bad carpentry from good carpentry or poor schooling from excellent schooling.

That much can be achieved in life with high standards is understood by most parents. That children in grade one should be able to read and write simple sentences is a standard accepted by most communities. That the English used by these students should reflect and honour the standards set by the King James Bible, Alice Munro, William Styron, Charles Dickens and William Shakespeare is also understood by most parents.

Wendell Berry, a farmer, poet and English professor, makes three important observations about standards.

Low expectations in community colleges and universities, he says, have the effect of lowering standards in schools. When universities and community colleges teach high school grammar or math, they merely relieve high schools of their responsibility to do so.

A school that individually adjusts standards to meet individual students debases the standard as well as the possibility of real teaching and learning. "If we shape education to fit the students, then we clearly can maintain no standards; we will lose the subjects and eventually will lose the students as well."

If standards are to have meaning and are to be respected, they must be upheld in common, and fairly so. "There must be no discrimination for or against any person for any reason," writes Berry. "The quality of the individual performer is the issue, not the category of the performer. The aim is to recognize, reward, and promote good work. Special pleading for 'disadvantaged groups'—whether disadvantaged by history, economics, or education—can only make it increasingly difficult for members of that group to do good work and have it recognized."

Many educators, however, don't share these views. As committed relativists they regard fixed standards as limiting relics. Paraphrasing a progressive educator from the 1920s, an assistant education professor at York University recently wrote that "education must always look forward to tomorrow's horizons rather than backwards to yesterday's standards."

Thus, standards should be fluid, diverse and individual, say modern educators. If a child isn't reading in grade one, just step back and adopt a whole new set of expectations for the child.

Such views ultimately undermine faith in public schooling and should be rigorously challenged by all parents.

See also **STANDARDIZED TESTING**.

SUMMERHILL   The name of an alternative private school founded in 1921 by A. S. Neill, one of the fathers of child-centred education and therapeutic schooling. Depending on one's point of view he was either a genius or the perpetrator of a great deal of nonsense. Educators either love or hate him.

With his libertarian views and extreme individualism, Neill was really the Milton Friedman of education. While the Chicago economist still champions unfettered markets as the cornerstone of democracy, Neill upheld free students as the true engine of emotional development. Wrote Neill in his 1960s best-seller *Summerhill: A Radical Approach to Childrearing*: "When my first wife and I began the school, we had one main idea: to make the school fit the child—instead of making the child fit the school.... Well, we set out to make a school in which we should allow children freedom to be themselves. In order to do this, we had to renounce all discipline, all direction, all suggestion, all moral training, all religious instruction ..."

Summerhill is still a secular Bible for progressive educators more interested in the emotional life of children than in their intellectual development. Neill, in fact, took no interest in teaching methods or even what was taught at his school. He didn't care much about books, either. His laissez-faire approach, however, was very much an over-reaction to the relentless rote learning and harsh discipline that characterized British public schools at the time. If most schools looked like prisons at the time, Summerhill was a zoo.

At Summerhill freedom meant freedom from authority and tradition, whether good or bad. Students were free to come and go as they pleased, free to do nothing, free to be rude, free to read pornographic books and free to have premarital sex.

A study of fifty Summerhillians found that ten really thought the place had been good for them, while seven said it had been harmful. (The rest held no strong opinions one way or the other.) All the graduates complained about a lack of good teachers and a dearth of academic content.

Because most of the students were refugees from middle class homes and schools that were often cold and uncaring, Neill's school appeared as a welcome oasis. But as the great child psychologist Bruno Bettelheim once noted, Neill never really appreciated that his program worked for a small number of overly repressed students. In trying to sell his philosophy as some kind of universal truth, Neill merely repeated the mistake of other educational innovators who claim to have discovered the Holy Grail of happiness and enlightenment.

Neill's beliefs place him among the ranks of upper middle class liberals who have always felt that the best kind of child-rearing is no child-rearing. Most of the so-called free or alternative schools that were developed in his name during the 1970s and 1980s failed rather dramatically. In many cases parents and teachers demanded their closure. Spoiled children, it seems, are not happy students.

A researcher visiting one Summerhillian preschool typically found the kids bullying each other and their teachers. The moral climate of the institution was summed up as "the survival of the fittest." Ideologically committed to "creativity" and "free expression," the teachers stood around like ornamental shrubs, never offering an emotional response to the chaos that reigned.

If Neill's vision had one redeeming virtue it was that

children, particularly adolescents, should have a role in the governance of their school. At Summerhill, where there were never more than forty to sixty students, every pupil had one vote.

Some Neillisms

The aim of education is to work joyfully and find happiness.

Make the school fit the child.

The absence of fear is the finest thing that can happen to a child.

Lessons are optional. Children can go to them or stay away from them—for years if they want to.

Children should not be compelled to respect property, for it always means some sacrifice of childhood's play life.

Keep your child as far away from his grandparents as possible.

If your child refuses to do her homework, she is showing a healthy criticism of the system by refusing to take part in it.

There are no problem children, but only problem parents.

TEACHER TRAINING   Most teachers admit that attendance at a faculty of education is akin to enduring a boil on the behind for an entire year. Not much gets accomplished other than learning how to cope with excruciating situations and maddening educators. Consider, for example, the all-too-common story of Suzanne X. In 1991 she attended the University of Toronto's faculty of education (FEUT) and found, as most teachers know, that the nation's education faculties offer a disappointing menu of "Mickey Mouse courses" and a grinding anti-intellectualism.

"I am fifty-five years old, a parent, middle class, and have had the same husband for thirty years. I am straight, square and as dull as you can imagine. I have often voted NDP.

"I was fifty-three when I entered FEUT. It is a difficult place to get into: only one in ten applicants is ever accepted. The average age of students was twenty-nine and most had already had considerable experience in the classroom. Most were bright-eyed, bushy-tailed and idealistic.

"Yet, in spite of some well-intentioned instructors, my year was a nightmarish wasteland.

"The compulsory course in one of my two high school teaching subjects was hopelessly taught, and the optional courses (of which we had to take three) were as vacuous as their descriptions in the calendar. Their intellectual content was close to zip, their relevance was questionable, and I learned very little of what I am now discovering a teacher must know in order to teach effectively.

"One of my electives was 'Developing a Personal Philosophy of Education.' I naïvely thought it might provide a historical review of educational thought and explain how we arrived where we are today. But it really turned out to be a course on creating a personal philosophy with lots of chats, discussions and the keeping of a 'personal narrative.' I can't tell you how annoying and paternalistic it was. In the end, we all presented a diary on our 'personal development,' and we all got an A. It might be difficult to get into the faculty, but it is extremely easy to get out.

"My course on evaluation was a similar travesty. I thought it might help me set and mark tests and explain the theory behind such tasks. Yet, it turned out to be so theoretical and abstract that I had no idea how to sit down and fairly mark a stack of essays by the end of it.

"My English as a Second Language course was another exercise in frustration. It was so highly political that it childishly painted all refugees as good people and most racists as trashy white folk. Instructors decried the Canadian Establishment as cruel and vicious, and championed multiculturalism as a new cult to be embellished and expanded. Myself and several other beginning teachers lodged a complaint about one of the instructors.

"Because I had less actual teaching experience than most other students, I was keen to learn methodology and to pick up some practical wisdom. To my alarm, there wan't one practical course designed to help me set up and run a class. All the things that a beginning teacher should know before being turned loose in a classroom were absent: no basic principles, no practical guidelines, no discussion at any time about lesson plans or about the opening, closing and pacing of a lesson.

"It seems that the faculty leaves all of this important training, by default, to the experience gained in the four practice-teaching periods that lasted only two weeks each. Fortunately, I was lucky enough to be placed with four excellent teachers. But even good fortune can't provide all the crucial material a new teacher needs, and I still get angry when I think back on it.

"In retrospect the whole ideological thrust of the education faculty seemed woolly and self-indulgent. We were constantly in small groups, either picking lint out of our navels or going through fatuous activities aimed at encouraging us to be responsible for our own learning. When we were not interacting, we shared our thoughts by engaging in group work and peer tutoring. Any fool knows that this kind of curriculum ultimately loses sight of the everyday realities of teaching ordinary teenagers as well as the importance of a teacher as a leader.

"Even the word 'teach' now has dirty connotations at the faculty because it has, God forbid, nasty overtones of one person maybe knowing more than another. And as for acquisition of knowledge, forget it. That takes second place to vague theories about personal growth.

"Although I love teaching very much, I cannot say the same of teacher training. Lengthy internships followed by some instruction in theory would be much more meaningful than the current zoo. The old normal school approach of getting prospective teachers into classrooms, fast, was a good one. And as heretical as it might sound, I no longer believe a degree is at all necessary to teach."

When I first wrote about the revelations of Suzanne X on the nature of teacher training a great many people—including the dean of the faculty, Michael

Fullan—went to their typewriters. Fullan vigorously defended new reforms at FEUT in a piece he wrote in *The Globe and Mail.*

Not surprisingly, many of the letters came from Ms X's fellow graduates. Most found her graphic depiction of the faculty's program "one-sided" and unfair. But mail from other educators across the country confirmed that teacher training is, indeed, neither a high art nor a revered science.

With the authors' permission I share a sampling of their correspondence as a small window on the ongoing and uncertain debate about the quality of teacher training at the nation's education faculties.

Let's begin with Ken Stone, a forty-six-year-old father and high school history teacher who graduated the same year as Ms X. He writes that Ms X's experiences "may not have been as common as you claim." (I still maintain that they are standard fare across the country.) He recalls that most of his professors were "on the cutting edge.... They were proponents of active learning in the high schools; that is, hands-on education in which students get away from the nonsense of sitting in straight rows and regurgitating reams of facts and dates."

Ken Stone also has some criticisms of the faculty. There was far too much busy-work and too little practice-teaching. But he still concludes that "it's too bad Mrs X, unlike the Faculty of Education, was unable to move with the times."

Paul Van derHelm, a twenty-six-year-old award-winning elementary teacher, also graduated from FEUT with good feelings. He admitted over the phone that most of his colleagues still regard teacher training as a matter of "putting in a year until you get into the classroom" and "were amazed" that he got anything out of FEUT.

But he took advantage of a new pilot program aimed at making teacher education more responsive to classroom realities. He writes that it was taught by experienced teachers and "packed full of useful ideas and information" such as "co-operative learning" (a fancy term for student teamwork). FEUT also set up and paid for an in-service support program "that equipped every member of my class with a computer and a modem for electronic mail and conferencing.... What other Faculty shows such dedication to helping teachers develop so fully?"

The answer, it seems, is not many. Another letter, for example, contained an unflattering 1991 brief by the British Columbia Principals' and Vice-Principals' Association to the British Columbia College of Teachers. The review found that teacher education may look good on paper, but it fails to deliver because the faculties "are isolated from the real classroom (too theoretical), resistant to input from the field (don't want to get chalk dust on their hands) and unresponsive to the demands of public policy (just do what they want to do)." It adds that many faculty members "are poor models of good teaching and lack recent classroom experience."

The confessions of Ms X also rang true for Robert Bryce, the former dean of the faculty of education at the University of Regina. The sixty-year-old professor of educational administration reported that Ms X's experiences "mirrored mine of nearly four decades ago." Discontent is widespread, he adds, and "I've found that dissatisfaction with teacher preparation is a common denominator amongst most educators."

His four-page letter also notes that the wall between most schools and education faculties is "made of concrete." He knows of "professors of education" in some universities "who haven't been in a K-12 school in twenty years or more." When combined with the low esteem most universities hold for effective teaching, anyway, education faculties often become "handmaidens to their own misfortunes."

This, however, is not the case at the University of Regina's celebrated four-year program, where budding teachers work with well-trained mentors and their education professors in real classrooms, says Bryce. "Student teachers are not dumped into the schools with both teacher and practising teacher left to sink or swim," he writes. "Extensive preparation is the norm." In contrast to the six or nine weeks of classroom experience that graduates of FEUT and other one-year programs might receive, Regina's students get twenty-three weeks in a monitored classroom with loads of feedback.

You just can't get efficient teacher training, adds Bryce, without expecting teacher trainers actively to work in the schools. "And if you don't have well-trained horses, you are not going to have much of a race."

Although educational faculties have their defenders, I'm not one of them. My own experiences at York University were dismal, and I have rarely met a teacher who will give his or her training a B minus. Perhaps the best way to reform the faculties is to close them. Nursing, journalism and teaching all began as apprenticeships and should be restored as such.

Leon Botstein, an American school critic, has long suggested that the undergraduate degree in education should be wiped out. Individuals who want to teach English, math or history should study their major and how to teach it in English, math or history departments. Educational psychology should move to the psychology department. And so on. After majoring in a subject, potential teachers should serve long apprenticeships in the schools under the watchful eyes of excellent teachers. (In Ontario a beginning teacher usually has no more than eight weeks of classroom experience—less on-the-job training than a hairdresser.)

Such radical changes might end the unhealthy indoctrination in voodoo psychology and sociology that passes as enlightenment in too many faculties of education. Among the teaching profession it might also restore a respect for ideas and subject matter. That Canadians should tolerate a training process that allows 60 percent of grade eight math teachers in some provinces never to have to study math at university is remarkable.

See also **EDUCATORS**.

TELEVISION

It is more important, more decisive, to solve the difficulties raised by technology, the dangers coming from technology, than to solve purely political issues.

—Jacques Ellul

Ask most primary teachers to identify the single greatest bane of their existence and they'll probably answer television. The idiot box, they'll argue, is an unmitigated evil. It shortens attention spans and it robs young souls of imagination. They are right on both accounts.

In most homes television has replaced the hearth. Rather than sit around the fire and listen to earthy, moral or humorous stories, modern families surround a glowing tube. In just thirty years this new technology has done much to silence family conversations. It has also replaced imaginative play with a flood of brutal, sexy and amoral images. But the very same educators who despair of television's colonization of the home will unwittingly pull out audio-visual aids at school, subscribe to Chris Whittle's *Television One*, and use the box, as many parents do, as a convenient baby-sitter.

These virtuous television critics will also champion whole language readers, such as the Impressions series, which present kids with the following bedtime rule: "Ask to watch one more television show."

Here are the perspectives of three social critics on the medium's conquest of childhood and its invasion of our schools.

Jerry Mander

According to the fifty-six-year-old media critic and celebrated author of *Four Arguments for the Elimination of Television* (published by William Morrow), "the school system still believes that more and more computers are good. That audio-visual information is good. Yet TV watching at home is not good. That's hypocrisy."

Now, Mander deeply sympathizes with the plight of teachers who must deal with primary couch potatoes and their debilitating TV addictions. But if society really wants creative and vital kids, he argues, then it has to understand that watching hours of television at home or at school is just going to make the job more difficult.

He also thinks that Waldorf Schools, a 400-strong movement of private schools established by Rudolf Steiner, have the right attitude: most request that parents lock their TV sets away. That's because Waldorf teachers value playground discourses on good fables and fairy tales, as opposed to Ninja Turtles. "I approve of that, and I don't think kids should watch television at all until they are twelve." (See also **WALDORF**.)

Mander's popular critique of the tube (his book has sold 150,000 copies since 1978) begins with the assumption that all television is educational, and that most of this education is inimical to families and communities. The monolithic technology hourly instructs

kids and adults how to live and what to think, and pro-
pagandizes that buying is the primary purpose of
being. In so doing, television systematically steals from
ordinary people opportunities for living and reflection, while at the same time limiting their exposure to
wholesome ideas.

But Mander also believes, as do a great many social
scientists, that TV harms the minds of children the
most. For starters, it demonstrably speeds up nervous
and perceptual systems to the degree that societies
that watch a lot of TV suffer corresponding epidemics
of hyperactivity among their kids. "If TV is a drug,"
adds Mander, "it is speed, not valium."

When fed a hypnotic diet of ever faster and faster
images children also lose their ability to be calm as
well as to relate to the different rhythms of the natural
world. "It induces hyperactivity and that's what educators are faced with," adds Manders. "And on top of
that come the walkmans, computers, videos and sug-
ary foods."

But when confronted with a young audience high
on TV and other electronic gadgets, weary teachers,
like weary parents, often resort to the easy solution, by
providing more of the drug. "I sympathize with teachers who want these kids to calm down," says Mander,
but he doesn't think schools should be tuning out real
education in order to tune in the "technovoids."

Mander doesn't have any specific solutions for the
effects of television addiction, but he doesn't think
schools should become pushers of mind-numbing
technologies, including computers. These tools
haven't made much of a pedagogical difference, and
they never show up in the research as prerequisites for
an effective school. In fact, the opposite is probably
true: good schools tend to use electronic gadgets spar-
ingly or not at all. (See **COMPUTERS**.)

Not only should schools switch off their television sets, but they should also inform parents of the dire effects a television addiction will have on their kid's schooling. Requesting parents to adopt the Waldorf model or to restrict home viewing is also an entirely sane idea. (Mander suggests a half-hour per day with a parent.)

To combat the epidemic of hyperactivity that teachers routinely complain about, schools should take note of the Japanese habit of following each lesson with ten minutes of rigorous and playful exercise. Schools that place the purchase of audio-visual equipment or computers ahead of their physical education programs are probably self-destructing, warns Mander.

"The more that kids relate to television and computers," concludes Mander, "the less they relate to teachers and other human beings."

Jerry Mander would never have written *Four Arguments for the Elimination of Television*, he says, if most people watched the damn thing one hour a week. But television, together with the computer, has become such an intrusive force in most homes, and many schools, that it has intolerable social and political consequences.

The point of Mander's argument, however, is not to totally eliminate the neon beast, but to become its active master rather than its passive slave. "We probably have to withdraw from the drug altogether before we can find a new balance," he says.

To help work towards a more equal relationship with television, Mander has drawn up a list of recommended attitudes about technology. It appears in his most recent book, *In the Absence of the Sacred* (Sierra Club Books). His homilies are as useful for parents as they are for school boards, which often purchase unnecessary gadgets and multi-media toys without ever examining their utility or consequences.

Mander's list is designed to make adults more conscious of their relationship with the realities of technological society.

1. Be sceptical of all claims about new technology. Abandon "the gee-whiz reflex" and regard technological innovations as "guilty until proven innocent." The negative attributes of a new technique are always slow to emerge.
2. Remember that no technology is value free. Every technology, including television, computers and calculators, has "inherent and identifiable social, political and environmental consequences." The telephone killed the art of letter writing and decreased the emphasis placed on writing in schools; the television subverted the grace of family conversations and replaced homework; the computer, in turn, has banished the study of ideas by drowning teachers and students alike in a flood of meaningless data.
3. "Never judge a technology by the way it benefits you personally." Seek a total view of its impact on your children, neighbours, community and school. The question, says Mander, is not whether it benefits you, but Who benefits most? To what end? Does it weaken or strengthen democracy?
4. When society's leaders and the media argue that the benefits of new technologies always outweigh harmful outcomes, think of Lewis Mumford's summary of such claims: "bribery." And if you think the dismantling of families, communities and schools is not directly or indirectly related to the inroads television and computers have made into everyday life, then think again.
5. Last but not least, make a distinction between technologies that solve problems for our children (solar

energy) and those that leave insoluble problems for them (nuclear energy).

By adopting this critical stance, individual parents and teachers can become, in Ellul's words, "mutants." To be a mutant, "a person needs to become someone who can use the technologies and at the same time not be used by, assimilated by, or subordinated to them."

Mander doubts that this is a proper curriculum for primary schools unless the local community has given the school such a mandate, and Ellul definitely believes that schools are too much a part of technological society to foster such critical attitudes. Teaching children the limits of technology, he advises, can be done "only in communities of parents."

Joseph Pearce

As a distinctly New Age lecturer and a writer, Pearce proffers some very provocative ideas. His latest book, *Evolution's End* (HarperCollins), graphically describes television's effect on the development of a child's imagination. By flooding a child's mind with discordant images, television stunts a child's capacity to make his own images of the world. According to Pearce, television actually saturates the mind "with a counterfeit of the response the brain is supposed to learn to make to the stimuli of words or music. As a result much structural coupling between mind and environment is eliminated; few metaphoric images develop; few higher cortical areas of the brain are called into play; few, if any, symbolic structures develop."

Unlike storytelling, which engages the brain on a number of neural fronts, television electrifies the brain in one field such that no creative response can be made. This addictive posture, known as "habituation," means that the six thousand hours of television assaulting a young brain by the age of five "might as well have been all one program." So it really doesn't matter whether a child watches Barney the Dinosaur or Big Bird any more than it matters whether an adult drinks gin or vodka: either one gets you drunk. This habituation response also explains why both adults and children "have difficulty turning away," even when they hate the programming.

Being robbed of the power to imagine is a tremendous loss for a child—and for the culture. To Pearce "it means children who can't see what the mathematical symbol or the semantic words mean; nor the chemical formulae; nor the concept of civilization as we know it.... They can sense only what is immediately bombarding their physical system and are restless and ill-at-ease without such bombardment."

Studies also show that children whose imaginations are stunted are far more prone to violence than imaginative children, "because they can't imagine an alternative when direct sensory information is threatening, insulting, unpleasant or unrewarding." When the child of television will lash out, the imaginative child will imagine an alternative solution. "Thus imagination gives resiliency, flexibility, endurance, and the capacity to forego immediate reward on behalf of long-term strategies."

Neil Postman

As a long-time communications critic, Postman has decried television's effects on children and schools. He contends that kids raised by television prize what television values: fastness, flashiness, emotion and immediate gratification. The school system, of course, is founded on none of these principles. Because the people who now design textbooks and write curricula have watched a great deal of television, their books predictably celebrate images and their study guides eschew history. In the end, television threatens to reduce teaching to a form of entertainment in which engaging and keeping an audience in a self-satisfied stupor is more important than learning. "What worries me," writes Postman, "is that if school becomes so overwhelmed by entertainment's metaphors and metaphysics, then it becomes not content-centered but attention-centered, like television, chasing 'ratings' or class attendance. If school becomes that way, then the game may be lost, because school is using the same approach, epistemologically, as television. Instead of being something different from television, it is reduced to being just another kind of television." This partly explains why so many parents raised on little television find so many modern schools discordant, incoherent and tied to values that are quite bluntly neither parent-friendly nor respectful of children. A print culture appreciates sequence and history; a culture wedded to images, however, worships the present and actively banishes context.

Every family should set firm rules for television watching and every member, including mom and dad, must abide by them to make them fair.

V

VALUES CLARIFICATION Developed in the 1970s by colleagues of the famed psychologist Carl Rogers, values clarification entered North America's school system as a new way to teach values. According to Kathleen Gow, a Canadian educator, this approach holds that the direct teaching of such values as honesty, justice and compassion is moral indoctrination and a violation of children's moral freedom.

In such a program, according to one values clarification guide, the teacher "avoids moralizing, criticizing, giving values or evaluating. The adult excludes all hints of 'good' or 'right' or 'acceptable' or their opposites." The program merely encourages children to go through a process of thinking about values and then advocates that they pick one value the way a person might pick a car or a television set. Not surprisingly, one values textbook even states that "it is not impossible to conceive of someone going through our seven value criteria and deciding that he/she values intolerance or thievery. What is to be done? Our position is that we respect his/her right to decide upon that value."

Although values clarification is no longer used as widely as it was during the 1980s, it still remains a prominent feature of most drug and sex education programs. The research on this approach has been overwhelmingly negative, and many of its philosophical mentors have denounced it. (See **CHARACTER EDUCATION**.)

A Clarifying Example:

The following dilemma-plagued lesson is a typical values clarification exercise used in sex education programs in Toronto schools; it recently appeared in the *Journal of Health Education*:

The Alligator River Story

Once upon a time there was a woman named Abigail who was in love with a man named Gregory. Gregory lived on the shore of a river. Abigail lived on the opposite shore of the river. The river that separated the lovers was teeming with man-eating alligators. Abigail wanted to cross the river to be with Gregory. Unfortunately, the bridge had been washed out. So she went to ask Sinbad, a river boat captain, to take her across. He said he would be glad to if she would consent to go to bed with him preceding the voyage. She promptly refused and went to a friend named Ivan to explain her plight. Ivan did not want to be involved at all in the situation. Abigail felt her only alternative was to accept Sinbad's terms. Sinbad fulfilled his promise to Abigail and delivered her into the arms of Gregory.

When she told Gregory about her amorous escapade in order to cross the river, Gregory cast her aside with disdain. Heartsick and dejected, Abigail turned to Slug with her tale of woe. Slug, feeling compassion for Abigail, sought out Gregory and beat him brutally. Abigail was overjoyed at the sight of Gregory getting his due. As the sun sets on the horizon, we hear Abigail laughing at Gregory.

In other versions of this bizarre tale the sex and/or sexuality of the characters is varied: Gregory yearns for

Abigail and sleeps with Sinbad or Sinbad becomes
Cindy and Abigail sleeps with her. After twenty minutes of discussion in which the teacher provides character summaries, the students are asked to rank the
five characters in the story "from the one you most
respect to the one you least respect in terms of
his/her behaviour."

Diane Malott, a Toronto parent, reviewed this exercise and found seven things wrong. She asks parents to
rank them from "the one you most respect to the one
you least respect":

1. It turns an otherwise meaningless exercise into an
   armchair philosopher's math problem by requiring
   students to rank the characters according to
   respectability, of which each has none.
2. It forces students to think only "inside the box."
   Abigail or Gregory could have enlisted a group to
   build a bridge or a raft, taken a cold shower, reported the boat captain to the police or someone who
   could actually do something about it, instead of
   Ivan the nudnick.
3. Any meaningful discussion is cut off by the structure of the process and is finally precluded by the
   teacher presenting the specious character summaries ("Abigail—Romantic love as a powerful
   emotion and its influence on decision-making").
4. Versions two and three are homophobic because
   they stereotype homosexuals as having nothing better to do with their time than extort sexual favours
   from horny, hapless heterosexuals.
5. Versions two and three are heterophobic because
   they stereotype heterosexuals as slaves of their emotions, weak-minded and weak-willed.
6. Illustrates the new barbarism/tribalism rampant
   today and the need for character education in our

schools.

7. All of the above and worse.

See also **CHARACTER EDUCATION** and **CHILD-CEN-TRED LEARNING**.

WALDORF

> It is "aliveness" that must be the guiding principle. Aliveness in the teacher must pass over to aliveness in the children.
>
> —Rudolf Steiner

The Waldorf movement is the largest and fastest-growing non-sectarian educational system in the world. With more than five hundred schools world-wide (and six opening every year in North America), Waldorf's anti-materialistic and overtly spiritual curriculum has struck a chord with many parents.

The first Waldorf school was established nearly seventy years ago by the Austrian philosopher and writer Rudolf Steiner. Steiner, who dabbled in a great many fields including organic farming, had some very elaborate beliefs about human growth; his schools reflect his concern that the minds, bodies, hearts and souls of children be engaged with wholesome activities. His first school was for working class children in the Waldorf Astoria cigarette factory (hence the name).

The movement has always been popular in northern Europe, particularly in Germany and Holland, where many Waldorf schools are part of the public school system. There are Waldorf schools in the slums of Sao Paolo and Johannesburg. The city of Milwaukee sponsors an inner-city all-black Waldorf school. Although there are a few Waldorf schools in Canada, most notably in Ontario, Alberta and British Columbia, the movement has grown slowly here.

In a Waldorf school, art, music and handicrafts are as important as reading and writing. A teacher may start with a class in kindergarten and remain with the students for eight years (Steiner valued consistency). The object was never to create consumers or television addicts (Waldorf schools shun most high-tech gimmickry and ask parents to do the same) but decent, self-reliant human beings who could run the long mile.

Peter Dodwell, a psychology professor educated at a Waldorf school in Britain, and his son Nicholas Dodwell, a Waldorf teacher, describe the philosophical tenets of Waldorf in this way in this unpublished essay:

> Steiner held that education should aim at more than the intellectual and vocational needs of the child. Of vast importance is the provision of conditions which further social, personal, emotional and physical development so that talents can flower that allow young people to take their places in life as self-confident, creative and fully independent beings. To this end Waldorf Schools are organized differently from most schools.... Each morning starts with two hours of "main lesson" in which the class teacher teaches. There are many distinctive facets to this instruction; the teacher takes a very active part in formulating the lessons and gearing them to the enthusiastic participation of the pupils. Text books are not used, but pupils make their own "main lesson books," in which written text, sometimes from dictation, partly produced by the children themselves, diagrams, pictures and other imaginative displays are combined. In the lower school the emphasis is always on meaningful artistic creation, mostly under the guidance of the class teacher; although the material covered is quite conventional from one point

of view, there is always a focus on fostering individual artistic feeling and understanding. This is true even of such apparently dry subjects as learning to write, mastering a multiplication table, or making a geometrical construction.

It is a surprise to many to discover some of the subjects that are taught in the lower school, and the way in which Main Lesson time is arranged. Rather than the conventional division of the timetable into a five or six-day rotation for all subjects, blocks of time, typically between two and four weeks, are devoted to a single topic, such as some particular aspect of history, biology, or mathematics. In addition, main lesson blocks are devoted to the myths of various cultures, legends and ancient history. To many people such matters are the stuff of phantasy, and not to be taken seriously in the contemporary world. According to Steiner they instil in children an indispensable appreciation for the wisdom and dignity of humanity, and a feeling for the cultural evolution whose products we are. To know about Persian and Greek mythology, Roman history, and the transition to the modern world is as important for the child as to find out about the local history and geography of the part of the world in which he or she lives, topics that are also covered in Main Lesson. Some subjects, like foreign languages that require constant application—even drill!—and gym and sports, are taught according to a more conventional daily and or weekly timetable. The Main Lesson is, however, the core of the school day, and from one point of view, the most distinctive feature of the educational system.

Parents usually have one of two concerns about Waldorf. Some complain about its heavy arts emphasis theme, which is undeniable. In the wrong hands the elementary program can lose its balance and bore some children. (Steiner strongly believed that the introduction of too much academic material at an early age would result in premature sexuality.) But in good Waldorf schools (Toronto has one) the children will be engaged on a number of levels.

The other central concern focuses on the schools' resolute idealism and avoidance of machines. Will Waldorf grads be able to face the real world? ask many parents. The answer is an unequivocal "Yes." A study in Germany several years ago looked at the graduates of a Waldorf school and a public facility and found no difference in their community standing. Many Waldorf grads do go on to university and do quite successfully there. They have the reputation of being fine citizens who have a deep and rich sense of cultural history.

Some Thoughts from Rudolph Steiner

For it is essential that we should develop an art of education which will lead us out of the social chaos into which we have fallen during the last few years and decades. And the only way out of this social chaos is to bring spirituality into the souls of men through education, so that out of the spirit itself men may find the way to progress and the further evolution of civilization.

We know in our hearts that this is true, for the world is created in spirit and comes forth out of spirit, and so also human creation can only be fruitful if it springs forth from the fountainhead of spirit itself. But to achieve such fruitful creation out of spirit, man must be educated and taught in the spirit also.

The teacher must be a person of initiative in everything that he does, great and small ...

The teacher should be one who is interested in the being of the whole world and of humanity ...

The teacher must be one who never makes a compromise in his heart and mind with what is untrue ...

The teacher must never get stale or grow sour...

Sources

Steiner, R. *Kingdom of Childhood*. Hudson, N.Y.: Anthroposophic Press, 1982.

Steiner, R. *The Child's Changing Consciousness*. Hudson, N.Y.: Anthroposophic Press, 1988.

Books on Waldorf education may be ordered from Rudolf Steiner College/St George Book Service, telephone 916-961-8729, and the Anthroposophic Press, telephone 518-851-2054.

For information on Waldorf schools in Canada, call the Rudolf Steiner Centre in Ontario, telephone 416-881-1611.

See also **MONTESSORI, TELEVISION** and Appendix 10.

WHOLE LANGUAGE   This reading approach has been adopted in most Canadian and American public school classrooms. Billed as a philosophy rather than a methodology, whole language began as a broadly based critique of the mindless worksheets and dull Dick and Jane readers that characterized a lot of reading instruction in the late 1950s and early 1960s.

As an alternative, the critics sought to provide children with material that was worth reading and that respected their interests and intelligence. They also sought to make reading and writing something that mattered right across the curriculum.

Some of these critics thought that phonics should play an important role in early reading instruction, although others did not. To this day some whole language teachers teach phonics and some don't. The controversy, and it's a big one, concerns whole language's lack of consistency and its appropriateness for all children.

In its best and purest form whole language is about reading good books, daily writing and discussing literature in groups. A number of cognitive scientists have advocated more writing in the classroom and the reading of high-quality literature. Whole language has helped spread these ideas, but does not hold a patent on them. "The history of reading instruction," writes Jeanne Chall, "teaches us that literature, writing and thinking are not exclusive properties of any one approach to beginning reading."

By the early 1980s whole language had become the chief form of reading instruction in New Zealand, England, the United States and Canada. Canadian teachers now glibly talk about children "interacting" with texts, while education ministries in Quebec and Nova Scotia support whole language as "official policy." In Ontario and Alberta, only whole language books get approved for primary reading.

The Origins

The philosophy was first articulated in the late 1960s by linguist Ken Goodman, now a professor at the College of Education at the University of Arizona. Goodman says that he didn't found whole language; "whole language found me." But for thirty years Goodman has made a good living by peddling whole language books (*What's Whole In Whole Language*) and accessories such as "miscue analyses."

Goodman started his career by analysing the reading errors of young children to demonstrate that good readers use context or meaning to help make sense of words on a page. He built his career on this belief and still contends that his "miscue" research shows "that a story is easier to read than a page, a page easier than a paragraph, a paragraph easier than a sentence, a sentence easier than a word, and a word easier than a letter." As long as reading is meaningful children will figure it out, says Goodman.

Goodman defines reading as "a process in which the reader constructs a text parallel to the published text. It is this text the reader comprehends, and it is one that incorporates the reader's beliefs, knowledge, values, and experience. This model is very different from the popular notion of reading as identifying and pronouncing words."

Goodman's personal philosophy is also very much tied to his views on whole language. "I am a social realist and educationally a social reconstructionist.... For me culture and the social community must not only prepare people for their future social roles, it must prepare them to reconstruct society and make it better. For me research is never neutral. It is always for or against something or somebody. It always benefits or hurts someone." (Perhaps this explains why Goodman ignores a lot of research that contradicts his theories.)

In Canada, the main advocate of whole language has been Frank Smith, an Australian-born writer, lecturer and researcher. His books, *Reading Without Nonsense* and *Insult to Intelligence*, argue, like Goodman's work, that reading is a "psycholinguistic guessing game." The only rule that any teacher needs for reading instruction is this: "make learning to read easy—which means making reading a meaningful, enjoyable and frequent experience for children."

Perhaps the major contribution to whole language that Goodman and Smith have made is their disavowal of phonics. Goodman has characterized the direct teaching of phonics as "racist," while Smith calls phonics instruction "meaningless." You can't keep a language whole or meaningful if you teach the sounds of letters, argue the two academics.

In the seventies and eighties, books by Goodman and Smith were mandatory reading at most faculties of education and sold hundreds of thousands of copies. When ministries of education began to make whole language "official reading policy," publishing companies realized a good profit could be turned and published "whole language readers" such as *Impressions* and a host of "real," "authentic" and "big picture" books for the elementary grades.

In sum, the philosophy's central tenets, as pinpointed by Marilyn Jager Adams, are the following: "(1) teacher empowerment, (2) child-centred instruction, (3) the integration of reading and writing, (4) a disavowal of the value of teaching or learning phonics and (5) the subscription to the view that children are naturally predisposed towards written language acquisition (in other words, they will learn to read in the same way they learned how to speak: without teaching)."

Educators of different stripes can accommodate points one, two and three, but four and five are not only unsound but incorrect. According to Adams, who completed a monumental study on beginning reading instruction for the U. S. Senate in 1990, "the positions of the whole language movement on teaching and learning about spellings and sounds are historical artifacts. Although they are central to its rhetoric and focal to its detractors, they may well be peripheral to the social and pedagogical concerns that drive the movement." In other words, whole language's weaknesses may ultimately cancel out its strengths.

Whole Language in the Classroom

Because whole language is a philosophy about reading, it comes with no guide other than a call to expose children to "texts." Some schools use whole language basal readers such as Impressions and others just use a wide assortment of books, which may or may not be classic literature. In many whole language classes students choose their own books; in others the teacher makes a point of having all the children study a good sampling of the world's best writers.

Whole language writing programs, which usually consist of journals, writing workshops and invented spelling, may be structured or unstructured. The only two fair assumptions that parents can make about a whole language class is that there will be a heavy emphasis on reading fiction as opposed to science or history, and a strong focus on writing fiction stories, the most difficult genre in English and the one least likely to benefit most students.

Older teachers who have taught whole language for a long time tend to teach phonics systematically and get the job done in quick order. But many whole language programs will still be fiddling with phonics as late as grade four. Others will never address the issue.

Anita Dermer, a former elementary teacher at a working class school in Ontario, taught whole language with phonics. But she was repeatedly stunned by the inconsistencies in whole language instruction from class to class:

> In my school there were five senior kindergarten classes taught by three teachers. I used strict phonetics. The second teacher used whole language

with some phonetics. The third taught no reading skills at all and didn't even put much effort into having children learn to print their names.... Another used the scribble method.... Imagine the typical child. In all likelihood he had problems that might slow his progress: poverty, neglect and broken families.... Now he had the additional burden of having to cope with radically different teaching methods every year.

The whole language people always put the best light on these inconsistencies. Of course we teach phonetics, they claim. What they don't discuss, however, is the difference from class to class in the amount of time spent doing so. One teacher may teach phonetics several times a week, assign regular phonetic drills, keep those who have not mastered a particular point after school. Another may teach phonetics once a month. A third may never do it. Parents are complaining about the latter two types of teacher.

And when the whole language people claim success for their methods, I also have to wonder whether they consider how unscientific their studies often are. Pupils may well be doing brilliantly in whole language classes. But I wonder how many of them are receiving instruction at home from either a parent or tutor to compensate for the lack of phonetics at school.

The Research on Whole Language

There has been little good comparative research on whole language. Even the American authors of a recent book called *Research on Educational Innovations* concluded that "advocates continue to tout their approach on the basis of enthusiasm and testimonials."

Michael Pressley, a respected educational psychologist, says that "there is not a substantial body of evidence that would compel a person with conventional scientific values to conclude that Whole Language instruction is more effective than alternative forms of beginning literacy instruction." What little research is available is muddled and poorly designed. To the extent that such research is readable, whole language does not appear to outperform a basal reading program or even a traditional look-say approach. So whole language is another educational innovation with little applied classroom research to prove its efficacy.

Whenever the reading achievement of pupils attending whole language schools has been measured with standard achievement tests, the effects have not been good. After three years of whole language in Great Britain, test data on 450,000 seven-year-olds showed a 50 percent rise in severe reading problems. After eighteen months of whole language in San Diego the percentage of kids who scored above the median on district achievement tests dropped by 50 percent.

Although California prizes its designation as a "whole language state," literacy there hasn't fared well by the philosophy. With 90 percent of its grade four teachers reporting that they do whole language, the state's grade four students scored last in a national assessment of reading. Whole language defenders responded, "Hey, we have a lot of diverse learners here!" But even California's white fourth graders scored near the bottom of white fourth graders in the United States.

Whole language enthusiasts, however, contend that their philosophy cannot be evaluated by standardized tests or other scientific measures that assess a student's ability to read or comprehend. According to Goodman the results of such tests should be ignored because they break down reading into subskills, which in his world view do not constitute reading.

The competencies that whole language advocates value include interpretations of books and enjoyment of literature; they count books read, books withdrawn from the library and amount of writing produced. All of these characteristics are eminently measurable and important. But comparative studies of such things have yet to materialize in the whole language camp, an omission that still hobbles the philosophy. This avoidance of scrutiny and fair study ultimately prevents whole language from making a strong case for itself. Notes Pressley: "To claim ... that measurement of Whole Language effects is impossible is to place the study of reading instruction on par with the pseudo-scientific pursuits of UFOs, out-of-body experiences, and poltergeists."

In spite of this lack of research many whole language advocates claim that their approach works best with disadvantaged kids and will help achieve "a democratic state of free, autonomous, empowered adults." Lisa Delpit, a black activist and former teacher from Mississippi, challenges these notions: "There is little research data supporting the major tenets of process approaches (such as Whole Language) over other forms of literacy instruction, and virtually no evidence that such approaches are more efficacious for children of color."

What Teachers Think

Teachers have mixed views on whole language. This is largely due to its inconsistent and individualistic practice. The fact that whole language fails a great many children, particularly at-risk children, also explains why so many teachers dispute the philosophy's wholeness.

From Mary Osler, a reading specialist with a private practice in Toronto:

Every time I enrol yet another child, illiterate after two or three years of so-called education, every time I read yet another report labelling a child as learning disabled rather than teaching deprived, every time I read a recommendation that expectations be lowered, self-esteem raised and "modalities" addressed in order for a child to learn, I mean to write [the perpetrators of this nonsense]....

I have read countless reports on children subjected to batteries of tests to determine why they have not learned to read. Among amorphous terms and questionable "diagnoses" applied to place the blame squarely on the child is frequently that of "low self-esteem." These children's self-esteem is indeed shaky, as a consequence, not a cause of failure. My job is to teach them to spell, read and write. Their self-esteem blossoms. They bound in the door twice a week, at lunchtime, after school, before school. They give these sessions priority over birthday parties and hockey games.

My method is simple; the goals are clear. Thus, the children's attention is absolute and enthusiastic. The responsibility for their learning is mine: their job is to work hard, and this they do with great verve. Every child becomes a competent reader. On average, they gain $8/10$ of a grade in oral reading, $9/10$ in silent reading and $7/10$ in spelling for each ten hours of instruction....

My approach draws on theory, experience and common sense. Children used to the practice of "whole language," and mired in a Goodman/ Smith swamp, rarely LOOK AT a word, let alone examine it for information its structure might contain. I teach phonics and classification and their direct application to word attack. Guessing and memorizing are replaced by logic. When the children read from a story book, I sometimes cover the illustrations until the page is read—this vital mechanical stage is not a "guessing game."...

From Sharon Palermo, an elementary resource teacher in Halifax:

What whole language teaches, in fact, is that children learn to read by using the "whole" language, of which phonetics is a part, but only a part. Together, interest, need and semantic and syntactic context play a more important role. The latter two of these, along with pictures and story line, are necessary for the interpretation and prediction of meaning, and can often be used more easily and sensibly than can phonics....

Thousands of students are not learning to read, and thousands of conscientious teachers are looking for methods that work. In some cases phonics does work. In others it doesn't. We have a very large adult population of illiterate people who came up through phonics. We also have a current population of students with "conscientious" phonics teachers who are not learning to read. But for some reason their teachers continue in the way they think best. What they are ignoring are the two most basic principles of whole language: interest and need. If the interest is not there, if children do not have some need to read—i.e., they love books, they want information, they see reading as something valuable to them—then phonics is going to be one more horribly boring, authority-imposed, educational stupidity in their minds....

The Great Debate

In academic circles the whole language controversy largely boils down to three important issues—reading is meaning, reading is natural and phonics is unimportant—and the lack of solid research to support these assumptions. Hence the controversy.

Phonics is unimportant. The research says that instruction—phonics and sound-letter matches or what some educators call "the code"—makes the learning of beginning reading a sure thing for most children.

In a 1967 review of reading research from 1912 to 1965 Dr Jeanne Chall at Harvard University found that phonics worked better than "look-say" or whole word approaches that emphasized context first. Noted Chall: "A code emphasis method, one that views beginning reading as essentially different from mature reading and emphasizes the learning of the printed code for the spoken language—produces better results at least up ... to the third grade.

"The results are better, not only in terms of the mechanical aspects of literacy alone, as was once supposed, but also in terms of the ultimate goal of reading instruction-comprehension and possibly even speed of reading."

Ever since Chall's ground-breaking report, study after study has reconfirmed her results. In 1990, after reviewing more than six hundred studies on beginning reading instruction, Marilyn Adams concluded that phonics matter a great deal and that presenting phonics first works: "When developed as part of a larger program of reading and writing, phonic instruction has been shown to lead to higher achievement at least in word recognition, spelling and vocabulary, at least in the primary grades, and especially for economically disadvantaged and slower students."

Reading is natural. Many whole language advocates contend that reading is as natural as learning to speak. Surround a kid with books and he'll read, they say. Their reasoning goes as follows: written language is language—babies acquire language, like magic, by casually using it; oral language is learned incidentally; therefore, written language is learned incidentally.

Respected linguists, psychologists and educators do not agree. For starters, written language is not language but a symbolic representation of language and as such is a rather recent cultural invention. They also argue that babies learn how to speak with the help of some very direct instruction provided by special tutors: Mom and Dad. Withdraw those teachers and not much language is learned.

So reading, like tying a shoe, another cultural invention, requires some instruction if it's going to be mastered, and some children will need more teaching than others. Nearly half a dozen studies in the last ten years have proven that children who are given early training in phonemic awareness (that's the ability to handle sound units smaller than a syllable) will become good readers and spellers. One famous Danish study found that early kindergarten training in phonemic awareness totally reversed one school's dismal track record in reading achievement.

Outside of whole language circles, the reading-is-natural argument no longer has much life. Writes Michael Pressley: "In the 1990s no one with an informed opinion takes seriously that humans evolved to be able to read and write, given print and literary experiences. Reading and writing are clearly piggy-backed on to other psychological functions that developed in humans for different purposes. In fact biologists who have thought hard about the issue are convinced that explicit instruction is required if people are to learn to read and write."

Reading is meaning. Ken Goodman's contention that beginning readers rely on context to figure out words is fiction. Several studies have shown that only poor readers, who don't have the skills to sound out, will compensate by making wild guesses, miscues and predictions. In contrast good readers decode so fluently that they don't need to depend on the context for word recognition. Concluded a 1985 study of barely literate adults: "What is true of children learning to read is true of adults.... Adults who have never acquired skill in phonemic segmentation will remain poor in decoding and will not develop in reading and spelling beyond an elementary level.... They remain poor readers despite general cognitive maturity, experience with written language, and adequate general intelligence."

Keith Stanovich, one of Canada's foremost reading researchers, says the context or meaning theory is dead: "Over ten years this finding is one of the most consistent and well replicated in all of reading research." So learning how to read depends on one's ability to decode or sound out letters. Guessing is really not part of the game unless you can't read.

Politics

Most parents aren't aware that when they question the effectiveness of their school's reading program they are walking into a minefield. In fact, few issues in education have become as politicized as beginning reading.

Monopolies generally don't welcome dissent or criticism, and whole language is no exception. Great publishing fortunes and academic careers are at stake. As a consequence, education professors quote Frank Smith or face ostracism in many universities. In many schools, principals transfer first grade teachers caught using phonics to higher grades. And in many communities parents who politely request phonics instruction for their children often receive excuses instead.

The monopoly also ensures that teachers are poorly trained. Few faculties let teachers know that there are many alternative reading programs that might make a difference in the classroom. The kind of explicit instruction required for Reading Recovery, Robert Slavin's Success for All or any Direct Instruction program, of course, is not favoured by whole language trainers. So, too, is the explicit teaching of comprehension strategies. But a good reading teacher needs to know that there is more than one way to teach reading.

It seems that many whole language enthusiasts do not believe in pluralism when it comes to reading instruction. They repress data and opinions critical of their own. They champion supportive testimonials and ignore studies critical of whole language. They dismiss critics as "phornicators" and phonics as "thalidomide for the mind." They mandate one approach for teachers and castigate those who dare challenge it as being "right wing" or politically naïve. Even researchers haven't escaped the name calling. According to Pressley, those who differ are labelled "uncaring political manipulators who engage in repression." One prominent whole language guru even publicly suggested that the only way to deal with respected researchers like Marilyn Adams was to "forge a silver bullet, for that is what is needed to kill a vampire." Such behaviour makes a mockery of whole language's fuzzy commitment to "dialogue and emancipation," and marks many whole language advocates as academic bullies and hypocrites.

The insensitivity of the whole language monopoly has not escaped the attention of the Canadian Psychological Association, which represents more than four thousand psychologists. In 1993 the CPA released a five-page position paper on the subject that ruefully notes that one reading approach dominates the provincial lists of approved elementary school textbooks. (The only readers approved in British Columbia, Manitoba, New Brunswick, Newfoundland/Labrador, Ontario, Prince Edward Island and Quebec belong to the whole language camp. Alberta and Nova Scotia each list one phonetic series, while Saskatchewan lists two.)

The Association has adopted two sensible positions: that all ministries of education provide school districts with a balanced selection of phonics and whole language readers, and that teachers and primary consultants carefully select beginning reading materials that match children's needs. As the position paper correctly states, "children at risk for reading failure" and children from homes poor in language development often "require more structure and greater emphasis on phonics than most whole-language programs provide."

Copies of the paper can be obtained by writing the CPA, Chemin Vincent Road, Old Chelsea, Quebec JOX 2NO. Telephone 819-827-3927.

Whole language and phonics are entirely compatible. There is no reason why daily writing, good literature (fiction and non-fiction) and systematic phonics instruction in grade one, for those students who need it, can't be part of the same program.

Whole language has its legitimate successes: the integration of reading and writing and the emphasis on good books. But these practices now suffer from gross inconsistencies from grade to grade, poor assessments and little accountability.

By clinging to nonsensical practices that penalize many normal and at-risk children, the whole language establishment not only discredits what is whole in whole language but also undermines faith in the public school system. Ordinary people expect schools to teach their children how to read, usually by the end of grade one. When bad whole language practices fail to achieve this end with any consistency, the public school system loses supporters it can no longer afford to lose.

Parents can't fight this issue alone. But as members of reform groups they can press provincial governments to adopt the recommendations of the Canadian Psychological Association. And they can lobby school boards to combine the best of whole language with excellent phonics instruction and one-on-one remediation, if necessary, to ensure that all children leave school highly literate beings.

See also **IMPRESSIONS, PHONICS, PHONEMIC AWARENESS, READING, READING DISABILITIES, EFFECTIVE SCHOOLS** and Appendix 7.

Sources

Why Johnny Still Can't Read by Rudolf Flesch is still the best and most readable book on this issue. But if parents presented only one article to their school boards or trustees, I'd suggest "Romance and Reality" by Keith Stanovich. It appeared in *The Reading Teacher* 1993 (47, no. 4). This journal is available in most main public libraries. (Dorothy Pullan's "Whole Language—Exploding the Myths" also makes good reading and is in Appendix 7.)

To get a taste of Ken Goodman, go back a few years in *Reading Teacher* 1992 (46, no. 3) and check out "I Didn't Found Whole Language." It speaks volumes about the holes in whole language.

YEAR 2000

PHILOSOPHY is a big word. Sometimes, too, it is a dull word. And all too often, sadly, a hollow one. Not so the PHILOSOPHY OF THE PRIMARY PROGRAM.

—Year 2000 document: FD:357

The *Lumby Valley Times,* a small community newspaper in British Columbia's dry interior, recently ran a report on an imaginary Year 2000 track meet. Most parents know Year 2000 as a controversial multi-million-dollar program to reform the province's public school system. With an eye to the future and "changing societal conditions" it aims to "serve the interests of all students" with a novel mix of non-graded classrooms, co-operative activities, anecdotal reports and a commitment to "lifelong learning."

Reflecting this bold design, the newspaper's Year 2000 track meet strangely eschewed standards and competition. As a result, the high jump came with no bar, because hitting it "could produce an attitude of failure." The sprint came with no set distance, because participants should feel free to run in any direction and as far as they wish. Ball throwers merely placed the ball in the spot where it "felt right." And so on. In the end, everyone received a big trophy with everyone's name on it. "This is to better prepare our young people to be successful in our non-competitive society," concluded the *Times.*

The paper's ruthless mocking of Year 2000's educational philosophy reflects two sober realities: that educational reform in British Columbia has definitely gone off in the wrong direction, and that many parents with children in the school system feel mightily betrayed. Although educators still champion Year 2000 as "the biggest educational change in 150 years," the program has become so mired in paper (450 documents in one year alone), politics and notoriety that even the ministry of education admits that the future of Year 2000 remains problematic. "Nothing is written in stone," now cautions Jerry Mussio, the province's director of school programs and one of the program's key bureaucratic guardians. "The need for clarity is a major issue.... We are still modifying a lot of proposals."

The public has also modified its initial response, from one of polite confusion to open hostility. While more than thirty ad hoc groups have sprung up across the province opposed to the plan's child-centred approach to learning, private schools report huge increases in enrolment. Many teachers, wearied by the program's "fatuous buzzwords and phrases," openly predict its *demise* by the year 2000, if not sooner. "A lot of people are unhappy with the educational system," notes Ron Adams, a school trustee and investment broker in Salmon Arm. "Year 2000 has become a catch-all for what's wrong in our schools."

Promoting preposterous classroom practices was never the intent of Year 2000. The program is, in fact, a part legitimate and part bastard child of the 1988 British Columbia Royal Commission Report on Education. Headed by the late Barry Sullivan, a respected lawyer, the broad-ranging study lamented the province's high school dropout rate (34 percent) and recommended a series of "adjustments" to help the system better serve those students not destined for university.

According to Thomas Fleming, the commission's editor and chief researcher, Sullivan prescribed no "Royal Road to Learning" and made no calls for "ambitious new social or educational engagements." He did, however, suggest that schools focus more narrowly on educational objectives than at present, and that there be a common curriculum for grades one through ten. Sullivan believed that educators must make room in the school system to accommodate different educational ideologies within the context of serving the public will.

More important, the commission recommended a system with "loose and tight properties": loose in the sense of giving schools greater freedom and choice to decide how best to meet the needs of the local community; tight in the sense that the government would set the standards and assessment procedures. Sullivan clearly wanted a results-driven school system that would "free the great human resources found in and around schools from the weight of conflict and uncertainty."

In this regard the commission never made specific proposals, but instead recommended giving local schools the authority to try new approaches "on an experimental basis" without having to come, cap-in-hand, to Victoria for permission. In retrospect, Fleming now admits "that it may be argued that the commission's recommendations about curriculum and instruction were not as well balanced intellectually as those in other areas."

The result: an effort to encourage diversity and higher standards simply became another monolithic and badly executed attempt by government to change an entire school system with centralized directives that no one understands. Adds one disgruntled educator: "The real purpose has just been blown away."

This dangerous and dramatic shift in purpose partly reflects uneven leadership. Since its inception, Year 2000 has passed through the hands of three education ministers (two Social Credit and one New Democrat) and four deputy ministers. None of the originators remains anywhere on the scene.

The drift away from Sullivan's original proposals also reflects the program's new, heady ambitions. Supporters and critics alike agree that Year 2000 has become a highly complex menu of theory, practice and jargon all geared to replace the shape and focus of education from kindergarten to grade twelve with three ungraded composites: primary (kindergarten to grade six), intermediate (grades seven to ten) and graduation. Based on the theoretical works of modern psychologists including John Bradshaw (*The Inner Child*), David Elkind (*The Hurried Child*) and Jean Piaget (*The Playful Child*), the primary program has noisily colonized most of the province's schools with non-graded "environments" where groups of children of varying abilities and ages now playfully collaborate.

Though the intermediate program has been launched in fits and starts, the ministry has sent it back to the drawing board because of its profound lack of meaningful content that, as one reviewer noted, threatened to reduce the program to "the Trivial Pursuit model of Curriculum." The graduation program, when completed, will be likely to include little Year 2000 philosophy because neither secondary teachers nor universities can stomach it. Declared a review of Year 2000 by the University of British Columbia's Faculty of Arts: "The philosophy of the program erodes attempts to achieve academic excellence."

The child-centred dogma driving Year 2000, primarily that children can learn great things in a vacuum of

standards and expectations, is not new but a mishmash of progressive ideas that have been floating
around schools for nearly thirty years. Some tenets are
harmless, while others read like a Social Darwinist
recipe for penalizing children who need structure and
good teaching. One Year 2000 primary resource guide
explains that learning is simply a natural and enjoyable activity that demands "examining one's beliefs
and knowledge." Each and every child should be able
to proceed at his or her own pace in an individual
style, adds the guide. It also suggests that learning is
really a matter of students constructing their own
knowledge and reasons for learning. To survive in
such a progressive milieu a child needs to be a highly
motivated self-starter with good language skills. Given
the child-centred bias and the guide's total avoidance
of standards (it offers only "developmental
sequences"), one teacher recently wondered in a
provincial union journal if "there is a place for the
teacher in the Primary Program."

In the absence of consistent stewardship, and given
the haphazard manner in which school policy is made
today, the process managers won the day. So, too, did
the dynamics of democratic consultation. In the interest of fairness, the government took into account
every special-interest group with a stake in education—some twenty associations in total. But the actual
task of writing school programs for the primary, intermediate and graduation levels fell to three distinct
steering committees, composed largely of teachers,
social workers and school administrators. Because of a
profound lack of leadership, these three groups largely operated without regard for the public interest.

"They came in without reading or understanding
the Sullivan commission and served their own interests," notes one observer of the consultations. "They

didn't balance the left or right, the progressive versus the traditional, and so the entire process tilted to the child-centred and progressive side...." Asked if public policy hadn't unwittingly become too much a captive of the people responsible for its implementation, Jack Fleming, a former assistant deputy minister of education who oversaw many Year 2000 developments, simply responded: "I don't totally disagree."

The self-interested, if not self-absorbed nature of the exercise became readily evident in the government's 1992 review of the primary program's design and philosophy. Not only did three members of the primary steering committee also serve as members of the Primary Program Review Consulting Group, but five of the seven reviewers appear as key sources in ministry documents supporting Year 2000. Not surprisingly, these reviewers commended the government "for an extraordinary document ... very up-to-date," one "which embodies the very latest findings." Notes Doug MacDonald, the chairman of the Vernon chapter of Concerned Adults for Responsible Education, a new group opposed to Year 2000: "There just wasn't any objectivity. The reviewers of this thing just fed off themselves."

What the reviewers missed in their blissful "congruence"—another Year 2000 buzzword—appeared in a seven-page article last year in the *Journal of Curriculum Studies*. After commending the program's stated goal of making schools more "learner-focused," the author, Roland Case, found that Year 2000 suffered a bad case of "vagueness, ambiguity, redundancy, contradictions and jargon." The program's assumption that intellectual development was simply a matter of building on the knowledge and experiences that children brought to school, he wrote, was "flawed," "misleading" and a contradiction of the very meaning of the word *education* ("to lead out"). Added Case, an assistant professor in the faculty of education at Simon Fraser University: "Absent from their view of learning is an appreciation of the public standards that govern intellectual inquiry. Significantly, the document acknowledges that the term *challenge* is mentioned rarely, if ever, because it connotes a summons from without, not from within." (The words *study* and *student* also don't appear.)

Blinded by self-serving reviews, the ministry pressed on with an avalanche of pronouncements ("a paper thunderstorm," noted one rueful teacher) that obscured a number of important distinctions. The government, for example, never mandated non-graded classrooms or multi-aging as compulsory reforms. They were merely "suggested options," says Jerry Mussio. He adds frankly that the current program has been compromised by "a confusion of ends and means" in the system. (Critics say it's more a matter of the program being captured by means, with the ends omitted.) But the sheer proliferation of blue and green documents on suggested classroom practices—a field that education ministries in most provinces have wisely left to teacher discretion—led many educators to believe that non-graded classrooms were the new Holy Grail. Administrators, eager to appear progressive or improve their chances for promotion, quickly impressed the "suggested options" into their schools.

In the resulting flurry of innovation, the ministry also neglected two tenets of good school reform: quality control and control groups. Although some six hundred lead schools initially received special funding in 1988 to adopt a child-centred program, these beacons for Year 2000 were never matched with an equivalent number of schools pursuing academic excellence through alternative or traditional methods. Nor did the implementation of Year 2000 come with a quality control mechanism to ensure that the innovations were actually improving teaching and learning on a weekly basis. Without such controls the ministry will never be able to say with any accuracy how well the progressive theories embodied in Year 2000 really serve the interests of children or society. But in the absence of proper controls, supporters of the experiment, such as Simon Fraser education consultant Patricia Holborn, continue to ask parents to be incredibly forbearing about their children's future: "I hope everyone will let this system run for eight years and then decide if it works."

Another omission comes in the difficult but important realm of assessment. Even though Year 2000 arrived in many primary classrooms more than five years ago, the province still has no formal method for evaluating student or teacher performance, let alone the program's own strengths and weaknesses. Although one of the program's original documents came with the subtitle "A Curriculum and Assessment Framework" and a commitment to stating "intended learning outcomes," the testing and measuring component got waylaid. Even Jack Fleming, who retired from the ministry six months ago, can't understand the delay. "The assessment process has lagged a bit ... and is not well developed," he says. Others familiar with the ministry say that the British Columbia Teachers' Federation's long-standing mistrust of testing or quality control (an attitude not shared by many teachers) accounts for Year 2000's missing assessment component. Consider, for example, this statement by Steve Naylor, past president of the B.C. English Teachers' Association: "Teachers feel that the notion of levels of reading and writing is inappropriate because it leads to the assumption that some students cannot perform certain tasks and that something must be done about language instruction to correct these deficiencies."

Contrast British Columbia's assessment process with Kentucky's. With one of the worst school systems in the United States, Kentucky has revamped kindergarten to grade three with a "learner-focused" program, borrowing much of the B.C. curriculum in the process. Nevertheless, it won't introduce any more innovations until the state has good reason to do so on the basis of two kinds of assessment. The first, a so-called authentic testing system, requires students not only to solve problems (say, in math), but to explain their reasoning in writing.

In conjunction with achievement tests and other formal or informal monitors, the authentic tests are then carefully graded against a common standard. (This system can become highly subjective and inconsistent unless teachers are well-trained and the testing carefully standardized.) The state has also given each school a "benchmark" based on test scores, dropout rates and attendance, and the percentage of students who make a successful passage to the workplace. Schools that improve their benchmark performance get monetary bonuses; those that fail either receive intense supervision or get shut down.

No such system of accountability exists in British Columbia and none seems poised to give Year 2000 teeth or purpose, even though a version of authentic assessment for writing, at least, is in the works.

What is most damning about the Kentucky comparison is that British Columbia could easily adopt the same level of accountability. The province keeps profiles on all its schools that include the results of tests that all students take in grades seven, nine and twelve. It also tracks 20 percent of the student population that moves from school to school. But without any leadership or will the assessment component of the educational system has been left in limbo.

Because the primary program was chiefly designed by teachers, and often very good ones with twenty or thirty years of experience, it comes with a formidable built-in vulnerability. Much of what is suggested in Year 2000 can work, but only with the kind of energy and expertise that would severely test the average teacher or novice. Notes Susan Hargraves, the former principal of Sundance Elementary School in Victoria: "A system that depends on people with twenty years of experience in order to succeed is not going to work."

Hargraves has a unique perspective on Year 2000 that is now lacking in most educational quarters. Her school experimented with many progressive tenets, such as multi-aging and integrated lessons, long before they became provincial fads—only to learn their real limits. For starters, her school discovered that self-esteem does not spring from accentuating the positive or avoiding comparisons. "We had a kind of conspiracy of what we would tell the kids by over-exaggerating the good things." But ten-year-olds who couldn't print numbers one to ten or identify upper-case letters of the alphabet knew that "our enthusing didn't match their feelings. They knew they weren't measuring up." The result was that progressive theory achieved the opposite of its intentions: low self-esteem. "Year 2000 shouldn't mean you don't give children honest feedback," argues Hargraves.

The other lesson that Sundance took to heart was that learning doesn't occur magically. "It isn't enough to remove desks and group children together and somehow expect learning will occur. You need a framework.... I think direct instruction and whole class teaching are still two of the best ways to help children move ahead." Hargraves, a maverick, would like to see public schools committed to the best of traditional and progressive methods. "It's not one or the other."

Such common sense could have surfaced long ago had Year 2000 been rigorously debated among educators instead of becoming a religious enthusiasm with utopian ambitions of helping children become "life-long learners" for the new millennium. (Fads in education take on the appearance of evangelical revivals.) Dissent is simply not welcome in the Year 2000 camp. "In my opinion," recently wrote Penticton high school teacher Peter Kruse, "the Year 2000 and its proponents are imposing a form of tyranny where criticism is met with the despotism of righteous indignation, where dissent is suppressed by intolerance and ridicule, and where the ultimate effect on the dissenting voices is the harshness of alienation and stress. As a result common sense has become the victim and we all need to be concerned."

Even school trustees, the system's elected watchdogs, "got blitzed with the gospel of Year 2000," says Ron Adams. When the trustee suggested at one annual general meeting of the British Columbia School Trustees Association that there be a debate on the pros and cons of Year 2000, he was abruptly told that "a debate would be inappropriate" because trustees were 100 percent behind the plan.

Many school administrators have expressed similar fears of democratic discourse free of "educanto" and other jargon. "Instead of answering the concerns of citizens with respect, certain educators take questions as a form of criticism, with the result that the questions go unanswered and more parents' groups are formed," says Moyra Baxter. As the president of the B.C. Confederation of Parent Advisory Councils, she supports much of Year 2000 but believes that educators have failed to talk to parents honestly and directly about the program. Even though the councils have the authority to advise schools on any matter—another Sullivan recommendation—Baxter finds that "the parents are being told that they can't bring certain things to the table.... It's a conundrum."

The ministry of education is now keenly aware of the maelstrom it has unwittingly unleashed among the province's schools. Jerry Mussio, who has been responsible for shepherding Year 2000 for only a year, promises there will be more clarity and consistency in future Year 2000 documents. The failure of anecdotal reports to report anything meaningful is under review, he says. The government also plans to get out of the business of telling teachers how to teach and provide instead what government is good at: guidelines on expectations, standards and ways to measure them fairly. "The ministry has done a poor job of communicating things in simple terms," admits Mussio.

It is unlikely that such changes, however laudable, can restore the trust that has been lost in the public system or honour the truly subversive spirit of the Sullivan Commission. Perhaps the real reason Year 2000 degenerated into a silly track meet characterized by psychobabble about no winners and no losers is that Sullivan intended his adjustments to identify some definite losers in public schooling. In fact, his vision of a "tight and loose" school system would probably have ended the need for school boards, centralized bargaining units or one big teachers' union—all educational players that have supported Year 2000.

A school system that truly respected the different needs of different children by offering both traditional and progressive ways of teaching would also have killed public education as a monolithic enterprise addicted to fads, enthusiasms and bigness. But in letting educators set public policy, the province allowed them to detect and derail the true intent of Sullivan's recommendations. Instead of diverse community-based schools meeting challenging provincial standards, as Sullivan intended, parents suddenly found their schools participating in a uniform Year 2000 track meet. In the process, supporters of the status quo conveniently and quite predictably put self-interest ahead of the public interest and the province's future.

See also **CONTINUOUS LEARNING** and **"INNOVATIONS" vs. "REFORMS."**

Update: In response to public criticism, the government of British Columbia has amended parts of Year 2000. It has scrapped the name as well as anecdotal report cards. It has reintroduced traditional grade levels and "structured written reports for parents." It has also reaffirmed the importance of "strong basic skills." The program's core, self-paced, co-operative learning with an integrated curriculum, and all of its attendant weaknesses remains intact.

YEAR-ROUND SCHOOLING   In any debate about school reform, parents and business leaders inevitably call for a longer school year. North Americans can't improve or sustain good academic achievement, the argument goes, if our school year averages only 190 days, compared to 200 to 240 days in Europe and Japan.

Although extending the school year may sound like a quick way to foster better learning, the solution treats a very complex subject far too simply. At issue is not only the number of days spent in school for different categories of children (many pupils have much greater learning needs than others) but the very quality of teaching that now occupies traditional timetables.

The charge, however, that most Canadian schools offer much less instruction time than they advertise is sadly correct. In 1992, a New Brunswick commission on education (Schools for a New Century) reported that the schools in that province rarely honoured their mandate of 182 days. Test schedules, professional development days, winter storms and other day-eating school events reduced the average school year to an "unsatisfactory" 161.

But such subtractions also occur in Japan. Its much-praised 240-day school year owes its venerable length to a variety of school trips, national festivities and half day classes on Saturdays. Harold Stevenson and James Stigler, two American experts on Asian schools, maintain that the actual time Japanese spend in class, although not as low as New Brunswick's, is quite comparable to the North American average.

Where European and Japanese schools really differ, though, is in actual time spent on learning a task. Japanese schools have six fifty-minute periods in junior high and five forty-five-minute classes for elementary students. During these periods Japanese pupils concentrate for 80 percent of their lesson time because teachers are well prepared, engage the whole class and allow nothing to interfere with the lesson. No hard data exist for Canadian schools, but the same study showed that U. S. children barely focus on their work for half of the lessons. Idle chitchat, poor organization, intercom messages, individualizied instruction, busy-work or discipline problems rob most American lessons of their punch.

In fact, a Japanese scholar, upon examining Stevenson and Stigler's data, expressed praise for the ability of American children to learn what they do given how little time they actually spend in academic activities.

The erosion of learning time in Canada, though not as well documented as the American experience, also has its origins both in and outside the classroom. A disgruntled high school teacher in Scarborough, Ontario, recently compiled a dismal list of time stealers in a typical day at her school. They included forty-five-minute-long conference periods (for extra help that was rarely requested), seventy-five-minute lunches, thirty-five-minute spares, sports events, special assemblies, fund-raising rock concerts and career days that featured a hockey player and a witch.

Once a teacher actually gets to class, he or she is often greeted by no more than half the students, while field trips, bouts of flu, work programs or plain old truancy claim the rest. Whether to introduce a new idea or rehash an old one in such trying circumstances is often a weekly concern. In turn, teachers may miss as many as two school days a month as a result of work-related stress, administrative hassles and professional development (questionable teacher training lectures).

In conclusion, this same teacher calculated that thirty years ago she received nine 38-minute periods of instruction each day, for a 342-minute total in high school, whereas today's students get only four or three 75-minute periods, for a paltry total of between 210 and 300 minutes. "The gap in my mind amounts almost to a fraud," she writes. "The only glaring problem with lessons given to most Ontario students is their infrequency."

Given such a common scenario, a thoughtless lengthening of the school year might very well result in more days filled with more "nonsense, trivia and truancy." This is why any move to extend the school year should follow other basic reforms that first improve the quality of teaching and the content of the curriculum. To do more of the same is probably not a healthy prescription for any school in North America.

But in addition to examining how effectively schools respect learning time and treat their teachers and students, educators should consider paring down the educational system's crowded social curriculum. Ask any teacher and they'll quickly admit that they cannot teach parenting skills, AIDS education and drug awareness programs without stealing from the already limited hours for reading, math and history.

Few educators and even fewer parents understand that every time another interest group or political agenda adds another social mission to our school curriculum—no matter how noble or good—nothing is ever done to make room for it. The lamentable result sees harried and exhausted teachers trying to do too much poorly instead of trying to teach a few things well.

For inner-city schools, however, the key issue is not only time spent "on task" but also extending learning time in ways that work for the local community. Many research studies have shown that a longer school year with fewer and shorter breaks (perhaps divided into three terms, as in Japan)—along with a longer day and week—can help disadvantaged students bridge the distance with their middle class peers by greatly boosting their retention of ideas and skills.

For the last three decades many schools have repeatedly failed children from poor and troubled families because inflexible schedules geared to disappearing rural routines didn't provide what these children needed most: more care at an earlier age and more time with proven and varied teaching approaches to mastering the rudiments of learning.

Although a longer school year in conjunction with better teaching tools is a long-overdue idea for helping inner-city school districts, other school boards might do well to give this reform less priority. Until Canadian teachers and parents have done their home-work on how local schools now use the day and to what end, then adding to the school year may simply be a matter of taking more trips to the zoo.

APPENDIX 1

Letter from a Principal

Percy Ciurluini is the principal of St. Norbert Catholic School in Downsview, Ontario. He characterizes much school administration today as a case of the "blind leading the bland." He and his staff have always strived for good schooling. This is his account of what it is like to be a school principal in modern society:

St. Norbert Catholic School
60 Maniza Road
Downsview, Ontario
M3K 1R6
393-5309

Jan. 29, 1993

Dear Mr. Nikiforuk:
This is my twenty-fourth year as an administrator, seventeenth as a principal, and the most interesting year thus far. This is not because of curriculum innovations or program changes or exciting things of any description. Rather it is because of a growing general disenchantment with school systems across the country. Media responses to the "malaise" have highlighted the feelings of thousands of people and given publicity to many "advocacy" groups. I say, "More power to the groups!" Anything which brings the most important part of our lives to public attention is fine with me. I can only respond with a personal viewpoint coupled with varied experiences in this, the most dangerous profession on earth.

I'll try to explain.

Loren Eiseley, in a Dewey Memorial Lecture some years ago, said that if teachers really thought about what they do, their hands "would become paralyzed on the classroom door." I agree with the late Professor Eiseley and would go further. We teachers are responsible for the future and that frightens the hell out of me. In my small school here in Metropolitan Toronto, I am responsible for 240 hostages to fortune. The debates raging everywhere give me pause to ponder the spectre of some future anthropologist studying our culture and concluding that, as a society, we abused our children by not preparing them for the world.

Everybody is an expert on schools because everybody has been to school...just ask them! I don't know how many conversations with parents are prefaced by: "When I was in school..." followed by comments about how good things were then and how much better schools were. I'm not about to compare but I can comment about "then" and "now."

Over twenty years ago, I was part of a staff which was at the "leading edge" of curriculum implementation and, I suppose, curriculum design. We were working together in teams to plan and explore new programs and ways of delivering those programs. Whole language was called language experience and was extremely demanding of teachers but very rewarding. Phonics was not ignored but taught as needed. Creative writing was encouraged and corrected copies only were displayed. Group work and cooperative learning were normal procedure. The school was an open complex building with all attendant problems...but we solved many of the problems through hard work, cooperation and planning. Many, many hours were spent after school and in the evenings planning and dissecting ideas, lessons, etc. The time was a magical experience, not without difficulties of course, but tremendously energizing.

I do not want to laud us for doing what we were supposed to do but rather to juxtapose that time with the present flap about educational programs. The present debate/discussion saddens me greatly. Seemingly out of nowhere whole language and active learning and student-centered learning have taken precedence...but teacher training has lagged behind. This is not news, obviously, but bears mentioning. Principals were not trained either. Of course, we are middle management and not to be trusted by our superiors about anything. Ask them.

In the classrooms good teachers will use everything at their disposal to ensure that their charges learn as well as they can. This has been going on since teachers and students first began meeting, whether on mountain-sides or in city classrooms. Good teaching goes unnoticed for the most part and I find this sad. The effective teacher is one who follows that most wonderful paradigm: "Test; Teach; Test." I think that covers it pretty well. Find out how much the kids know. Teach them. Test them to see if they learned. If they haven't grasped it, teach them.

Elegantly simple, isn't it?

It's becoming increasingly difficult to do that, though. It has been stated many times that we have more to do in schools now and I won't go into that to any great extent, except to say that it's true. A great deal has been added to the general curriculum but to my certain knowledge, not one item has been dropped from the curriculum. Yes, we have to be social workers and counsellors and surrogate parents and meal providers and, very often, the only stability for many children in a world gone awry. My response to that is to say, "All right, if that's the way it is, give me the tools and the time and get out of my way. If we must make up for society's shortcomings, help us, don't hinder."

We have our share of fools and incompetents, those who take the money and run, who are members of the Three-Thirty Track Club, who perform their duties in rote fashion....who don't care. The vast majority of the teachers I know are caring, careful individuals who consider themselves fortunate to be doing something they love. Their focus is always the child, that wonderful creature who presents a continuing challenge and a warm acceptance every day. Even the troubled kids know when someone cares. Some of the stories we hear are shattering and give us pause to wonder what happens to kids in the name of love.

I believe my job as a principal is to support my staff, to provide the logistics, to eventually work myself out of a job by making teachers independent, to take the flak which heads our way, to make the school accessible to the community as a whole, to provide opportunities for teachers and parents to develop their knowledge of the system...to do everything in my rather limited power which will increase the possibilities of children succeeding.

The Education Act says that the principal is the curriculum leader in the school, the master teacher. My colleagues and I find that ironically humorous in that it's generally the last thing that fills our time. Actually tops on the list is transportation. Problems with the large school buses, the mini-buses which transport kids to and from special classes, the kindergarten buses which provide noon hour transportation, buses for excursions, etc.

There are of course other areas of school life which drain the time from educational pursuits. I'm not sure I should even bring them up here because I don't want this letter to be seen as carping or complaining. The point to be made is essentially that the complications of modern life in our changed society have radically altered the educational system and of course, the role of the principal. Perhaps at another time this can be pursued.

Thanks again.

Percy Ciurluini

APPENDIX 2

Speech from a Teacher

Walter Scott has been teaching history for twenty-nine years and garnering numerous awards in the process. His perspective on education has been shaped by life experiences that take him far from chambers where edu-jargon passes as talk. Most of his friends are farmers or carpenters. "I have the skills and would, could I afford it, likely farm or build homes. As a result, I empathize with those who want cost-efficient, measured and measurable education and are frustrated by what they see as a lack of accountability there."

He gave the following address in 1993 while accepting a Teacher of the Year Award from the *Toronto Sun* and the Ontario Institute for Studies In Education:

"Education in the 90's—Is it Working?"

I am personally a very optimistic person who has a lifetime of reasons for feeling positive about education in Ontario's past, present and for the foreseeable future.

Please bear this in mind because I intend to use the bulk of my allotted time to focus upon what I see to be serious flaws in our educational system that require our immediate and concentrated attention.

Many of the strengths in our system stem from the fact that the vast majority of students that our society produces are great kids who are motivated and have good work habits. We have as well, in spite of the virtual absence of effective on-site quality control, a very large proportion of our teachers who are hard working, dedicated and effective, and the market has been giving us large numbers of great teaching prospects in recent years.

There are, as well, two 'keepers' in the wave of new initiatives inundating North American education today. The first of these is benchmark testing, providing that this testing isolates upon generic skills and clearly indicates to students, parents, teachers and administrators the level at which the student is reading, writing, thinking and the like. The second of these is tied closely to and is even more important that the first. It is the much more elusive intention that educational program and instructional design pivot upon cross-curricular student skill development.

I am, however, deeply concerned that we are likely to bury both of these vital initiatives under a host of peripheral priorities which frequently will not reinforce these primary objectives, and, in fact, in some instances, will run at cross purposes to them. I will return to cases in point later.

One of the most pressing concerns for teachers today is the question of the efficacy of much of what is presented to them as educational research. I and many of my classroom peers often feel that expertise in education must increase exponentially with time and distance away from the classroom, because we often have difficulty making many of these new highly touted schemes work.

Part, of this, no doubt, is the product of ineffective communication between our theorists and practitioners. It is true that we have a great deal of professional material circulated to our schools, but the in-school follow-up is minimal. Intensive in-servicing, as distinct from brief laid-on programs or voluntary workshops, is almost non-existent in most of our educational jurisdictions. Perhaps medicine can count upon its professional publications to retool and reorient medical practice—although I am not entirely confident that this is the case—but the evidence I see around me in education suggests that this is not so here. Furthermore, any business faced with the drastic product line changes we are now committing to in education, had it any concern for effective customer service and bottom line performance, would almost certainly involve a significant proportion of its personnel in a far more comprehensive retraining process than we here have even begun to contemplate.

Even more ominously, this failing is compounded by the fact that education, as an academic discipline, is, in relative terms, still in its infancy. When one advances new ideas in the sciences or established humanities like history the idea has to run a veritable gauntlet of criticism before it is accepted. Unfortunately, neither much of the apparatus, nor tradition to ensure that this happens to educational research is in place. Therefore, when many of these new and seemingly tested ideas appear to contradict common sense you have very good reason to be sceptical. In fact, you as trustees, educators and concerned community members had better take a very critical approach and require that the promoters of these ideas deal clearly and directly with your common sense concerns. Far too often, should you do this, you will be providing the first real resistance that many of these ideas will have encountered.

Normally the field testing that is done for these ideas has been conducted either by stakeholders in the new approaches, or by enthusiastic, talented and optimistic volunteers who can normally make almost anything work in the classroom. Consequently, most of these initiatives need both cross-sectional testing spanning a realistic spectrum of classroom settings and the adequate equivalent control testing of alternative approaches.

Destreaming offers us a case in point here. We need to see it in operation in schools which have not either been deliberately staffed for the experiment, or where the teachers have not volunteered to serve as pilots. We need, as well, to have parallel streamed controls which offer integrated, skill-focused programs. We then need to do the testing to assess comparative skill development, maturation, and the like. Even here the assessment would have to be external and neutral because the reporting processes, the pass rate policies and the testing approaches that I have seen to date used for the destreamed settings appear to be self-fulfilling.

The course of action we have, unfortunately, committed to will see us engaging in a province-wide experiment with no effective control options.

I am not defending the status quo here however—far from it. We shouldn't lose sight of how tremendously flexible our existing credit system can be. For instance, we could readily design and implement two credit compulsory core programs for grade 9 students in language skills (reading, writing and keyboarding) and in applied arithmetic and scientific logic which would require hands-on shop experience, or for a Self and Society program which would use the student's immediate milieu to develop the thinking skills necessary for situational analysis. These programs could and probably should be staffed and operated independently from existing departmental structures. Parallel sequential programs could and should be devised for grade 7 and 8 as well.

Ironically, it is the coupling of destreaming and this skill focus that gives destreaming much of its allure for educators and it is even more ironic that the mechanics involved in creating and operating the requisite instructional design for these destreamed classes will likely, in spite of benchmark testing, undermine this intent. Indeed the task focused, co-operative learning format should be and is becoming a major instructional component for streamed classes. Here, this format runs much less of a risk of being resented by students and, as a result, being severely compromised or abandoned by teachers.

Unfortunately the process that many of our educational jurisdictions are using to create these interdisciplinary programs is likely to make a bad situation here much worse. These programs, at least in the intermediate term, appear to be shaping up as collages of these centred topics contributed by a variety of competing disciplines, smothered in a myriad of objectives. The resulting experience for students, teachers, parents and the community at large may prove as uncomfortable as our earlier 'open-concept' scenario. Sadly, real, coherent, truly 'transitions' programs which offer reasonable prospects for success even in a destreamed environment seem destined to get short shift here.

An obvious case in point is the Self in Society transitions component which could and should, at the grade 9 level, be built around the existing Living in a Changing World course. This program starts with the student, his or her immediate surroundings, the people, the customs, the jobs, career opportunities, the institutions, etc. found here and the value systems generated by this milieu. This program is naturally and necessarily interdisciplinary in its own right. Student interest and focus could be assumed here and integrated skill development could be readily given centre stage. However, what we are most likely to get in most of the province will be some eclectic combination of Family Studies, Health, Guidance, Business, Twentieth Century Canadian History, Canadian Government and Canadian Geography content and teachers will be scrambling to rationalize and deliver the product.

In sum, what we need to do, if there is any way we can manage it at this late date, is to step back from the proscribed time lines for this province-wide destreaming experiment and allow *properly* scrutinized pilot schools, rather than all of our schools, to work through these difficulties.

As indicated earlier, I welcome benchmark testing, but the format we utilize must avoid the pitfalls I have seen in the existing T.I.P. (OAC assessment) approach. Our T.I.P. programs have tried to do far too much. They are intended to control the quality of the OAC programs we deliver, to test teaching quality and to ensure and to assess student mastery of a range of requisite skills and course content. Ironically this attempt to ensure minimum standards in all of these areas, apart from the justified criticism that can be levelled at some of these standards, tends to lead, too often, toward these minimum standards from both ends of the performance spectrum. No doubt skill and process deficient programs are jolted, but ominously, many very good and some outstanding programs have had to be seriously compromised, or jettisoned in the interests of conformity. This complex testing process has also invited the type of abuse that is unacceptably unprofessional.

We need province-wide tests that are straightforward, that isolate upon generic skills and that tell students, their parents, their teachers and the community exactly where the student stands. The implications of this type of testing for programs and teaching will be obvious. But these tests should not be the final exams, or even mid-term tests for programs which should be tailored to accommodate unique community and classroom needs.

As serious as the concerns that I have focused upon to this point are, they pale in significance in comparison to the last three areas I wish to address. These crisis situations are made much more ominous because they have attracted so little of the attention requisite to even beginning the process of change.

We must, particularly for our secondary schools, define in real and workable terms the expectations that we as a province and as individual communities have for student commitment and behaviour in our schools. We must, as well, spell out the approaches that we will be taking when these expectations are not met. Simply put, we need to design 'bottom line' criteria for student behaviour and effort and to create more effective and much more cost-efficient alternatives for the students who fall short. Almost all, if not all, classroom teachers would agree that a few behavioral problems in a class can virtually neutralize the efforts of your best teachers and almost totally undermine the programs of your average and weaker teachers. In all of these cases the academic cost to the vast majority of our pupils is unacceptably high. Our existing approaches address only a small minority of these situations and are very costly in teacher, vice-principal and resource personnel time and too frequently offer little more than 'bandage' solutions.

We need something akin to 'in-school' correspondence programs for these students who routinely disturb their classes. The existence of this type of program and the blunt choice that it presents to the student might, in itself, reduce problem behaviour and confrontation. The upshot of removing behavioral problems from the class setting would pay massive educational product dividends. In particular, general level programs, which too often have to contend with far more than their share of these problem students, would have a far better chance of meeting the objectives they were designed for.

Secondly, as a community, a system and as a profession we have paid virtually no attention to effective on-site quality control for education delivery.

We, too often, have 'revolving door' administrations whose primary focus is the system rather than their school. The two normal three to five year 'postings' to a school makes long term ownership for staff profiles and the matching of professional development with individual needs well nigh impossible. In fact serious problems here are far too often simply overlooked. This situation, as well, virtually mandates consensus policy-making of the lowest common denominator kind. In sum, in this setting it is rare indeed for the principal to be the 'principal teacher'.

The reverse side of this same coin has seen the building of expensive administrative superstructures which spend much of their time and effort defining and defending their 'raison d'être' and remove too much of even routine decision making one or two steps further away from the students, the teachers and their schools.

Better that we have principals who are, on one hand, empowered to be principal teachers and, on the other, are held accountable for their and their school's performance.

We also need a small second management level in our school which is directly responsible for curriculum and teaching performance. Our existing secondary school department structures are far too fragmented and our department heads exercise little more than moral leverage. Here we should both reduce their numbers drastically and turn the five or six that are necessary in a secondary school into administrators who are responsible for and given the means to ensure the quality of programs and classroom teaching.

The ministry, in turn, must re-examine our Board of Reference parameters and the legal constraints which hamstring administrators when they try to deal with poor teaching. Our students and the system should never have to put up with less than adequate teaching. The possibility that all of us should be hired on performance-specific terms contracts should at least be considered. It is indeed ironic that a profession which tells its students to prepare for career changes seems unwilling to countenance this for teachers even when it is in the best interests of almost all concerned.

Finally, we must make room for the excellent new and potential teachers that the market is currently offering our schools. To shut them out now and over the next few years will almost certainly divert this flow of outstanding talent not only for the next three years, but for years to come. The damage here to our system may well prove even greater than any of the other problems that we have focused upon to date.

In review, we have a significant number of strengths in our existing scheme of things, even though, unfortunately, many of these are more the product of fortunate 'happenstance' rather than conscious design. This situation, however, offers us the luxury of time to deal with the concerns raised in this address.

All of us owe it to the positive course of educational reform to take a much more constructively critical approach when we scrutinize the various proposals before us. We have, also, to look at what really happens in a typical classroom to realize just how important student behaviour and work ethic is to what can begin to be accomplished here. If we do we won't be able to ignore the imperative that the system must do much more to provide the wherewithal to modify or neutralize negative classroom behaviour. Lastly, we owe it to our society, our kids, and, indeed, our teachers to effectively monitor and ensure consistently good teaching, to deal directly and effectively with inadequate teaching and to, at the same time, find ways to bring the wealth of new, very good teachers into the field that are presently on the doorstep. These are the issues which are at the real hub of effective educational reform.

APPENDIX 3

Essay from a Parent

Elsje de Boer, a native of Holland, lives in the mountainous interior of British Columbia, where she runs an informal community daycare for several children. One of her charges is learning disabled and another has fetal alcohol syndrome. De Boer, who was educated in a Montessori school, makes this candid analysis on where so much progressive schooling has gone wrong:

Why are Children such Animals

Much is said and written these days about why and how children should be taught. Radio and television, books, magazines, all carry programs and articles about education. While parents for the most part still expect their children to learn "the basics", that is, basic literacy and numeracy skills, and maybe a smattering of science, history and geography, those in the teaching professions now claim that the primary purpose of the school is to socialize the child and to foster creativity, cooperation and self confidence. Happy, self-directed students are motivated to learn at their own pace, they argue.

Those who contend that the free-wheeling, unstructured and ungraded child oriented schools of today fail to give their students a sufficient grounding in the basic literacy and numeracy which are so essential in our increasingly technological society are asked indignantly if they would prefer to return to the old method of rote learning. Usually, this effectively shuts down the dialogue because the question is based on a false premise. It is like asking if you want your house painted pink or purple, as though those were the only options.

Any discussion on how children ought to be taught without a thorough examination of how children learn is, in my view, as pointless as a discussion of treatment plans for a patient before a diagnosis has been made.

Few today would deny that man is a social animal. Like the buffalo, the goat, the sheep, the lion, the zebra, the wolf, the elephant and the howler monkey, man lives in groups. This necessitates some very significant modifications of his behaviour.

In herds accumulated knowledge can be passed from one generation to the next. In moving with the herd, young animals learn where the best grazing/hunting is, where the watering holes are, which routes to take. Jackdaws must learn from the flock which animals are predators constituting a danger, and monkeys learn which foods are edible and which poisonous. It is essential for their very survival that young animals learn these lessons and learn them quickly. The compulsion to act in concert with the herd and do exactly as the others do is therefore very strong. This compulsion to do what the herd or group or society does constitutes a powerful motivation for a child to learn.

Robert Ardrey in "African Genesis" shows that systems of dominance are characteristic of all animal societies. This was extensively documented by Konrad Lorenz in the case of jackdaws. Lorenz shows that dominance or rank supersedes feeding, nest building and mating instincts in importance. Robert Ardrey confirms this from research with other species. For the human species, "the roles of territory, of dominance and of society (herd) in the play of our ancestral animal instincts exist without question" (African Genesis p. 169).

The basis of rank can differ from species to species and even in different populations of the same species. No one would deny that the feudal system was one of rigid rank decided by the accident of birth. Once a lord, always a lord, once a serf, always a serf, with only minor opportunities for change. In escaping this system North America's pioneers vowed to do things differently. No more class system: there would be equality for all. There are still people who argue that whereas Europe has a class system, North America does not. I suspect there are many who would vehemently disagree with this assertion. Natives, Blacks and Mexicans come to mind.

Even in Europe the feudal system with its inherited rank has fallen into disrepute. This does not mean there is no ranking system. Respect (which is merely another word for rank) in Western Europe comes to those with learning. In Holland, my best friends are farmers both with a grade 6 education. When their children were small, they would point out my father, a professor: "See, there's the perfesser in his study. You learn good in school, one day you'll be smart like the perfesser." This seems to be the prevailing attitude. It isn't here.

Our educators are quick to contend that competitiveness in academics may be good for those who are doing well but is devastating for those who are not. They should stop kidding themselves. The kids know. They don't need a teacher to tell them they are not learning as well as the rest of the class. In fact, the duplicity of the teacher who assures them they are doing fine when they know very well they are not may well compound the problem. Besides, those at the bottom of the pecking order do not compete with those at the top. No golfer has yet quit because he could not compete with Arnold Palmer, and no skier stays home because he is not as good as Alberto Tomba. Most of us try to keep up with the Joneses, not with the Conrad Blacks. Children, like athletes and animals, compete only with those closest to them in rank.

Students in Dutch schools and probably in other Western

European countries as well actively strive for good marks because good marks and a good education are the measure of rank. Consequently, their school drop-out rate is considerably lower than it is here, but there are other consequences as well. Teen pregnancies are rare and school violence is unheard of except on American television. The incidence of child alcoholism and drug abuse is also significantly lower than it is here.

Canadian schools have made a concerted effort to eliminate academic competitiveness. All students are supposed to be equal. And so prestige or ranking in the class room is no longer established by academic achievement, but ranking is a biological imperative.

Deprived of the opportunity to establish rank by means of academic excellence, our kids have to find other ways, and they will look to the society they live in to see how these things are done. For the majority of our children, such information is obtained from the television. What matters on television is power. Raw power. The power of money, of "pull," of brute force, the power of weapons. There is a premium in our society on being the Macho Male, and it is not lost on school children. What about the girls? Simple. What matters for girls is looking sexy, being desirable, and getting laid. And that, too, is not lost on school children.

Now here is a paradox. In our attempt to lower the drop-out rate we have de-emphasized academic achievement and rendered it irrelevant. Rather than encouraging school attendance this may well be at least a contributing factor to an increasing drop-out rate: there is little incentive to learn when learning is irrelevant. In our attempt to promote non-violence we have tried to eliminate competitiveness from academics and in doing so we have forced students to find other ways to establish rank or pecking order. We should not be surprised if, following the example they see on television, they reach for switchblade knives and fire arms to do so, nor should we be surprised at the lengths to which girls will go to be sexually attractive.

What we see is that the propensity for violence in schools is inversely proportionate to the demand for academic performance. This is borne out by a number of inner city schools in the United States. Situated in some of the worst neighbourhoods and operating under some of the worst conditions, these high schools reinstituted discipline, dress code, respect and emphasis on academic achievement. Students are required to say "Yes Sir" and "No Sir," wear a shirt and tie and do their homework. Violence, truancy or non-compliance result in expulsion. Period. Few expulsions were necessary. Students now take pride in their school and in their work, violence and drug abuse in the school have vanished. Deprived neighbourhoods and disfunctional families notwithstanding, academic results are excellent.

These schools give their students precisely the sense of belonging and the values by which to establish a pecking order which they might otherwise have sought in a youth gang, a cult, or a Neo-Nazi group. It is fashionable to say these youths are searching for an "identity;" perhaps it would be more apt to say they are looking for "identification." They need to belong somewhere, be accepted by a group on any terms rather than not belong at all, and to adopt the values and customs of the group and its ranking system. There is an obvious social advantage to having that ranking established by intellectual braggadocio rather than switchblade knives and promiscuity.

Even a cursory look at the statistics shows that something in our educational system isn't working. Illiteracy is on the rise, the drop-out rate isn't dropping, violence is on the increase and there is no let-up in teen pregnancies. Maybe it is time for a change, maybe even something as radical and revolutionary as a renewed emphasis on academics.

Fauquier, Jan. 15, 1994.

APPENDIX 4

A Brief to Ontario's Royal Commission On Learning
Jack McCaffrey and Lorne Hicks are two very articulate Ontario high school teachers. Trained by Northrop Frye, they understand the meaning of a good curriculum and have lived the consequences of a bad one.

No Possum, No Sop, No Taters
(No Curriculum, No Standards, No Hope)
by Jack McCaffrey and Lorne Hicks

Preamble
The writers of this brief are two teachers, not educators. Educators are often teachers who escape the classroom and shortly thereafter begin to have brilliant ideas which they would like other people to carry out. We have both had the experience of getting away from teaching for a half year or so, and have found that after a few weeks two things happen: we forget what it is like to be in the classroom, and we start to see with startling clarity just what teachers should be doing. Upon returning to the classroom, we find that the ideas which seemed so clear and obvious are difficult, if not impossible, to carry out. This latter experience is unknown to the educator, and is one of the key things that separates an educator from a teacher. The following analysis and suggestions, therefore, will differ from those of educators in our having come to them while still in harness.

We have both taught English in the same high school since 1970. Coincidentally, while working on our master's degrees, we both studied with Northrop Frye, a great teacher whose ideas are out of fashion with the truly hip. As a result of such limiting experiences, we cannot claim to speak for anyone other than ourselves.

Outline
Our brief will make the following points:
1) There is no curriculum in English in Ontario;
2) There are no standards in English in Ontario;
3) The response to these problems has been nothing but an expensive exercise in public relations;
4) These problems are not insoluble.

1) No curriculum
When we were in high school—a time which now seems to us as remote as Dr. Arnold's at Rugby—Ontario had a curriculum in English. It specified which texts a teacher had to teach in each grade. It included composition and traditional grammar, for which specific amounts of classroom time were set aside.

Some educators found this restrictive and even fascistic. In the late sixties the famous Hall-Dennis report changed everything: Presto—no more curriculum. Teachers were not free to respond to the individual needs of their students. This often took the form of analyzing the poetry of the Beatles.

Operating from a different perspective, Frye, in spite of the new dispensation of Hall-Dennis, devised a complete curriculum in English which was incorporated into a series of textbooks by Harcourt Brace. This curriculum—quite different from the old traditional Ontario curriculum—emphasized the teaching of myth and poetry, as Frye believed that they were at the heart of all literature. He insisted on the primacy of literature because it is the repository and highest form of language of imaginative possibilities. Frye also believed that literature is based on certain structures and principles which could be taught to anyone. But he was certain that to do so, a teacher would need a sequential curriculum, which he spelled out in detail.

But Hall-Dennis and the sixties revolutions had already intervened, and Frye's wisdom was jettisoned without ever being tried. Instead of a structured, sequential curriculum, we have had a series of guidelines, which carefully avoid mentioning any literary works or any specific body of knowledge of any kind. Instead they list long series of seemingly worthy, but vague, goals which students and teachers "should" work toward.

As the study of English in Ontario since 1968 has required the mastery of or even nodding acquaintance with no particular content, it has been possible—and too often the practice—that students have graduated without ever having read any Canadian book or any poem whatever. For many students, English has consisted of a random heap of novels chosen at the whim of the individual teacher.

When all content is optional, any particular knowledge is unnecessary. Students rightly wonder why they should study hard stories of the olden times by Dickens when their friends down the hall are playing with pipe cleaners to learn non-verbal communication.

Teachers continue to try and teach English, but without any firm principles or definite knowledge to be communicated and mastered, they sometimes feel as if they are blundering along in the dark. In our school, each grade has a book list, from which teachers are free to choose as many—or as few—texts as they please. Each teacher makes up his own exam. Only by means of random lunchtime conversations do we ever know what our colleagues are doing. Some of us get the definite impression that no one really cares what we do.

Along one wall of the English office stand shelves of novels. If you were the fly on the ceiling, you would from time to time see grown men and women studying this wall of books. This is the planning of the curriculum.

If other schools do things differently, it is purely by chance, as no particular content, methods, or procedures are absolutely demanded.

The only thing you can count on in the Ontario English curriculum of the last quarter century is the abandonment of any ordered or sequential learning of grammar. Grammar is held to be a choker of creativity. All the studies, we are repeatedly told, show that a knowledge of grammar is useless, although very few teachers that we know have actually read these studies, nor have we heard of any studies that show that grammar is harmful.

Instead of specific poems and novels, instead of a sequential, structured study of grammar, instead of any specific knowledge of any kind, the Ontario curriculum in English consists of aimless reading and writing, with no knowledge of the terms necessary to discuss or improve either. In other works, we have no English curriculum.

2) No standards
With the abolition of external exams, we have had no particular standards in English for 25 years. Of course, when you have no curriculum, you don't need standards: teachers do not have to teach or students learn anything in particular, and so there is nothing to test.

With no definite content to master, and no particular abilities to acquire, students do not know what they are aiming for, except a "credit." With the absence of any external check on what goes on in our classrooms, we should not be surprised that many of our graduates are illiterate. Many of them cannot write a short paragraph of correct sentences. With no knowledge of grammatical terms, teachers cannot point out and help the students to correct deficiencies in their writing. We are reduced to saying, "You can't write that. Try this instead."

Even native speakers graduate knowing very little of a precise nature of their own language—they have no control over it. Even if they can read and write in a basic fashion, many of them cannot do so in a sufficiently critical and competent fashion to function successfully as citizens and as workers.

Even if teachers attempt to teach and grade according to some personal notion of a standard, their efforts are negated by night school and summer school, where students typically earn much higher marks for work of less quantity and quality than they do in the regular classroom.

Students at night school and summer school howl with outrage if their marks are below 80%.

WHY DO WE HAVE NO CURRICULUM AND NO STANDARDS?

The Ontario Ministry of Education has 2000 bureaucrats who promulgate endless guidelines, but never absolutely demand and ensure that anything in particular happens.

From the board and the ministry we have had no leadership during our entire careers. Perhaps any attempt at leadership at this time would fail, as teachers have no reason to have any faith in the Ministry, which has not once provided anything of use. Neither has the plethora of superintendents and coordinators at the board level. We do not even know what they do, except hold meetings.

3) Public relations as an attempted solution to the problems

School boards know that the public is suspicious and unhappy about what goes on in schools. But no board would want to say that there is something wrong about what it is doing. Neither would teachers' unions. To do so would mean accepting responsibility for the errors and working to find a solution.

Instead, both boards and teachers' unions have engaged in a war of PR, advertising, and propaganda, with endless prattling about excellence in education. Everyone claims to be doing the finest possible job. No overt admission of error is allowed. But the storm of "mission statements" and advertisements and the installation of mall-like signboards outside schools might betray something more than just an ardent desire to communicate with the public. Oddly enough, when curricula and standards existed, none of this public relations effort was necessary. Perhaps the existence of curricula and standards communicated the schools' purposes.

Strangely enough, the universities don't believe any of the propaganda. They find themselves bewildered about how to admit students, knowing very well that an 80% from one school is the equivalent of a 90% from another. In the absence of any known standards, the universities are faced with two possibilities: the creation of a giant database linking marks of students from each school with the university marks of the same students, or the institution of university entrance exams. Before 1968, no one would have contemplated the need for either.

Neither do businesses believe the tales of excellence. On the contrary, much anecdotal evidence suggests that businesses find our graduates illiterate.

But the public relations campaign continues.

4) Possible Solutions

Perhaps it is time to abandon the grand experiment of "individualized" education and attempt once again a provincial curriculum in English. As one of our colleagues has remarked, the relations between teachers and the Ministry of Education have been characterized by growing acrimony. Accordingly, for a curriculum to seem to have any validity, it might have to be created by actual working teachers rather than educators, bureaucrats, or administrators.

We are aware that to prescribe an exact sequence of texts in the old way would seem downright bizarre, with visions of Nazi goose-stepping arising in the brains of some teachers and educators. But a curriculum could specify types of literature to be studied, while giving considerable latitude in actual titles. Perhaps one specific novel and a dozen specific poems, at the least, might be demanded at each grade level, if only to create the impression that some things matter. Students would at least share some elements of culture beyond television.

Would some minimum knowledge of basic terms and rules in grammar actually harm students? Could we perhaps experiment and find out if some specific knowledge of this kind might be useful in the discussion and improvement of student writing?

Might even spelling once again be formally taught?

Whatever the minimum requirements in each grade, we will need a specified allotment of time for these requirements— perhaps half of classroom time, leaving the rest for optional content.

We cannot see how we can have a real curriculum without standards enforced by external exams. Otherwise, how does anyone know whether the curriculum is being taught, let alone how well?

Conclusions
New benchmarks or standards without a curriculum and external exams will change nothing. And nothing has changed in the last 25 years in our teaching experience, except that teaching English has become increasingly hopeless, dramatically so in the last couple of years.

APPENDIX 5

A School Vision

Calgary's Woodman Junior High School is exactly the kind of high school to which most parents would like to send their children. It is bright, smart and responsive. Lead by the charismatic Larry McIntosh and a dedicated staff, Woodman could well become a charter school. The following documents represent what administrators should be doing and what parents should be looking for in good schools:

WOODMAN JUNIOR HIGH SCHOOL
A VISION FOR A SCHOOL

Over the past decade, there has been new research into the fields of teaching and learning that suggests that we must shift our focus from that of being transmitters of knowledge to being facilitators and enhancers of learning; that not only are the students learners, but also the adults within that school. Each school is now encouraged to look at education from the standpoint of the student, to relate to the unique needs within that school. At Woodman we believe that a change has to occur. Business wants it, but hasn't yet forced it; legislators want it, but haven't yet mandated it; parents and communities want it, but haven't yet demanded it. Teachers and administrators at Woodman, however, not only want it, but are ready to make it happen. This change will meld the unique needs of our students with our own beliefs about teaching and learning.

We perceive a need on the part of our parents to be assured of quality, structure, and discipline, in the education of their children.

We have high expectations for all our students. We have high expectations for achieving academic goals and standards. We have high expectations for behavioral performance. We believe that a healthy, caring school climate that is SAFE for everyone is the responsibility of educators, students and parents.

We want to present a school in the academic mold where great importance is placed on achieving high academic goals for all students, whatever their ability level. Learning and teaching are the focus not only for students, but also for all adults in the school community. Woodman is a school which values and celebrates learning and teaching in all areas of the curriculum. QUALITY PROGRAMS, based on the Alberta Education Program of Studies, are offered in all subject areas. Teachers are using innovative and creative ways to engage students actively in the learning process. Students and teachers work collaboratively to integrate subject areas where appropriate, thus breaking down the traditional fragmentation of disciplines. Students see connections and relationships among the skills and processes being taught in different subjects. Some of the units developed by our staff are being used as models by teachers from other schools. We want to continue with the high standards we have so far achieved (47% of our students had an average above 75% during the year).

Woodman students will find success at what they do and will strive to do their best. They will be in a SAFE ENVIRONMENT where they will be able and will be EXPECTED to do their best. Woodman will present itself as a high achieving, committed, highly motivated school in academics, athletics, and citizenship.

In order to achieve our vision of Woodman School, a SIGNED CONTRACT between parent, student and the school will see that the concepts we present will be followed.

A values contract will be featured. Students will see that clear expectations, a sense of responsibility, self-evaluation, team spirit, a sense of challenge/purpose, where students are seen as individuals, and values that are about striving, serving, and caring, will lead to an outstanding education.

The Calgary Board of Education has a process whereby students may apply to a non-designated school by mid March of the school year. We see the process continuing for Woodman applicants.

We feel that it would be necessary to "close" the school as of June 30 and "re-open" around the concept we have presented, in September.

There must be a committed staff to make a true alternative work, and this can only be achieved by an open selection of staff. We would hope that any staff could apply to teach at Woodman and that all staff would be in place by April 1 for the following year.

With the students' help, and the help of their parents and the community, we will strive to make Woodman a truly outstanding, effective, caring school.

WOODMAN JUNIOR HIGH SCHOOL

CARING FOR STUDENTS IN A STRUCTURED LEARNING ENVIRONMENT

FUNDAMENTAL CONCEPTS AND ORGANIZATIONAL FEATURES

1. PERSONALIZED EDUCATION FOR ALL STUDENTS
CONCEPT: All students, as individuals, will be challenged

and supported to reach their full potential.

FEATURES:
- Individualized student support by means of the same teacher/advisor throughout the student's junior high years
- Remedial and enrichment clinics to provide academic support and challenge concept
- Comprehensive diagnostic and standardized testing/feedback program to determine individual academic abilities

2. A STRUCTURED LEARNING ENVIRONMENT

CONCEPT: Most students learn best when clear expectations for achievement and behaviour are given.

FEATURES:
- A code of behaviour will be presented to each student, and a contract signed agreeing to abide by this code
- Achievement expectations and assessment procedures will be clearly defined at the beginning of each term
- Teachers will give homework and will monitor it closely
- Supervised, after-school, homework hotel and resource areas for research and for students falling behind in their work
- Compulsory physical fitness monitoring

3. CURRICULUM PACKAGING FOR A COMPREHENSIVE EDUCATION

CONCEPT: Students are best prepared for the future demands of society when they study a broad range of subject disciplines.

FEATURES:
- Quality courses in the fundamental subjects of mathematics, science, language arts and social studies
- A study habits module that is integrated into academic subjects
- Pre-international Baccalaureate and advance placement programming
- Integration among subject areas

- Thinking skills and problem-solving skills and process skills integrated into subject disciplines

4. CLOSE LIAISON WITH PARENTS

CONCEPT: Schools function best when parents and teachers work closely together.

FEATURES:
- A strong parent-advisory council
- Progress reports on each student issued 6 times/year
- Parent/counsellor meeting concerning specific family impediments to learning, including family therapy if necessary
- Parent volunteer program

5. SCHOOL SPIRIT PROGRAM

CONCEPTS:
1) The development of personal, social and leadership skills is critical for life-long learning
2) School spirit and a sense of affiliation with the school are essential for high student morale and motivation

FEATURES:
- Specific training for student leaders
- Active student activity council program
- Teacher sponsored extra-curricular sports, clubs, and fine arts opportunities
- Teacher/parent sponsored field trips and activity days
- Personal dress requirements designed to foster a sense of responsibility and pride in one's appearance

6. MAXIMIZING PROFESSIONAL RESOURCES

CONCEPTS:
1) Teachers deliver the most dynamic programs when they are professionally challenged, supported and trained on an on-going basis
2) Teachers are most effective when they work as a collaborative team that establishes and maintains a common in-

school learning culture
FEATURES:
- Teaching practices will focus on the development of the total student
- Guest lectures and community resources will be utilized to the maximum to support curriculum
- The counsellor will institute a program designed to raise self-esteem and reduce emotional impediments to learning

7. DIRECT LIAISON WITH OTHER INSTITUTIONS
CONCEPT: Curriculum should flow smoothly from elementary school, through junior high, to high school
FEATURES:
- Direct liaison with elementary schools to ensure student readiness for this program
- Liaison with high schools to follow the progress of former Woodman students, thus ensuring that curriculum is more than adequate to prepare students for secondary school
- Close links with community resource agencies when in-school programs do not provide sufficient help for the student
- Articulation between Woodman and community schools: Science Buddies—Eugene Coste; Leadership Haysboro; Science Fair—Woodbine; Fine Arts Performances—Wise Wood

WOODMAN JUNIOR HIGH CONCEPTS

Some of the concepts and features that will make Woodman Junior High School experiences unique are:
1. Individual challenge and support for students
2. Clear expectations and consequences for achievement and behaviour
3. A well-rounded education where the program reflects a broad range of skills and subject disciplines

4. Close liaison with parents so the school program will be responsive to their priorities
5. A structured extra-curricular and school spirit program where students can experience high motivation and develop social skills
6. A safe, orderly school environment where students are encouraged to achieve to the best of their ability

---

WOODMAN JUNIOR HIGH
VALUES CONTRACT

WE CARE
- About ourselves; our personal achievements, our appearance, our conduct
- About other students and adults in our building as individuals and as groups and teams
- About our school, the school program, the school atmosphere, the school building
- About our families and community

WE STRIVE
- To achieve to the best of our ability in all subjects
- To prepare ourselves for the world of work
- To pursue personal physical and mental fitness
- To become quality Canadian citizens
- To establish positive relationships with our peers and adults within Woodman

WE SERVE
- Ourselves by taking personal ownership for our education
- Our fellow students by participating in leadership groups and/or supporting their activities
- Our families by assisting in quality communications between home and school

WOODMAN JUNIOR HIGH SCHOOL
CODE OF BEHAVIOUR

ATTENDANCE AND PUNCTUALITY
Regular, punctual attendance is essential to academic success. Students are expected to attend all of their classes. Students who are absent are required to provide documentation and take personal responsibility for completing assignments and activities missed.

ACADEMIC EXPECTATIONS
In order to reach their academic potential, students must bring required materials to class, participate actively and positively in class activities, and complete assigned homework.

RESPECT FOR OTHERS
Cooperation, mutual respect and trust create a positive school environment for growth and learning. Students are expected to be courteous to and tolerant of others.

RESPECT FOR PROPERTY
Students are expected to respect and care for the property of others. Damage to, theft of or misuse of school or personal property is unacceptable behaviour.

RESPECT FOR SELF
Junior high students are not old enough to legally purchase tobacco or alcohol and the use of tobacco, alcohol or drugs impairs the student's ability to make sound judgments, to concentrate and to learn. Users of these substances will not be permitted to attend Woodman.

WOODMAN JUNIOR HIGH SCHOOL

AN ALTERNATIVE CALGARY BOARD OF EDUCATION PROGRAM

LETTER OF UNDERSTANDING AND AGREEMENT

After carefully reviewing the Woodman brochure, we, the undersigned, accept the concepts and features as defined in the brochure and commit ourselves to these conditions. Some of the conditions are:

1. All Woodman students will study an approved Alberta Ed. curriculum package and follow an approved timetable as defined. As part of student responsibilities, students must do homework and use the student planner.
2. All Woodman students will comply with personal dress requirements in keeping with goals of developing employment readiness and a unique school culture.
3. All Woodman students will be required to pay a student activity fee which covers membership and special services related to the co-instructional program. (Cost - $50.00 per year)
4. All out of area Woodman students agree to comply with the conditions of alternative attendance as stated by the Department of Planning, Calgary Board of Education.
5. All Woodman students will be required to attend regularly and be punctual for all classes.
6. All Woodman students will "Strive, Care, and Serve" as part of the Values Contract.

SIGNATURE OF UNDERSTANDING AND COMMITMENT

DATE OF COMMITMENT:
STUDENT SIGNATURE OF COMMITMENT:

PARENT SIGNATURE OF COMMITMENT:
TEACHER/ADVISOR/MENTOR:

WOODMAN JUNIOR HIGH SCHOOL

INSTRUCTIONAL MANAGEMENT
BY MOTIVATION

1. Clear expectations for student decision making are
   defined within a structural framework
   EXAMPLES:
   A. Understanding and agreement on the conceptual
      framework of Woodman by both parents and students
      is achieved by a formal contract
   B. Specific evaluation expectations are spelled out at the
      beginning of each course and printed on report cards
   C. Student planners are required and homework is to be
      completed
   D. Compulsory requirements are periodically reviewed
      with students by their teacher-mentor

2. Students are taught a sense of responsibility by providing
   opportunities for them to take ownership in their educa-
   tion
   EXAMPLES:
   A. Providing a timetable in which students seek enrich-
      ment/remediation
   B. Requiring students to make self-assessments on report
      cards

3. Students are taught to perform self-evaluation or intro-
   spection and make adjustments based on feedback on an
   ongoing basis
   EXAMPLES:
   A. Individual progress is assessed on a regular basis in
      mentor-monitor group
   B. Individual progress is assessed by each student and
      confirmed by the teacher each semester

    C. A one-on-one interview is completed with each student once per semester

    D. Exhibitions of student work provide integration and self-evaluation

4. Students are encouraged to develop a feeling of belonging or team spirit
   EXAMPLES:
   A. Participating in the same mentor-monitor group throughout their junior high careers
   B. All students are encouraged to join co-curricular activities
   C. Regular participation in cooperative learning

5. An on-going sense of challenge or purpose with appropriate strategies for students
6. Emphasis is placed on the importance of students as individuals
7. Values are fundamental principles upon which the entire motivation structure is based

WOODMAN JUNIOR HIGH SCHOOL

EXTRA CURRICULAR

A wide variety of opportunities for co-curricular involvement is offered in the fields of sport and culture. Woodman students are encouraged to balance their school experience with a variety of co-curricular activities. All clubs and teams depend on student commitment.

CHECK YOUR INTERESTS AND PLAN AHEAD
Aerobics
Art Club
Band

Cheerleading
Cross-country
Drama
Environment
Fashion Show
Fine Arts
Grad Committee
Jazz Dance
Skiing Trips
West Coast Trip
Stage Crew
Student Council
Gymnastics
Newspaper
Reach For The Top
Badminton
Basketball
Chess
Choral Groups
Fitness
French Club
Athletic Council
Library
Photography
Radio
Recycling
Science Club
Track and Field
Volleyball
Yearbook
Leadership
Wrestling

APPENDIX 6

Notes from a School Reformer

Jennifer Logan, a Calgary mother with three children assembled these random notes. Her quirky and sometimes funny observations express a deep frustration with the assumptions made by progressive educators. Her notes also show to what extent the direction of modern schooling has already alienated many good parents:

THINGS I WISH I HAD KNOWN
(instead of having of learn them the hard way)

AGES 4, 5, 6 ARE CRUCIAL

With each subsequent child it becomes more and more apparent that the ECS (ECS means Kindergarten in Alberta) experience (as it currently exists in my children's elementary and probably most others) is far from satisfactory. The children all seem capable of so much more than the free flow between different play centres. In fact, some seem to crave "real school work" (daughter #3's words during ECS).

I now realize that there are windows of opportunity when it comes to children learning the basics. When these windows are missed the effort to learn the basics more closely resembles remedial learning than that excited new learning that occurs when the child first shows she is willing and ready and wants some help.

I have been told repeatedly that repetition is boring, worksheets are dull and boring, that direct phonics instruction is uninspiring and unnecessary but my young children consistently show me otherwise. I am always amazed at the quiet intensity with which they attack these sorts of activities with me at home or while playing school with their bigger sisters. These repetitive activities seem to comfortably reinforce the learning that has already taken place.

MEMORIZATION IS A SKILL THAT NEEDS TO BE DEVELOPED. I don't believe that learning to memorize anything impedes "real learning." If anything, it sharpens the mind and enhances other forms of learning. Opportunities to memorize are becoming extremely rare at any grade level.

EVEN ECS AND GRADE 1 STUDENTS NEED TO BE CHALLENGED. It is almost insulting the way the school assumes that the children (particularly the younger ones) can't withstand the rigours of intellectual stimulation. They are also protected and insulated from frustration and failure by not experiencing any "right answer" learning.

While receiving our training a few years back in preparation for volunteering in the ECS classroom, we (the parents) were told that when we were working with the children on any writing exercise they like to ask after having written a word, "Is it spelled right?" We were instructed that under no circumstances were we to answer in the negative (no matter how creative the spelling). The appropriate response was, "that's wonderful ECS spelling." Needless to say, most of the children were not impressed with that approach. They asked a simple question expecting a simple answer.

I BELIEVE TEACHERS SHOULD EXPEND MORE TIME AND ENERGY ACTUALLY TEACHING THE CHILDREN TO READ INSTEAD OF WAITING FOR THE MIRACULOUS EVENT TO OCCUR "WHEN THE CHILD IS READY." This waiting for the child to learn rather than teaching the child is much like a swimming teacher informing the parent of a nonswimming child that the child will not be taught water safety rules. Nor will the child be taught the basic stroke and kicking techniques. The child will simply be surrounded by all that lovely, inspiring water and the child will not only learn to swim on her own when she is ready but she will learn to love to swim and will be a lifelong swimmer.

I now become very uncomfortable when the school informs me that teachers no longer teach anything to the children. That is not their job. Their job is to facilitate learning. Children are to be responsible for their own learning. While I encourage and support the development of a responsible attitude in my children I realize that no child should shoulder that kind of responsibility on their own. Encouragement, praise, challenges, assessments, etc., need to come from the teacher. This does not impair motivation, responsibility, creativity or anything else. It simply clarifies the student/teacher role and allows the child to experience the sheer joy of learning something new.

Unfortunately, I realize that it is essential to school-proof your child prior to grade one. I would never consider letting the school get their hands on my child without first doing my best to teach the child to read and handle numbers with confidence. So much is missed when the child has to wait to enjoy the learning that takes place using reading as a tool.

CHILDREN NEED STANDARDS AND CLEAR EXPECTATIONS. No damage is done to the young ego by simply showing the child the correct way to hold a pencil or the correct way to form letters with printing. The expected move to cursive Division II is almost impossible when the child still can't print with any ease. My nine year old daughter informs me that this all comes down to just "getting off to a good start."

I believe there are CHRONOLOGY PROBLEMS with the strong emphasis on problem solving and higher level thinking skills before the child has had a chance to learn the basics. This becomes very obvious in math. What kind of meaningful problem solving can take place without some kind of grounding in the basics.

BEWARE OF RESPONSE JOURNALS. School practise indicates a near obsession with the child's feelings. When your child spends more time writing about feelings about math than actually doing any math she seems more likely destined for the therapist's couch than a science lab or a business boardroom. I have discovered that my children sometimes feel quite uncomfortable continually having to share their personal feelings. Their privacy is not being respected.

ASSESSMENT seems to have become an incredibly complicated issue. We are led to believe that the problem is so complex that it is near impossible to tell how a child is doing with any certainty (or objectivity). Too many variable factors coupled with uncertain standards leave parents in the dark much of the time. When report card time rolls around we learn about our children's enthusiasm (my daughter bubbles according to her teacher) and about how much her teacher enjoys having her in her class. Precious little information is given about her academic performance. The school seems more comfortable dealing with her emotional, personal and even her physical development than the one area where a parent really needs help monitoring—her academic progress. I believe that any teacher of experience has a very good idea of the academic goals appropriate to the particular grade level. Those goals in concert with the curriculum expectations could conceivably lead to a detailed checklist that could be systematically worked through over the course of the school year. At any given time a parent or teacher could tell what the child has accomplished and what is yet to be accomplished.

I question also the constant self-assessment that the student is supposed to do. All the self-esteem building exercises come into play at this point. Every child is doing great!

THE BELL CURVE IS NOT OBSOLETE. It is merely human nature manifesting itself. To gear learning so that each student experiences the same level of success is to create artificially low standards. No longer is the pursuit of excellence a possibility. By ensuring equal (and meaningless) outcomes school celebrates mediocrity.

ARE WE ALL SPEAKING THE SAME LANGUAGE? Educational professionals have established an elite private society. Exclusivity is ensured by the constantly changing terminology. CLASSROOM has become the LEARNING ENVIRONMENT. CORRECT SPELLING (too judgemental) is now referred to as CONVENTIONAL SPELLING. Incorrect spelling is less alarming to parents because now it is just an expression of individuality. GRADE 1, GRADE 2, ETC. (again too judgemental) is now referred to as YEAR 1, YEAR 2. AUTHENTIC ASSESSMENT—as opposed to what? ACCOUNTABILITY is often confusing. Parents know what it means and how it should work in the educational setting. Most educators unfortunately have the line of accountability working in the wrong direction.

Whole Language's Seven Myths

Dr Dorothy Pullan is a psychologist with the Toronto Board of Education and one of the few educators in the province concerned about phonemic awareness. Her excellent essay on Whole Language originally appeared in a Toronto teachers' journal, *Role Call.*

WHOLE LANGUAGE—EXPLODING THE MYTHS
Dr. Dorothy Pullan

In the process of implementing a whole language curriculum and in the interest of fostering self-esteem, many myths have arisen that have impeded the attainment of literacy for many children. As a result, the media, parents and teachers have been voicing concerns and criticisms about the education system.

MYTH ONE: Learning should be seen as fun, not work. If children experience frustration, they will not enjoy learning.

DISCUSSION: In the Fall, 1992 issue of *The Whole Language Teachers Association*, Dr. Don Holdaway, a whole-language guru, points out that: "To teach most effectively demands a humane environment, but the educator's first responsibility as a professional is to specify with great detail and precision those strategies of teaching which lead to the mastery of literate activity."

In the same publication, Dr. Lilian Katz, Professor of Early Childhood Education at the University of Illinois states: "Enjoyment is a goal of entertainment, not education. Our goal is to engage the mind of the learner in predicting, exploring and understanding experiences in order to make better sense of the world. Enjoyment is a by-product of good learning, not a goal."

MYTH TWO: Reading is a "natural" process that occurs when the child is ready. The child learns to read when immersed in the whole language program, rather than being teacher taught.

DISCUSSION: Current research reveals that children who appear to learn naturally have had an average 2,000 hours individual instruction at home before entering Grade 1. They have been encouraged to pay attention to letters and words, to realize that the printed word carries a message and to learn to print. Early literacy skills are learned in the most part from others.

MYTH THREE: There is no place in a whole language classroom for basal readers. All books must be chosen from "good" literature by the students themselves, according to their own interests.

DISCUSSION: Many children need the structure and organization of teacher-selected stories in a basal reader to guide them through the beginning stages of learning to read. Graded passages are also useful for teachers to present to students in order to confirm their observations of children's reading abilities. Teachers are professionals. They must be free to use materials that further their goals of teaching students to become independent readers.

MYTH FOUR: Students should never read out loud unless they have practised the text and know it perfectly. Otherwise, other children may make fun of them, and damage their self-esteem.

DISCUSSION: While reading is primarily visually driven, it is an auditory phenomenon. Print is oral speech written down. Thus, it is essential that children learn to make sound-symbol connections between what they see written on the page and what they hear. If reading is understood in this way, then auditory rehearsal can more readily be perceived as providing critical reinforcement for beginning readers. Children should read out loud to teachers daily so that any confusion they are experiencing in learning to read may be clarified. Beginning readers who are afraid of experimenting with new words or of making mistakes should be helped to overcome their fears by meeting challenges, not avoiding them. If reading out loud in small groups becomes a daily occurrence, children will feel comfortable. It is the role of the teacher to create a classroom environment where children learn to encourage and applaud one another for all attempts and approximations they make. Reading out loud, far from damaging a child's self-esteem, can develop self-confidence.

MYTH FIVE: Phonics should be taught incidentally, and only if necessary.

DISCUSSION: In order to extract meaning from the English alphabetic code, children must learn to decipher it. Because the English alphabet is an abstract and complex symbol system, where the sounds of words do not map one to one to the printed word, many inconsistencies abound. It is, therefore, crucial to provide beginning readers with texts that emphasize the code's consistencies. Consonants, for example, are 90% consistent. Also, as Wiley and Durrell point out, nearly 500 primary grade words can be derived from a set of only 37 rhyme families. By selecting material which gives children experience with breaking the code, teachers can help them learn to use print efficiently and to derive meaning from the context. Research shows that in early grades, the amount of time students are engaged in teacher-led phonic instruction is a strong predictor of reading achievement.

Recent research has done much to clarify the place of phonics in whole language programs. Good readers strategically use all three language cueing systems—meaning, structure and graphophonic analysis—in a flexible, integrated way to derive meaning from print.

MYTH SIX: Groups should be heterogenous, composed of students of varying levels of ability so as to avoid drawing attention to children who are less competent readers.

DISCUSSION: It is doubtful whether mixed groupings truly mask the various abilities of students within the group. Students are very much aware of their achievements and the achievements of their peers. In fact, children may misinterpret the teacher's goal for creating mixed ability reading groups and come to believe that they must avoid drawing attention to their problems. Children need to accept their stage of reading development and be comfortable with direct instruction. They need to accept the various stages of their reading development and to feel comfortable being taught with youngsters who have similar needs. Contrary to the myth, recent research indicates that homogeneous groupings may improve both the achievements and the self-esteem of slower learners.

MYTH SEVEN: Spelling should not be taught until the child is ready, and then only in the context of the student's own written work.

DISCUSSION: Fluent reading depends on the ability to recognize, effortlessly and automatically, letters, spelling patterns and whole words. Moreover the goal of all reading instruction, COMPREHENSION, depends critically on this ability. Previously learned spelling patterns make it easier for the reader to translate newly encountered words or spelling patterns automatically because s/he is already familiar with some typical structures. Thus, spelling reinforces the attainment of independent literacy.

"Invented spellings" are approximations of the sounds children hear in words and indicate that their creators are able to associate sound and symbol. In the interest of promoting creativity, children are taught to write their initial drafts of stories using invented spellings. Students who are at this stage of print literacy are capable of learning traditional spellings of the words they commonly use. It is important for the teacher to encourage children to value correct spelling as early as possible in order to develop literacy in print. Incorrect spellings are difficult to unlearn, while reinforcing correct spelling by demonstration and feedback is essential for learning to occur.

Summary

During the last ten years, the Toronto Board of Education has helped to transform classrooms into more humane and nurturing environments by implementing the whole language curriculum. The too-general nature of this curriculum has created some confusion on the part of teachers. Our students come from many different backgrounds and have had diverse experiences. These differences with which children start school have not been accounted for in the curriculum. Teachers need to have a clear understanding of the tasks children need to learn in order to become independent readers. Because each child is unique, the degree of structured materials and the amount of direct teaching needed to achieve independence in reading will vary.

The priority of the Toronto Board of Education is to provide equity and excellence in education for all children. That is why it is important to dispel some of the myths that have arisen about the whole language program and the teaching of early literacy. A student who has not **learned to read** cannot **read to learn**.

APPENDIX 8

Parental Recommendations

The University of Toronto Schools (UTS) has 450 multiracial students, a rigorous curriculum and a model teaching staff. The UTS Parents' Association believes that many of the values and characteristics that make UTS excellent could be implemented in other schools. Their recommendations, recently presented to Ontario's Royal Commission on Learning hold much wisdom:

TO VALUE LEARNING

1. Foster a culture where learning is valued.

2. Create smaller schools. Carve out smaller administrative units within large schools.
   a. Instill a sense of community by pairing older and younger students in specified activities.
   b. Cluster timetables for students taking similar programs.
   c. Have a home room, or house system, that groups students in smaller, closer units.

3. Develop a core curriculum that concentrates heavily on the traditional liberal arts and sciences.
   a. Make art/music/drama/physical education integral parts of the curriculum, at all levels.
   b. Reduce the number of options available to students in grade nine.

4. Ensure that the curriculum is presented in a way that is continually challenging intellectually.

5. Eliminate the semester system and teach only year long courses.

6. Expect students to do well, monitor their progress closely, and make them accountable for their successes and failures.

7. Make parents and teachers more accountable to each other in the teaching of students.

8. Require students to perform a minimum number of hours of community service each year.

9. Ask parents to evaluate the schools their children attend and to articulate their expectations of their children's education, perhaps using the UTS questionnaire as a model.

10. Use UTS as a model school within the Metro System and have local tax funding support the students who are admitted.

UTS PARENTS' ASSOCIATION

APPENDIX 9

Some Model Report Cards

I've spent three years searching for a good report card that made sense to parents, reflected a strong curriculum and respected the hard work of students. St. Francis of Assisi, a model school in every respect, fits the bill. Here are samples from the primary grades. The following Montessori Progress Report from Ontario's Blaisdale Montessori School is also a model of clarity as well as a good window on the Montessori curriculum.

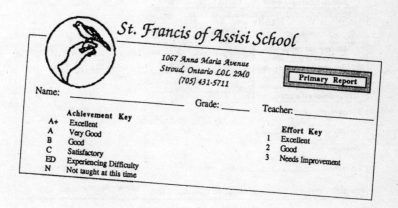

St. Francis of Assisi School

1067 Anna Maria Avenue
Stroud, Ontario L0L 2M0
(705) 431-5711

Primary Report

Name: _____ Grade: _____ Teacher: _____

Achievement Key
A+ Excellent
A   Very Good
B   Good
C   Satisfactory
ED Experiencing Difficulty
N   Not taught at this time

Effort Key
1 Excellent
2 Good
3 Needs Improvement

Core Subjects	Mid-Year		Year End		Mid-Year Report
	Ach.	Eff.	Ach.	Eff.	
English					
Listening					
Speaking					
Comprehension					
Word attack skills/phonics					
Oral Reading					
Grammar and Usage					
Creative Writing					
Spelling					
Penmanship					
Mathematics					
Concepts					
Basic Computations					
Problem Solving					
Science and Technology					
Knowledge					
Research Skills and Application					
French Language					
Oral					

Foundation Subjects					Times Late _____ Days Absent ____
					Interview Requested _____
Religious Education /Family Life					**Final Report**
Community Studies					
Music					
Drama					
Visual Arts					
Physical Education / Health					

Work Habits and Attitude

Courtesy and consideration		
Acceptance of responsibility		
Independence in work		
Work completion		
Attentiveness		
Neatness and organization		

Placement in September

Retained in　　_____

Transferred to　　_____

Promoted to　　_____

Principal's Signature _____ Date _____

Times Late _____ Days Absent ____

Interview Requested _____

Simcoe County Roman Catholic Separate School Board

EVALUATION KEY:
1. NEW PRESENTATION
2. HAVING DIFFICULTY
3. MAKING STEADY PROGRESS
4. MAKING RAPID PROGRESS
5. HAS MASTERED THE SKILL

A BLANK SPACE INDICATES THIS SKILL WAS NOT ADDRESSED THIS TERM.

PRACTICAL LIFE EXERCISES

CARE OF THE ENVIRONMENT
TUCKING IN A CHAIR ( )
CARRYING A CHAIR ( )
ROLLING/UNROLLING MATS ( )
DUSTING ( )
FOLDING CLOTHS ( )
POURING EXERCISES:
  (i) RICE-JUG TO JUG ( )
  (ii) WATER-JUG TO JUG ( )
  (iii) WATER-JUG TO 2 CONTAINERS ( )
      JUG TO 3 CONTAINERS ( )
      JUG TO A VARIETY OF CONTAINERS ( )
POLISHING:
  GLASS ( )
  WOOD ( )
  SILVER ( )
  BRASS ( )
  SHOES ( )
TABLE WASHING ( )
SWEEPING ( )
PLANT CARE ( )
FLOWER ARRANGING ( )
TABLE SETTING ( )
SPOONING BEANS ( )
SQUEEZING A SPONGE ( )
OPENING & CLOSING LIDS ( )
OPENING & CLOSING BOTTLES ( )
BASTING ( )
WHISKING ( )
CLOTHES PEGS ( )
TONGING ( )
TWEEZING ( )
WASHING CHALKBOARDS ( )
STRINGING BEADS ( )

CARE OF ONESELF
POLISHING SHOES ( )
FOLDING CLOTHES ( )
THE DRESSING FRAMES
  LARGE BUTTONS ( )
  SMALL BUTTONS ( )
  SNAPS ( )
  ZIPPER ( )
  BUCKLES ( )
  HOOKS & EYES ( )
  BOWS ( )
  LACING ( )
  SAFETY PINS ( )
  BRAIDING ( )
  HAND WASHING ( )

EXERCISES OF GRACE & COURTESY
OPENING & CLOSING A DOOR ( )
SHAKING HANDS ( )
GREETING ( )
SERVING ( )
WALKING IN THE CLASS ( )
THE SILENCE GAME ( )
WALKING ON THE LINE ( )

SENSORIAL DISCRIMINATION

THE KNOBBED CYLINDERS _____ ( )
THE PINK TOWER _____ ( )
THE BROAD STAIRS _____ ( )
THE RED RODS _____ ( )
THE COLUR TABLETS, BOX 1 _____ ( )
THE COLOUR TABLETS, BOX 2 _____ ( )
THE COLOUR TABLETS, BOX 3 _____ ( )
THE KNOBLESS CYLINDERS _____ ( )
THE BINOMIAL CUBE _____ ( )
THE TRINOMIAL CUBE _____ ( )
THE DECANOMIAL SQUARE _____ ( )
THE GEOMETRIC SOLIDS _____ ( )
THE GEOMETRY CABINET _____ ( )
    (I) PRESENTATION _____ ( )
    (II) TRAYS _____ ( )
    (III) CARDS - SOLID INSET _____ ( )
        CARDS - THICK LINES _____ ( )
        CARDS - THIN LINES _____ ( )
THE SMELLING BOXES _____ ( )
THE TASTING BOTTLES _____ ( )
THE CONSTRUCTIVE TRIANGLES _____ ( )
    RECTANGULAR BOX _____ ( )
    BLUE RECTANGULAR BOX _____ ( )
    TRIANGULAR BOX _____ ( )
    SMALL HEXAGONAL BOX _____ ( )
    LARGE HEXAGONAL BOX _____ ( )
THE TOUCH BOARDS _____ ( )
THE TOUCH TABLETS _____ ( )
FABRICS _____ ( )
THE MYSTERY BAG _____ ( )
THE BARIC TABLETS _____ ( )
THE THERMOS TABLETS _____ ( )
THE SOUND BOXES _____ ( )

LANGUAGE

CLEAR AND ENUNCIATED SPEECH _____ (
SPEAKS IN SENTENCES _____ (
KNOWS NAMES OF COMMON OBJECTS _____ (
USES NEWLY LEARNED WORDS _____ (
CLASSIFIED NOMENCLATURE _____ (

SOUND GAMES - ORAL _____ (
KNOWLEDGE OF ALPHABET SOUNDS _____ (

SHORT VOWEL WORDS W/MOVABLE ALPHABET _____ (
STUDY OF PHONOGRAMS _____ (
WRITES LETTERS ON CHALKBOARD _____ (
CAPITAL LETTERS _____ (
WRITING STORIES _____ (
PHONETIC CARDS _____ (
PHONETIC OBJECT BOX _____ (
PHONETIC PHRASES _____ (
PUZZLE WORDS _____ (

READING BOOKS _____ (
USE OF DICTIONARY _____ (
LABELLING THE ENVIRONMENT _____ (
CLASSIFIED CARDS WITH LABELS _____ (
DEFINITION BOOKLETS _____ (
SUFFIXES _____ (
PREFIXES _____ (
COMPOUND WORDS _____ (
WORD FAMILIES _____ (
ARTICLE GAME _____ (
ADJECTIVE GAME _____ (
LOGICAL ADJECTIVE GAME _____ ( )
DETECTIVE ADJECTIVE GAME _____ ( )
CONJUNCTION GAME _____ ( )
PREPOSITION GAME _____ ( )
VERB GAME _____ ( )
ADVERB GAME _____ ( )
LOGICAL ADVERB GAME _____ ( )
COMMANDS _____ ( )
SIMPLE SENTENCES _____ ( )

APPENDIX 10

A Waldorf Curriculum

As the world's fastest growing non-sectarian educational movement, Waldorf Schools must be doing something right. Here's a sample of their "lower school" or elementary curriculum. Note the attention paid to fairy tales, myths and history.

WALDORF LOWER SCHOOL CURRICULUM

In Waldorf education, teaching is regarded as an art as well as a science. This means that there must be freedom for the teacher to adapt both the form and the content of instruction to time and place in general, to the capacity of the particular children involved, and to the qualitative needs of each moment. In this sense, the Waldorf curriculum is created freshly all the time, and it can be studied not as a rule for the future, but only as a reality of the past. Following is an abbreviated curriculum outline.

Grade One

Main Lesson Subjects
Introduction to the alphabet
Introduction to reading
Introduction to the four processes of addition, subtraction, multiplication, and division, basic facts to 10
Fairy stories and nature stories (retold and dramatized by the class)

Special Subjects
French, German, music, eurythmy, handwork (knitting), games, form drawing, recitation, nature walks

Grade Two

Main Lesson Subjects
Spelling, reading, writing
Arithmetic (multiplication tables) & further work with four processes
Fables and legends (retold and dramatized, leading to composition in the child's own words)

Special Subjects
French, German, music, eurythmy, handwork (crocheting), games, form drawing

Grade Three

Main Lesson Subjects
Elements of grammar
Arithmetic
Introduction to cursive writing
Study of housing and farming
Old Testament stories (leading into history)
Measurement

Special Subjects
French, German, music (notation of rhythm & notes & rounds), eurythmy, handwork (knitting), games, form drawing

Grade Four

Main Lesson Subjects
Arithmetic (fractions)
Grammar, reading, spelling, composition, plays
Local geography & history
Study of humans and animals
Telling of Norse myths and sagas

Special Subjects
French, German (grammar and reading), music (two part songs & introduction of tenor & alto recorders), eurythmy, handwork (embroidery, cross stitch), gym, form drawing

Grade Five

Main Lesson Subjects
Composition, grammar, spelling, reading, plays
Mathematics
North American geography, Canadian history
History of ancient civilization (culminating in Greek History)
Botany

Special Subjects
French, German, music (four part recorder music), eurythmy, handwork (knitting with four needles), woodwork, gym

Grade Six

Main Lesson Subjects
Composition, grammar, spelling, plays
Literature
Mathematics, Geometry
Physics (sound, light & colour, heat)
Central & South American geography
Roman and medieval history
Mineralogy & Geology

Special Subjects
French, German, music, orchestra, eurythmy, handwork, woodwork, gym

Grade Seven

Main Lesson Subjects
Composition, grammar, spelling, drama
Literature
Algebra, geometry, mathematics

Geography of Europe & Africa
The Renaissance, the Reformation, and the Age of Discovery
Physics, astronomy, inorganic chemistry, physiology

Special Subjects
French, German, choir & orchestra, eurythmy, handwork
(handsewn garments), woodwork, gym

Grade Eight

Main Lesson Subjects
Composition, grammar, literature, drama
Algebra, geometry, mathematics
Meteorology & Climatology
American history, revolutions
Physics, organic chemistry, physiology

Special Subjects
French, German, Choir & orchestra, eurythmy, handwork
(machine sewn garments), woodwork, gym

APPENDIX 11

A Principal's Agenda

Matt Oberhofer once headed one of Calgary's top public schools. Now retired, he has lost none of his zeal and energy for upholding public education's mandate: an excellent liberal education for all. His "principal's bulletin" pretty well sums up the importance of instructional leadership in a school.

ANNEX 'A' TO PRINCIPAL'S BULLETIN 1

1. **AIM**

   The aim of this ANNEX to PRINCIPAL'S BULLETIN 1 is to emphasize and amplify the two CALGARY BOARD OF EDUCATION GOALS: GOAL 86—TO ENSURE INDIVIDUAL STUDENT DEVELOPMENT THROUGH EFFECTIVE EDUCATION and GOAL 87—TO ENHANCE STUDENT LEARNING AND TO EMPHASIZE STUDENT ACHIEVEMENT.

2. **GENERAL**

   All staff will endeavour to create a "positive climate" coupled with a strong sense of purpose in instruction. The instruction will take into consideration the different learning styles of the students and each student will be taught in a way so that the chances of him succeeding are greatest.

   All staff must work towards the development of a school which is characterized by the following features:

   1. Every person is considered to be important. His indi-

vidual dignity will be preserved at all costs. All persons in this school will be given the fairness and respect that is implied in our way of life and stated in our justice system.

2. The "whole climate" present in our school will serve to motivate every person to the upper limits of his/her individual potential. By encouraging students generally and by the encouragement of meaningful participation and by the communication of expectations will contribute to this desired "climate".

3. Encouragement will be given to all persons in the school to strive for quality of performance in carrying out their duties, tasks and responsibilities.

4. Assistance and encouragement are given to creative or gifted persons so that they might do the things of which they dream. New ideas and approaches will be supported with the resources and expertise available. Assistance and encouragement are given to those students who have a learning disability or who for some reason require remedial instruction.

5. Every effort will be made to emphasize that the learning process is meaningful and challenging. It does not necessarily have to be exciting and enjoyable but if it is, then all the better. Learning can be facilitated by effective teaching but it is important for the students to know that their individual efforts will play a major role in the degree of their success. They must be prepared to take ownership for their learning and realize that the staff will serve as catalysts.

The chances of achieving this kind of school are increased if teachers accept the following statements as having some validity.

1. At the early elementary level, the process of learning is more important than the content. By middle ele-

mentary the shift to the importance of content begins and by late elementary, content is more important than process.

2. All people want to succeed. They need but will not necessarily accept assistance.

3. All people start out a job with the intent of doing that job well.

4. When working with students, teachers must be aware of each student's personal motives—needs. These needs must be realized and attained before "teaching-learning" can take place.

5. Teachers who have a positive self concept are effective teachers. Principals must allow these people to remain the individuals they are.

6. Teachers with a strong positive self concept must be given the freedom to operate as an individual in the school.

7. Each teacher is the "principal" of his classroom.

8. A staff having varied backgrounds and interests is better than a staff of similar backgrounds and interests.

9. The Principal is more effective when he is "present" and "visible" in the school as opposed to being "visible" out of the school.

10. All people need to know "what's happening" and what is "going to happen".

11. People like to do activities that they do best and will select activities they do best.

12. When a child reacts, he reacts in the way that he learned from someone else or from a "trial and error" method that produced a reaction the child thinks he "needs" now.

13. Good example in word, dress and action is the most effective way of teaching children the socialization process.

14. All surviving societies and all Utopias depend ultimately on "work" and some of that "work" is not inter-

esting and is sometimes even boring.

15. Every subject taught must have the "thinking process" as its ultimate objective.

16. Direct contact with nature and taking part in basic physical labour helps shape a person's attitude about "life".

17. All people operate best in an atmosphere of respect, trust, openness and honesty.

18. Even in the hardest cases, all people want to "belong".

19. People feel more comfortable in a routine.

20. Not all students are bound by the same regulations. Those who are responsible, are given more freedom. Those who are not responsible, are given more structure.

21. Older students will not and cannot be expected to "do as teachers do" and "see as teachers see" or follow teachers advice BUT students do internalize teachers' actions, reactions and points of view and in later life, these students (now adults) will imitate and reflect those observed actions, reactions and points of view.

22. The younger one is, the less is the gap between "tolerating an act" and "endorsing an act". The gap widens as the student gets older.

23. People are NOT motivated by failure or the threat of failure.

24. When choosing a basic policy on student discipline and student rules, it is better to have a system that has common sense rules, endorsed by students and staff and enforced by ALL the staff. It is better to react to all violations and make the punishment very light as opposed to reacting only to serious violations and making the punishment very hard.

25. If a job needs to be done then "that" teacher will do it. There is no job in a school, if it needs to be done, that is beneath the duty of the teacher.

26. Teachers who stand up for justice and respect for

human dignity and whose lifestyle tends to side with those that have "no power", have the greatest chance of becoming successful educators.

27. The main objective when selecting staff for a school is to remember that there is a direct relationship between continuity, cohesiveness and success. The longer a group stays together, the more cohesive it becomes and therefore more successful in achieving a positive educational climate in the school.

28. Those teachers who like to listen to other people and who enjoy watching other people react as opposed to those who enjoy talking and being the centre of attraction, will become successful educators.

29. After mathematics, the most important subject is the study of history. By emphasizing history, students develop the concept of "democracy" and their responsibility in their world.

3. EXPECTATIONS OF STAFF—TEACHER'S ROLE

The professional teacher demonstrates competence in each of the following areas:

1. As a LEADER OF LEARNING, the teacher seeks to promote the educational growth and development. The teacher serves as a facilitator in the learning - teaching process, skilfully assisting each student according to his/her individual needs, abilities and interests.

2. As a MEMBER OF THE STAFF, the teacher is a participant in the total school program helping to develop overall objectives of the school and contributing to the program in such a way so these objectives can be achieved. This will involve working on committees and participating in the co-curricular and extra-curricular programs at the school.

3. As a MEMBER OF THE TEACHING PROFESSION,

the teacher has the responsibility for his/her own professional growth, and for contributing to the development of professional standards.
4. As a COUNSELLOR AND ADVISOR, the teacher, through developing an understanding of the student, will assist the student in developing self-understanding and positive self-image.

4. EXPECTATIONS OF STAFF ADMINISTRATION'S ROLE

The roles of the principal and assistant principal are leadership positions since they primarily involve accomplishing goals through the efforts of other people. Specifically, the process is working with teachers to bring about effective learning for the students. Thus, the main role of the school's administrators is to support the learning process and the role of the classroom teacher.

The administrative tasks are as follows:

1. Instruction and curriculum development
   - the assessment, development, implementation and evaluation of the total school educational program.
2. Pupil Personnel
   - the management of attendance, discipline and counselling services for all students.
3. School—Community Relations
   - the establishment and maintenance of effective communications between the staff and students in the school and between the school and the school's external audiences.
4. Staff/Personnel
   - the management of activities related to the interviewing, assignment and evaluating of staff
5. School Plant
   - the management of an efficient program of operation

and maintenance of the physical plant
6. School Auxiliary Services
   - the management of a safe and effective student transportation program and a well supervised lunchroom program.
7. Organization and Structure
   - the coordination of planning and scheduling for the purpose of complying with such regulations as CBE POLICY AND REGULATION, ALBERTA EDUCATION POLICY and ALBERTA EDUCATION PROGRAM OF STUDIES AND CURRICULUM and PROVINCIAL LEGISLATION.
8. School Finance and Business Management
   - the administration of all budgeting and accounting procedures for the school.

APPENDIX 12

Sensible School Board Reforms

Ron Wallace runs one of the poorest, smallest and best school boards in Alberta: Foothills Catholic School District. The superintendent's novel proposal that school boards cut loose their good schools while supporting their struggling institutions is probably one of the brightest ideas on Canadian school governance that I have read.

SOME IDEAS SURROUNDING
A REGIONAL CATHOLIC SCHOOL BOARD
Submitted by the Foothills Catholic School District

January 26, 1994

The major changes recently outlined by the Province of Alberta regarding school finances and school governance pose a whole series of perplexing problems for small Catholic school districts.

It would appear at this time that the six small Catholic school districts in Zone 5 will most likely be required to regionalize in some fashion within a six month time span. It is also a possibility that those who regionalize voluntarily in the first half of this time span are more likely to make arrangements suitable to their own needs and to the vision they have of Catholic education.

The traditional model of a school board which has developed in North America over the past 100 years basically has trustees involved with schools in which they have a personal stake, schools that their children have, are, or will likely attend. While there may be several elementary schools in a district, often there is just one high school, so trustees have a common focus. Students from outlying areas will eventually meet in the high school and the Board has a common sense of purpose.

This has been the universal model until recent times when, as cities grew, boards became more impersonal and removed from the every day experiences of school children. But the original model still exists in Catholic education in Alberta in all Catholic districts except for Calgary and Edmonton. Even in large systems like Lethbridge, all students eventually attend Catholic Central High School. The proposed regional Catholic Board in Zone 5 differs from both the urban experience of Edmonton and Calgary and the experience of all other Catholic Districts. Trustees from widely scattered communities will have little or no interest in most of the schools within the next district.

Considerations for a Regional Board

A new Regional Board, which would serve Catholics from a number of the current boards, has a unique problem. Trustees in one community some 50 or 60 miles from the next would have a very limited interest in the welfare of other schools. Long distances would have to be travelled with return journeys late at night after lengthy meetings. It would be very difficult to develop a community of interest and sense of common purpose in this district. Teachers in different communities would seldom, if ever, see one another and trustees would have little opportunity for social contact with most parents they serve. Any Super Board created would be seen by most of the staff, students and parents, as remote from every day concerns. It would be quite difficult to develop a sense of loyalty to this District using the traditional model of governance.

Attracting good quality trustees would be a significant problem. How many people from Drumheller would be interested in driving to a meeting in High River to discuss school maintenance problems in a school in Oyen? The only way to attract people with a traditional model of governance would be to pay high honoraria and trustees would serve more for the income provided than for dedication to students.

Compared to the present model where boards are close, informed of, and responsive to local needs, the new model with a centralized bureaucracy basically remote from most of the schools would tend to stifle local initiative and over time develop a certain cynicism.

Centralized hiring practices may lead over time to erosion of the current identity that the teachers have with our local community and Parish. Over time, fewer and fewer teachers may opt to live in the community. This will tend to alienate the school from the Parish. A centralized Superintendent can have little regular contact with the Parish Priest and with the local parents.

All of these people involved in small Catholic school districts may recognize these concerns as real ones and will see that if we simply take an existing model of the school governance and apply it to a Regional Board we will likely have considerably less than we do have now. We also recognize that we have little choice in amalgamating. Is there a way in which we can rethink the idea of school governance in light of the new realities? Are there possibilities here as well as problems? Are there ways in which we can maintain and even enhance high quality Catholic education with a different model or approach? Some outlines are put forward for your consideration.

Outlines of a Model

Many of the financial barriers to regionalization have been

eliminated by the removal of property tax from local school boards. Significant educational problems may well remain as outlined above. But the simultaneous arrival of three new ideas has made a new type of governance possible. They are

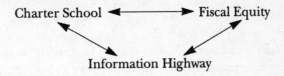

Charter School ⟷ Fiscal Equity

Information Highway

The information highway that is now a practical reality has made communications and the exchange of information on finance and student test results very easy over great distances. The traditional centralized administrative role of a school district may be carried over great distances with ease today. Fiscal equity enables various communities to come together without some being at a disadvantage. In particular the method of funding schools by the number of students enrolled makes collaboration much more possible. The third idea of the Charter School provides an opportunity for both administrative and business centralization and decentralization of instructional matters. Our model is for a significantly different type of school district operating three different kinds of schools.

First of all the District would operate in a traditional fashion in relation to TRADITIONAL SCHOOLS which are centrally managed and directed in all aspects of their operation as schools currently are. This would be very familiar landscape to all of us. The School Board that meets on a regular monthly basis would consist of Trustees from wards with traditional schools and would do the things that school boards currently do. They would be concerned about marks, religious education programmes, discipline and other matters. Schools that were recently established would be operated in this fashion. The role of the small central district administration would be

to nurture these fledgling schools from the concept forma-
tion phase to the acquisition of lands, the erection of facilities and hiring of staff and the first 3 to 5 years of operation.
Indices would be established which would measure progress
of the school in a predetermined fashion in the areas of
instruction, Catholicity and community support. At the point
at which schools had reached a predetermined level of excellence, had a common vision, strong leadership and good
community support, the school could apply to become a DIS-
TRICT CHARTER SCHOOL.

DISTRICT CHARTER SCHOOL

The Trustees representing the ward in which a charter
school was located would most probably become members of
the governing body of the Charter School (the Charter
School Council). They would be joined by the Principal,
some teachers, some parents and the Parish Priest to form
the directing group for a school. The Charter School
Council would have responsibility for all matters in the
instruction and operation of the school except for a small
core of services which would continue to be provided by the
central district. The trustees would no longer attend all of
the meetings of the District which mostly would be focussed
on the traditional schools and these trustees would be
involved at the Board level mainly for a period of several
weeks in the Spring to set the budget for the Charter School
and the District. The Charter School Council would have
authority to hire the Principal and teachers and to make,
within the regulations provided by the Minister, decisions
relating to all curriculum and instruction matters and, within
the guidance provided by the Bishop, to direct religious education. They would have complete authority over their local
budget and all matters not specifically reserved for the district. Basically the financial arrangements of the charter
school would be represented by

$$R - S = B$$

where "R" is the provincial per pupil grant multiplied by the number of students in the school and "S" is a fee collected by the district for its services. The amount "B" would be the local school budget which would contain the vast majority of the funds identified in R and this would be spent in accordance with a budget which was formulated each Spring by the Charter School council and approved or possibly amended by the District School Board. During the budget meetings of the district school board, trustees from the Charter School Council would sit on the Board as voting members. They would also participate in hiring the superintendent. All the monies (B) of the Charter School Council would be either spent directly by the local schools issuing their own cheques or disbursed directly by the District in the case of such things as payroll and utility bills. This would reduce the need for a large office staff in each local Charter School.

The services provided by the new district to the Charter Schools would be very restricted. The new district would be responsible for the global budget, both approving and exercising a general oversight to see that the approved budget was carried through and that bills were paid. The District would deal with new construction as well as modernization and additions to existing buildings and would hold debentures on capital expenditures. Experience in the United States with Charter Schools has shown that major problems occur when the Principal is diverted from his instructional role to areas with which he or she has little familiarity. At the direction of the local school council, the district could deal with the drawing up of contracts. It could look after payroll, benefits, sick days, safety regulations and matters relating to the construction and nurturing of new schools. The Superintendent could provide an outside opinion once or twice a year to each Charter School Council on how the school was doing academically. Direction, however, would be provided by the School Council itself. Advice to the School on technical and professional matters could be given by the District from time to time although the Charter School Councils would be free to get that service elsewhere should they so desire.

Should a Charter School fall away from its mandate, the District might have to assume a direct role. If there was a general perception that the school had lost its Catholic character or had adopted practices contrary to the teachings of our Church, the Bishop would have the right to ask the District to initiate an investigation. After a period of consultation, should the school not correct any real problems, the district could resume control of the Charter School for a period of time. Similarly should the Charter School lose the support of its community through a lack of confidence in the quality of its instruction or leadership or operating practices, and should the school council not be able to remedy this by itself, a petition by the majority of the parents would authorize the district to re-assume control of the Charter School for a period of time until it could be relaunched again.

Provision could be made for an intermediate phase between the traditional school and the district charter schools. Both new schools on their way to becoming Charter Schools and very small schools which would continue to need a significant measure of support and yet would like a measure of local autonomy could benefit from this.

Pros and Cons of the Model
Advantages of this model would seem to include the following.

1. Through the Charter Schools, strong local interest and influence would be maintained. Schools would quickly be able to respond to the changing needs of the community

and those responsible for the governance of the schools would live in and be a part of the local Catholic community.

2. The Parish-school communication would be maintained closely and the local Parish Priest would feel quite comfortable in the school. This in turn would promote closer relationship with the Diocese.

3. The model would also provide for centralization of some services where the economies of scale warrant it, and would give the Charter Schools the opportunity for a second opinion on instructional matters.

4. The model also provides for an opportunity to nurture new schools to imbue them with a vision and to guide them during the formative years.

5. Should abuses occur at the charter school level, the model provides for a means of correcting them. This model is particularly suited for a geographically scattered district.

6. This model would keep the central district administration at a very modest level and would concentrate financial resources at the level of the schools where they could be used to directly benefit students.

7. Should contract negotiations remain at the district level, it would remove this contentious issue from the level of the school and enable positive relations to be maintained there.

Cons
The most obvious drawback of this model is that it is new and requires thought and consideration. Some work would have

to be done to flush out the details regarding the relationship of the Charter Schools to the District. However, for those schools which are still operating in a traditional fashion, the landscape would remain very similar to what we have now.

A second drawback is that there might not be sufficient leadership at the local level to make a Charter School a success. That possibility takes us back to where we are now, to small districts controlling our schools locally. Whichever model is selected will fail unless there is good leadership at the local level. This is a limitation not inherent to this concept. Perhaps one of the roles of the central district would be to assist the Charter Schools in selecting a principal although the final decision would remain with the Charter School Council.

In the final analysis the model relies on good leadership especially from trustees and Councils in selecting good quality principals, teachers and other staff to provide high quality Catholic education. It needs to be coupled with a vigorous programme of achievement testing to give the Charter School Council benchmarks by which to measure success.

Conclusion
Where to go from here?

It should be stressed that these are simply some ideas concerning a Regional Catholic School Board. They could be seen, for those who are interested in pursuing them, as a starting point rather than a fixed set of concepts. Our aim in this process is to discern in the changing circumstances how we can continue to have Catholic schools that are committed to deepening the relationship of our children with Jesus and to giving them the skills and disposition necessary to be a success in this changing world.

APPENDIX 13

Expectations of a Parent

Born in Manitoba, Josef Macek has laboured long and hard to reform Manitoba's pallid science curriculum. His brief essay reflects his European upbringing as well as some very sound ideas.

EXPECTATIONS

As a parent, who knows his children well, I do not expect our schools to perform miracles. Instead I expect just three things to happen:

1. I expect that my child is not left to examine things on his own at random but is actually taught at school—and is taught in a systematic and structured manner.

2. I expect that the educational program which is offered to my child at school is free of gross errors, superficialities, amateurish conjectures and other nonsense, and completely free of any indoctrination peddled by various interest groups, of course.

3. I expect to be a full participant and partner in the education of my child, which means:
   a. To know precisely what is being taught in each subject every day;
   b. To be able to verify every day that my child understands the material taught in the school, and do so against a clearly defined Provincial or other standard;
   c. To be able to help my child as soon as the help is needed and to do so in accordance with the clearly defined

standards, Provincial or other;

d. To fully support daily efforts of classroom teachers in an informed, meaningful and very specific manner according to and with the help of a well-founded standard.

I do not think that these three expectations are exorbitant. These are only necessary conditions of any meaningful cooperation among the teacher, the student and the parent.

In order to establish these conditions right across our province, I urge that the Minister of Education and Training incorporates these two fundamental steps into his reform:

A. To gather the best disciplinary scholars from our University Departments of Languages, Mathematical, Arts and Sciences and ask them to create a new K-12 program for our schools. Then we can toss out our currently used, dated, meagre and mediocre program created by well-meaning but nevertheless semi-educated dabblers.

B. To write this new program directly for the students and incorporate all of it into very portable texts which will not only serve the student, but also become a binding curriculum for teachers and a detailed source of information for parents. In addition, it would become a clear Provincial standard fully defining knowledge to be taught and learned, out there in the open, for everybody to see.

Josef J. Macek, 79 Petriw Bay, Winnipeg, Man., R2R 1K2, Tel.: 632-7957.

APPENDIX 14

Spotting Violent Schools

The Toronto parents' group Outlaw Violence in Education Right Now (OVER) has published profiles on schools that are violence free and those that are plagued with misfortune and outrageous behaviour. Parents will recognize the differences immediately. The group has also created a useful checklist on the symptoms of pupils victimized by bullies or random violence.

SCHOOLS THAT WORK:
It's Simple, But It's Not Easy

Here's what people say about schools that work:

"It's simple—first we say what we will do, then we do what we say."

"Principalship is a benevolent dictatorship under the guise of a participatory democracy."

"It's our job to send the student home a little smarter, and with the same number of body parts in the same condition as when he left."

1. Schools that Work have principals who administer their schools for everyone's long term benefit, even if it must be done in spite of negative interference and lack of support from parents, senior bureaucrats and politicians.

2. Schools that Work clearly define expected standards of behaviour and the reasons for them, to be met by every student, regardless of the students' experiences. These

standards cover everything from courtesy, through manip-
ulative behaviour to criminal behaviour.

3. Schools that Work consistently enforce consequences for
failure to meet expected standards of behaviour every
time they are breached. Excuses for bad behaviour are
not accepted. Objectionable behaviour is not tolerated
because personal problems can only be resolved after the
misbehaviour ceases.

4. Schools that Work seek out and cooperate with police,
parents and the neighbourhood to develop preventative
measures to limit opportunities for unacceptable and ille-
gal behaviour, on and off school property. Decisive action
is taken to resolve minor difficulties before they escalate
into major problems. Mediation techniques are used only
BEFORE a violent situation occurs, not after.

5. Schools that Work expect and must receive the support
required to ensure student safety. Schools must have
police that come immediately when they are called, every
time. Good schools must have tangible support from their
school board by way of operational and adequate communications equipment and protection from negative political interference.

6. Schools that Work expect and assist the Community/
Street Crimes Unit officers to develop a rapport with the
students, and enable them to become educators. This
ensures that students feel secure enough to report problems.

7. Schools that Work require staff to know the students, the
school and the neighbourhood. Principals and Vice
Principals walk the halls, the streets, and talk to students
and residents on a daily basis.

8. Schools that Work are not afraid to talk about the violence/crime problems with the students, parents and public, and do not hesitate to call police whenever any school-related criminal activity occurs.

9. Schools that Work require all staff to present a united front when it comes to looking for and reporting problems. No staff member is exempt from this responsibility.

10. Schools that Work require staff, students, parents, police, and the neighbourhood to develop expectations for student behaviour and solutions to problems together. Each participant shoulders the responsibility to carry out the activities that are required to implement these standards and solutions.

11. Schools that Work expect cooperation and support from parents, but lack of same does not stop them from enforcing the rules. Good schools are not afraid to "inconvenience" parents who fail to support expectations for their child's behaviour.

12. Schools that Work resist political interference from sources who try to force them to back down on consequences applied to ill-behaved students. Good schools know that students must learn they cannot "get away with" bad behaviour.

13. Schools that Work require all their participants—students, staff, parents, police and the neighbourhood—learn from each situation they face. Good Schools know that every problem situation may be unique, and that new skills and remedies will be required to solve school problems.

14. Schools that Work clearly specify to victims and their

families what is being done to control and/or resolve problems by the school, police, the offender, and any other resources brought into play. Such resolution ensures that victims recover from the trauma, the school community can get on with their lives, and that students will report problems, knowing they will be solved.

SCHOOLS THAT DON'T WORK:
Don't See. Don't Tell. Don't Respond.

Here's what people say about schools that don't work:

"It's strictly a question of courage—but my principal doesn't have any."

"There's an unwritten rule—never call the police, and never see anything. Then, of course, we don't have to do anything."

"Around here, the perpetrator always gets back into the school before the victim."

1. Schools that Don't Work have principals who administer their schools for their own personal convenience, even if they must do it in spite of evidence that it causes unacceptable student behaviour.

2. Schools that Don't Work rarely define expected standards of behaviour. If fuzzy standards exist, reasons are never given for them.

3. Schools that Don't Work rarely enforce consequences for misbehaviour. They accept any excuse and tolerate any behaviour and manipulation by students in the name of "personal problems".

4. Schools that Don't Work won't cooperate with police, parents or the neighbourhood, and don't develop pre-

ventative measures to limit unacceptable behaviour. Bad schools deny any responsibility for student behaviour off school property, even if the problem started (or ended up) in the school.

5. Schools that Don't Work discourage staff from presenting a united front when it comes to watching for and reporting problems.

6. Schools that Don't Work discourage staff, students, parents, police and the neighbourhood from carrying out their responsibility to develop expectations for student behaviour and solutions to problems.

7. Schools that Don't Work routinely use the "Three D's" with parents of victims of school crime: denying the occurrence, deferring action, and dissembling about this dereliction of duty.

8. Schools that Don't Work tell parents of victims of school crime that they are the only ones complaining, and that it must somehow be their fault.

9. Schools that Don't Work rarely stop the re-victimizing of students on school property, and often threaten to "ban" parents of victims who try to protect their children at school.

10. Schools that Don't Work usually blame the victim and make him responsible for the offender's behaviour.

11. Schools that Don't Work make the victim and/or his parents take responsibility for the victim's safety, usually by requiring the victim to go 30 blocks out of their way to another school.

12. Schools that Don't Work accuse parents and victims of being unreasonable and won't take concerns seriously. The victim is told not to fight back, but to report the incident. When victims do so, the school often accuses the victim of "tattling" or tells him/her to "handle it yourself".

13. Schools that Don't Work, when confronted by a group of parents of victims of school crime, later call individual parents to attempt to "divide and conquer", accuse parents of undermining school morale and, in general, try to discredit parents who complain.

14. Schools that Don't Work fail to communicate to victims and their families what, if anything, is being done to control or resolve the problem by the school, the offender, or any other resources brought into play. This ensures that the victims do not recover from the trauma and that students won't report problems, knowing that they won't be solved.

SYMPTOMS OF A VICTIM:
Checklist for Parents and Teachers

1. Is the student engaging in sudden aggressiveness toward playmates and family members?

2. Is the student suddenly experiencing nightmares or insomnia?

3. Is the student experiencing mood swings: over-reacting to minor situations, angry and indignant one minute, nervous and fearful the next?

4. Is the student suffering mysterious recurrences of infan-

tile afflictions (asthma, breath holding when crying, respiratory problems, thumb sucking, etc.)?

5. Is the student experiencing unexplained bouts of crying and increased frequency of crying?

6. Is the student becoming reluctant to attend school?

7. Does the student have a growing desire to be escorted by a parent to/from school?

8. Is the student experiencing sudden or mysterious vomiting, stomach aches, breathing problems, headaches, etc.?

9. Is the student showing a loss of self confidence, appearance of timidness, "looking over their shoulder", etc.?

10. Is the student unwilling to go out for recess, no longer attending extra-curricular activities, social events, etc.?

11. Is the student arriving at school at the "last minute" or even late in the morning, or trying to leave early at the end of the day?

12. Is the student showing unexplained lateness in leaving for school and/or arriving home after school?

13. Is the student showing unexplained very early arrival at school?

14. Is the student showing unexplained very early departure from home?

APPENDIX 15

A Contract for Parents

Given the collapse of so many of our communities and the loss of a corresponding consensus on what our schools should be doing, some concerned educators have introduced contracts. The "letter of commitment" adopted by Woodbridge College, a public Ontario school, spells out what is expected of the school's participants. When used properly, a contract can bind a community together and renew purpose to the local school.

WOODBRIDGE COLLEGE LETTER OF COMMITMENT

Woodbridge College

LETTER OF COMMITMENT

Please review carefully the Woodbridge College requirements and expectations of students as you will be required to commit yourselves to adhere to them as a condition of enrolment. Some specific requirements are:

1. All College students will follow the compulsory program designed to provide "a well-rounded" education and will commit themselves to do their best academically. The compulsory program includes the remedial/enrichment period included on every student timetable. This period will be used, by the students, as directed by staff from time to time.

2. As stated in the school Homework Policy, all students are expected to complete homework assignments. Students are also expected to purchase and use a Woodbridge College Planner.

3. All College students will adhere to the code of student behaviour, attendance policy and other expectations and policies as set out in the school calendar.

4. All College students are expected to participate in the mentoring program while in the Intermediate Division (Grades 7 - 10).

5. All College students will be required to obtain a student activity card which covers membership in the Student Association and services in the co-curricular program.

6. All College students are expected to adhere to the College uniform dress code.

I _____have read, understood and accepted the conditions of
 Student's Name

enrolment and participation at Woodbridge College. I consent to the disclosure of my school-related personal information to my parents or guardians in accordance with the municipal freedom of information and protection of privacy act.

Date _____   _____
                                             Signature

I _____, the parent/guardian of
 Print Parent/Guardian Name

_____have read, understood and accepted the conditions of
Student's Name

enrolment and participation at Woodbridge College.

Date _____   _____
                                             Signature

On behalf of Woodbridge College, I accept this commitment.

Date _____   _____
                                             Signature

71 Bruce Street, Woodbridge, Ontario L4L 1J3 / Telephone: 851-2843

Mother Nature's Views on Spelling

Margarete Wolfram is a former student of Jean Piaget and a psychologist at York University. She is also the author of an excellent reading program that will be published this fall (for information call 905-294-0807). In her spare time, she talks to parents on a number of issues, including the teaching of writing and spelling. This essay is a classic eye-opener on educational foibles in these fields.

HOW TO TEACH WRITING— MOTHER NATURE'S WAY

My class in educational psychology is usually a lively one. Most of the students in this course either are in or want to get into the faculty of education and become teachers. But there are others who come from a number of different disciplines, such as economics, sciences, psychology, business or fine arts. I like to make use of this diversity in backgrounds by inviting students to express their views on different issues. While I provide them with factual information, research findings and different approaches, class discussions provide students with an opportunity to look at issues from a number of different angles and through the types of different interest groups. When I asked my students as to what they would do about the story of a seven year old child in grade two (page 437) the discussion became livelier than I had bargained for.

A couple of economics students are fast to provide their answers: "I would correct the mistakes."

1. Wuns Thre was a
   Teddy bear. hes
   name wus snupels.
   he lived in the
   weldrnes. one day
   the teddy bear
   wus in hes ckave
   eis uloo jewule
   but thes time
   he fawd a
   majk chast thut
   wed reafelevee
   eveatime it wus
   emtead.

"I would teach the kid how to spell."

One of the psychologists is not so sure.

"This is really quite a nice story, I mean ... what you can read of it. But he does need help with his spelling."

Three teachers in training look at each other knowingly. They smile and whisper as others voice their views. After a while one of them raises her hand and adds what was obviously meant to be the last comment:

"The spelling is fine. It is perfectly age appropriate, and it shouldn't be touched at all."

There follows a moment of silence; some people look puzzled. A mature student in the front row is rolling her eyes. She must have heard this before.

"You mean, you wouldn't tell this boy that his words are misspelled?" asks one of the business students.

"No, I wouldn't."

There follows another moment of silence.

"Well, how do you expect him to learn how to spell then?"

"He is only in grade two. He will discover the correct spelling as he runs across these words in the books he reads. Kids do a lot of independent reading in the classroom."

"How will he be able to read these words if he gets used to spelling them incorrectly?"

"Oh, he will." The teacher-to-be smiles reassuringly. "All children eventually learn to read."

"Yeah, I know, my brother did, after my parents hired a tutor," grumbles a fine arts student.

"Well, I can't afford a tutor. My son is in grade four and he still can't read. The reason I'm taking this course is to find out how I can help him. And—the mature student adds with a sideways glance at me—I sure hope I don't have to listen to much more of that discovery stuff, because it sure doesn't do it for my son!"

One of the top students in the front row has become visibly upset during this last exchange. She is usually calm and reserved, but now her face is flushed and she doesn't wait to be called upon.

"You know what, I was in grade eight before I finally learned to read. First they told my mother I wasn't ready and she should let me go at my own pace. Then they decided I was learning disabled. It was a good thing I went to a parochial school on Sundays and after school. And there they taught me to read and write in Hebrew. There they didn't talk about readiness and going at one's own pace and learning disabilities. Sure I didn't learn to read as easily as the other kids, but in Hebrew school they just put in more time to teach me. And you know what, if I hadn't had that wonderful grade eight teacher who spent all that extra time on teaching me, I probably still wouldn't know how to read and write in English."

Her classmates look shocked. They obviously find it hard to believe that this young woman, whose contributions they have come to value, could have been close to joining the ranks of the illiterates coming out of our school system.

"And why wouldn't you correct the child's spelling?" one of the business majors asks the student teacher.

"Well, this is a very creative story, and if you start correcting all kinds of things, it would inhibit the child's spontaneity. Even if he learns how to spell, he won't want to write anymore at all. And what have you gained then?"

Her neighbour looks at me somewhat impatiently, as if waiting for me to say something. When I don't, she resorts to her own defence:

"I really don't think one should correct children's spelling." The class looks at her, expecting to hear some justification, and she adds: "This is what we have been taught and this is what we believe in."

"And anyway", the third student in the group adds, "we aren't even allowed to correct spelling. It is against Ministry guidelines!"

These last comments really polarize the class. Some students seem to be dumfounded, trying to figure out how anybody who so blindly believes what has been taught can possibly teach critical thinking skills to her charges. A number of education students who have so far remained silent now speak up.

"You really can't believe everything they tell you in teacher training. There is a lot of stuff which to me makes no sense at all."

"The host teacher I work with corrects spelling. She simply closes the door and does what she thinks is right. And it certainly seems to be working. The children in her class love to write and they write quite well. And they are so proud of what they can do."

"My son's teacher couldn't care less how he writes!" The mature student sounds bitter and frustrated.

The exchanges have become so heated that I decide to break off the discussion.

There are really TWO questions here:
   Should one correct a child's spelling? and
   HOW should one provide corrections?

The first question can only be answered with a resounding YES for the very simple reason that we don't know of ANY skill which is acquired without feedback. It does not matter whether we talk about walking, talking, skating, pitching a baseball, riding a bicycle or writing. Some of these skills are called "natural skills" because it is Mother Nature who provides the feedback. There is no need to tip a beginning skater on the shoulder to tell him that he lost his balance. Mother Nature already did and much faster and more effectively than we could have. She also tells him when he misses the baseball. When his talk is unintelligible, she will let him know by people failing to respond. Mother Nature teaches a lot of skills, but she doesn't have any means of providing feedback on spelling. Reading and writing are inventions of civilization.

Couldn't the child be left to DISCOVER proper spelling? It may indeed happen that a person runs across a word in a reliable text and realizes that the spelling is different from the one he has been using and thus corrects himself. However, the likelihood that this will happen is not too big. A child may not encounter the word in written language for a long time. When she does, she may not recognize it, since she has gained practice in spelling it her own way. Or she may realize the difference and conclude that it doesn't matter, that these variations are all equally acceptable. Or—as was the case with the author of the little story presented here—the child becomes aware of the difference between his and the conventional spelling and requests that "they change the spelling in the books". This resistance to changing his own writing is not surprising if we consider that this child has been allowed to use unconventional spelling repeatedly without ever any hint that he should do anything differently.

Since feedback is necessary for correct spelling to be acquired, a second question is HOW this feedback should be given. In the past, feedback was often given in a punitive fashion. Over the years many of us have run across teachers who handed back our work covered with red ink marks, making us feel sorry we ever wrote anything in the first place. There is plenty of evidence that punishment is not an efficient procedure, because it does indeed tend to inhibit much more than it was meant to. Rushing in to "correct the mistakes" ignores the fact that this little story is far more than a string of poorly spelled words. There is a lot of imagination, a readiness to communicate, to put the story down on paper even though there may be uncertainty about the individual words. There is readiness to make use of whatever phonics is known and to venture some educated guesses. This is very important, because the perfectionist who stalls whenever he is not 100% sure and waits for somebody to provide him/her with the correct answer doesn't go very far. Marking each misspelled word with a red pen, tallying them all up to inform the child that he has made x number of mistakes and having him write each word correctly five times would be similar to blasting a series of small targets with a cannon. Not only the targets but a lot of what surrounds them would be destroyed too. There is indeed a high chance that the child's spontaneity will be inhibited and the pleasure and eagerness to write be lost. It is neither desirable nor necessary to proceed in such a heavy-handed fashion.

In the present case, the second grader, after having been duly praised for this nice story, could simply be invited to now write it in "grade three fancy style". The teacher would have to rewrite the story in conventional spelling before asking the child to copy it. Once the story has been put aside, the teacher can then introduce an occasion for children to solidify their vocabulary, using word games, pointing out rules or assuring that children discover these rules.

Would this be a lot of work for the teacher? Would the child resent having to copy the story all over? This would depend on the child's previous education. If rewriting a story in conventional spelling is a procedure which is used consistently right from the start, then the child will be used to polishing his/her work. And since unconventional spellings are steadily eliminated rather than being practiced, fewer words will need to be corrected. If however, children do not receive feedback early and on a regular basis, they will be much more reluctant to change their writing, especially since there will be so much more to correct and the errors have become more ingrained.

Mother Nature does not teach spelling, but educators would do well learning from her way of teaching. If she taught children to walk with the same halfheartedness and inconsistency with which our schools teach them to write, if she raised them in a greenhouse under conditions of weightlessness, if she waited until they had grown tall before introducing them to gravity and the real world, letting them crash down from a few feet rather than start early when they can only slide a few inches, I suspect that a lot of children would graduate from her school crawling.

APPENDIX 17

New Choices for Parents

College Place Elementary in Lynnwood, Washington, has solved the choice dilemma by offering parents three different programs or villages all under one roof. "Parents," says a school brochure, "are invited to select the village they believe is the best match for their child."

If more public schools followed Lynnwood's example, the public school system might have a more promising future.

ART VILLAGE

Envisioning the landscapes for tomorrow's masterpieces

ORGANIZATION: Self Contained
Students working with others similar in age in the same classroom with one teacher

FOCUS: Integrating Art Into Traditional Curriculum
Students creating a mosaic to demonstrate their understanding of patterns as they relate to math.

K-6 PROGRESSION: Progress Through Traditional Grades
Students progressing through grades 1-6

TEACHER/STUDENT ROLES:
Instruction Primarily Teacher Directed
Teacher provides instruction and directs most activities.

PARENT CONNECTIONS: Contribute to Individual
Classroom Activities
Work in individual classroom and organize village events

THIS STRUCTURE WORKS WELL FOR:
- Students who work well within clear structure
- Students who excel in the traditional classroom environment

C.O.R.E. VILLAGE

Creating Opportunities for Real Life Experiences: The world
in a classroom

ORGANIZATION: Multi-age
Students working with people of varying ages and with more
than one teacher

FOCUS: Connecting Learning With Real World Experiences
Students creating their own business in a way that reflects the
real world

K-6 PROGRESSION: Continuous Improvement With Formal
Assessment At The End of Years 3 & 6
Students working at their own pace as they demonstrate the
attainment of essential skills and learning

TEACHER/STUDENT ROLES:
Instruction Is a Combination of Teacher and Student Directed
Teachers facilitating opportunities for students to participate
in hands-on learning experiences

PARENT CONNECTIONS: Contribute to Village Projects
Share special interests and job related experiences

THIS STRUCTURE WORKS WELL FOR:
- Self directed students who work well individually and in
  groups

- Students who work well by creating their own structure to
  the task

COMMUNICATION VILLAGE
Communicating the present for the future

ORGANIZATION: Team Learning
Students working with others similar in age with more than
one teacher

FOCUS: Integrating Reading, Writing, Listening, Speaking
and Watching Throughout The Curriculum
Students writing stories to share with others by using both
sign language and reading aloud.

K-6 PROGRESSION: Progress Through Grade Levels With
Flexible Cross-Grade Level Groupings
Students progressing through age-level groupings with
opportunities to work with students of other ages.

TEACHER/STUDENT ROLES: Instruction Is Teacher And
Student Directed
Teachers facilitating opportunities for students to actively
participate in their learning

PARENT CONNECTIONS: Contribute to Grade Level
Activities
Share special interests while working in grade level class-
rooms

THIS STRUCTURE WORKS WELL FOR:
- Students who enjoy flexibility and working with a variety of
  adults and students
- Students who enjoy working with a variety of students, some
  of whom use sign language to communicate.

APPENDIX 18

Numerous non-partisan parents' groups have sprouted up across the country, and are useful sources of information. Some, such as Albertans for Quality Education and the Organization for Quality Education, produce excellent newsletters. Here's a partial listing:

Alberta

Albertans for Quality Education: 403-254-8333

British Columbia

Advocates for Education: 604-538-7438
Concerned Adults for Education: 604-545-5350
Teachers for Excellence in Education: 604-854-6608: Fax: 854-6530

Manitoba

Parents for Basics: 204-269-5900
Parents Concerned About Education Standards: 204-957-5518

Nova Scotia

Parents Against Reduction in Quality Education Networking Together: 902-434-4635

Saskatchewan

Citizens for Accountability and Excellence in Education: P.O. Box 886, Regina, Saskatchewan, S4P 3B1

Ontario

Citizens United for Responsible Education: 416-693-CURE

Educators Association for Quality Education: 905-884-5410

Ontario School Board Reform Network: 416-488-1125

Quality Education Network Northern Region (Unionville) 416-471-6491, Central Region (Hamilton) 905-521-8882, Eastern Region 416-509-2984, Western Region (London) 519-471-8184.

Parents Interested in Quality Education (Ottawa) 613-741-6934

Trustees National Standards Organization: 613-239-2211

Organization for Quality Education
Regional Contacts in Ontario:

Brant: Debbie André	(519) 448-1889
Dufferin: Rick Middlebrook	(519) 942-0245
Durham: Patti Charbonneau	(905) 286-2984
Elgin: Kathy Cronheimer	(519) 633-7587
Essex: Robert Cartlidge	(519) 326-2687
Etobicoke: Ilona Matthews	(416) 259-3572
Frontenac/Kingston: Lisa Moses	(613) 335-2001
Grey: Irene and Dave Ward	(519) 371-5069
Halton: Jennifer Brooks	(905) 827-8611
Hamilton/Wentworth: Judy Labate	(905) 643-3215
Hastings/Prince Edward: T. Johnson	(613) 395-3990
Lambton: Anne Khan	(519) 337-3520
London North: Bonnie Cumming	(519) 471-8184
London South: Craig Stevens	(519) 473-0802
London/Middlesex Separate: H. Bos	(519) 473-2078
Middlesex Public: Judy Sumner	(519) 666-0809
Niagara: Vic Mamchych	(905) 384-2293
Nipissing: Ann Fudge	(705) 472-5602
North York: Julie Wood	(416) 638-7595
Norfolk: Lesley Johnstone	(519) 426-5284
North/Newcastle: Cindy Chatterson	(905) 885-2028
Ottawa: Theresa Ziebell	(613) 722-1693
Oxford: Kathy Lubitz	(519) 684-7686
Parry Sound: Christine Dowell	(705) 342-5502

Peel: Karin Aucoin   (905) 453-4594
Peterborough: Maureen Beebe   (705) 939-2035
Scarborough: Steve Swigger   (416) 499-8706
Simcoe-Barrie: Wendy Cahill   (705) 734-2602
Simcoe-Collingwood: Robert Crysler   (705) 445-3512
Toronto: Catherine Daw   (416) 482-8487
Toronto French: Mireille Bealle   (416) 493-9014
Waterloo: Karen Mitchell   (519) 725-5420
Wellington: John Akin   (519) 836-2965
Windsor: Mark Weglarz   (519) 735-7913
York Region North: Bill Everitt   (905) 836-0533
York Region South: Rita Kavanagh   (905) 477-5397

Contacts in Other Provinces

Alberta
Grant Sikstrom   (403) 459-8692
68 Akins Drive, St. Albert, Alta. T8N 2Y7
British Columbia
Susan O'Neill   (604) 929-3069
3988 Hixon Place, North Vancouver, BC V7G 2R6
New Brunswick
Marjorie Gann   (506) 536-1794
Box 666, Sackville, NB E0A 3C0
Newfoundland
Jim Hornell   (709) 489-7538
15 Gardener St., Grand Falls/Windsor, Nfld. A2A 2T3
Northwest Territories
Laurie Didiodato   (403) 873-6564
19 Taylor Road, Yellowknife, NWT X1A 2L2
Nova Scotia
Randy Hoyt   (902) 462-0330
15 White Birch Lane, Dartmouth, NS B2W 6B4
Saskatchewan
Susan Wigmore   (306) 584-9249
3203 Angus Street, Regina, Sask. S4S 1P6

APPENDIX 19

Parents Councils

The popular call for more parental involvement in schools often includes site councils, democratic bodies designed to govern a school. Such proposals are usually fraught with hazards unless well defined. The Oregon Education Association has produced a fine handbook on what site councils can do well:

School improvement is problem-rich. Some problems are easily solvable; others almost intractable. A site council's success in school change efforts is much more likely if "easy" problems are solved first. Examples of such problems include understanding that:

Educational reform involves learning new skills to solve complicated problems in a setting already overloaded with demands. One of your site council's first tasks will be to develop a plan for increased collaborative planning time for the entire faculty and staff.

A site council does not make final decisions for a school, nor is it simply another advisory committee. The role of the council is to make school improvement recommendations to the entire staff based upon the careful examination of an educational approach. This assumes your school has an established process for discussing and approving recommendations.

Trust and Goodwill among site council participants is essential. Training in conducting meetings, conflict management, communication, and decision-making skills are important startup activities for all site councils. However, these activities are only important insofar as they contribute to the pursuit of better instruction.

Planning for change is based on knowledge. "Know thyself" is a good motto for beginning school improvement. This means your council must have a clear picture of its own school first. Develop or update your school's profile with demographic data and information about the school's existing instructional program.

INNOVATION AND REFORM

Check today's mail. It may contain a new educational innovation. Public schools are inundated with policies, programs, and methods all promising improvements in teaching and learning. Education on a large and small scale has hopped on and off many bandwagons as fads recirculate under new names. As a result, schools and teachers are frustrated by often meaningless changes. Your site council can avoid desperate leaps at instant solutions and stop this cycle if its members recognize that not every innovation in education is a reform. Only true reforms yield increases in student learning that are measurable.

The pace of innovation is increasing, and, unfortunately schools cannot always tell which innovations will be most effective with their particular students. This is especially true of schools with large numbers of diverse learners who have the most to lose when their school moves from one untested innovation to another. By the end of the sixth grade, a child of poverty, for example, would have to go to school an extra year and half to equal the academic involvement of more advantaged students.

Judging the Potential Value Of an Approach
Clearly, many important factors, such as a child's readiness

for school, are factors beyond a teacher's control, yet strongly influence student learning. Nevertheless, teachers need to be able to make the optimal contribution to student learning within their sphere of influence.

There is no cookbook for successful educational reform; however, your site council should have a plan for judging the potential value of an approach. The following framework presents six important questions a site council can ask to evaluate both existing and proposed educational practices.

1 Are the Approach and Its Outcomes Clearly Defined?

The first question your site council should ask when examining existing or proposed educational approaches is, "Are the approach and its outcomes clearly defined?" A clear description is easy to understand and comprehensive. "This innovative educational approach uses interactive holistic portfolios to enhance left-brain learning" sounds impressive but communicates little useful information.

A complete description of an educational approach provides a picture of what teachers and students will be doing, the instructional materials to be used, how teachers interact with students, and the amount of time devoted to instruction. Clearly defined approaches also convey what students will be able to do at the end of given periods of time and describe measures to evaluate whether these outcomes are reached.

If an approach is vaguely defined, it cannot be determined whether it has in fact been implemented, and consequently its effects are impossible to measure. Measures of whether an approach has been implemented should focus on determining whether a match exists between what teachers do in the classroom and the description of the approach.

2 What Evidence Exists the Approach is Effective?

People want to hear good news. "Adopt this program and your school will be transformed into a learning paradise." This claim may be true, or it may be wishful thinking. The point is that the effectiveness of an educational approach must be considered before your school decides to use it with students.

If your council proposes an approach, its effectiveness should be documented by research that demonstrates its effectiveness versus other approaches that have attempted to achieve similar outcomes. In the documentation, the explanations of the research should be clear enough for a layman to understand, yet detailed enough to be believable. If research shows only a slight gain in student learning in response to a large expenditure of money and effort, the value of the approach is questionable.

You must be cautious about how the word "research" is used. Much "research" in education is not actually research but the opinion of people in the field. Research should be of high quality and ample to justify widespread adoption of an approach and the accompanying expenditure of funds and effort. For example, the success of an approach used in one classroom with a very talented teacher would not justify the use of this approach in a large number of classrooms with teachers of varying levels of performance. Instead, the approach would need to first be evaluated with more teachers.

In general, the education field suffers from a lack of research on significant issues. If research is not available to judge if an approach is effective, one option is to visit schools using the approach, observe their students' performance in the program, and review its evaluation results.

3   Is an Accountability Process Built into the Approach?

Accountability is not a process for identifying scapegoats. A lot of promising educational approaches fail because they can't help teachers determine whether they are successfully implementing an approach and if the students are learning at a desired rate and level of proficiency.

An accountability system should respond to these questions:

- Have student and teacher measures been identified or created that will contribute useful information about a program's implementation?

- Does the program provide regularly scheduled observations for the purpose of supporting student and teacher performance in a timely and effective manner?

- Is there necessary personnel for providing such support?

- Are assistance procedures specified for teachers and students who need additional support?

- Are contingencies in place for teachers and administrators?

4 Is the Approach Sustainable?

School improvement programs do not run themselves. They require substantial time and effort for a good payoff. It makes no sense for a site council to recommend an educational approach that cannot be sustained. Sustainability depends on how practical and reasonable it is to expect to implement and monitor an approach.

An approach that makes unrealistic demands on teachers' time is doomed to failure. For example, many reforms assume that teachers will be responsible for developing new curriculum materials. This can be an unrealistic assignment unless teachers are given adequate time for writing the lessons, trying them out with a range of students and teachers, accumulating data on student performance, noting problem areas, then rewriting the curriculum and trying it out again.

Issues involving staff development are also critical. Helping teachers learn how to apply an educational approach should involve appropriate staff members for the same reason that baseball players aren't pulled off the bench and sent into hockey games: They may be skilled athletes, but their skills are the wrong kind. Advocates of innovative approaches often underestimate the amount of staff development needed to have all teachers reach a satisfactory level of implementation. Without adequate staff development and monitoring, the approach is likely to fail in many classrooms and ultimately be abandoned.

In judging if an approach is sustainable, a site council should ask these questions.

- What type of staff development is required to assure that teachers will perform successfully in the proposed approach?

- Has the success of the staff development been documented in terms of the ability of staff members to perform at uniformly high levels following the proposed training?

5 Is the Approach Equitable?

Educational approaches should not impede the progress of any group of students. Diverse learners — children of poverty and children with disabilities — are usually the ones hurt the most when well-intentioned programs do not work. A subtle form of discrimination often occurs when the same educational approach is mandated for all students despite evidence that using the same approach with all students results in high failure rates for diverse learners. There is no one-size-fits-all solution to the problems of education.

Unfortunately, some claim that educating all students in the same way represents equity. This claim ignores the reality of the high failure rate for diverse learners. Equal access to an education should mean more than simply using the same approach with all children; the goal is to use approaches that best meet the needs of particular children.

An approach intended for widespread adoption should be found effective with diverse learners. Also, a monitoring system to ensure that at-risk students are progressing adequately and backup plans should be an integral part of the approach.

6   Are the Costs of the Approach and its Implementation Reasonable?

You wouldn't buy a jet plane to make a trip across town because it's too expensive and the costs aren't justified. The same applies to educational reform. An approach may be capable of reaching your school's desired objectives but might be too expensive to be feasible. With tight school budgets, wise use of funds is critical. The total costs for an approach, including adequate funds for staff development, should be calculated and compared to the relative benefits expected. Approaches which are capable of bringing about significant improvement to the greatest number of children should be given priority.

Summary of Considerations for Selecting Educational Approaches

Answering these six questions can provide your site council

with a responsible decision-making process for judging the value of an approach for improving student learning.

1. Are the Approach and its Outcomes Clearly Defined?
   In describing philosophy and what happens in the classroom.
   In providing measure of teacher and student outcomes.

2. What Evidence Exists the Approach is Effective?
   Quality of research
   Amount of research
   Impressiveness of research results

3. Is an Accountability Process Built into the Approach?
   Monitoring teacher performance
   Monitoring student performance
   Back-up plan

4. Is the Approach Sustainable?
   Adequacy of staff development
   Reasonable expectations for teachers
   Reasonable expectations for administrators
   Coordination of instruction, assessment and staff development

5. Is the Approach Equitable?
   Effectiveness — research showing no adverse effects for any group
   Monitoring procedures and back-up plan

6. Are the Costs of the Approach and its Implementation Reasonable?
   Cost within a typical school's budget